REEL VULNERABILITY

REEL VULNERABILITY

Power, Pain, and Gender in Contemporary American Film and Television

SARAH HAGELIN

RUTGERS UNIVERSITY PRESS

New Brunswick, New Jersey, and London

Library of Congress Cataloging-in-Publication Data

Hagelin, Sarah.

Reel vulnerability : power, pain, and gender in contemporary American film and television / Sarah Hagelin.

pages cm

Includes bibliographical references and index.

ISBN 978-0-8135-6104-2 (hardcover : alk. paper) — ISBN 978-0-8135-6103-5 (pbk. : alk. paper) — ISBN 978-0-8135-6105-9 (ebook)

1. Vulnerability (Personality trait) in motion pictures. 2. Power (Social sciences) in motion pictures. 3. Pain in motion pictures. 4. Sex role in motion pictures. 5. Motion pictures—United States. I. Title.

PN1995.9.V85H34 2013
791.43'655—dc23

2012038529

A British Cataloging-in-Publication record for this book is available from the British Library.

Visit our website: http://rutgerspress.rutgers.edu

Manufactured in the United States of America

For my parents, Teresa Love Hagelin and Richard Hagelin

Contents

Acknowledgments

This book is the result of a long intellectual collaboration with friends, mentors, colleagues, and family members without whom this work would not have been possible. I am deeply grateful to them for their insight, kindness, and fellow-feeling, and it is a great pleasure to be able to thank them publicly.

Susan Fraiman, Eric Lott, and Sylvia Chong were a model dissertation committee—supportive, challenging, and intellectually generous—and they have remained important sources of encouragement and advice throughout the book's development. I am extremely grateful to each of them for their friendship and support. Ellen Malenas, Andrea Stevens, Michael Lewis, Jill Rappoport, Jolie Sheffer, Michael Lundblad, and Justin Gifford have been involved with this work since I first began thinking about these ideas, and I am deeply grateful to them for reading endless drafts of these chapters and sticking with the project and with me.

I owe a debt of thanks to my wonderful colleagues and friends at New Mexico State University, including the students in my courses on gender, violence, and war, whose deep ethical engagement with our course work challenged me to do justice to these texts. Elizabeth Schirmer, Jen Almjeld, Peter Fine, and Ryan Cull have read countless versions of the manuscript, and I could not have completed it without them. My thanks also to Tracey Miller-Tomlinson, Harriet Linkin, Joyce Garay, and Monica Torres for their help and support. Robert Paul Lamb has been mentor, friend, and family to me for more than a decade, and his encouragement, friendship, and example as a scholar and teacher have made my own career possible.

An earlier version of the work on *Saving Private Ryan* in chapter 3 appeared in *The War Body on Screen,* edited by Karen Randell and Sean Redmond (2008). I would like to thank everyone at Rutgers University Press, particularly Leslie Mitchner, Lisa Boyajian, and India Cooper, for their insight, support, and help with the manuscript.

Finally, I owe a tremendous debt to my family, who has supported me throughout this adventure. My thanks and love to the Loves, the Hagelins, the VanderSchoors, the Fraziers, the Huffers, and particularly to Suzanne Temple, Ben Temple, Grace, Joe, Caleb, Brian Hagelin, Alisa Burpee, Riley, and especially to Rich and Terry Hagelin. All that I have ever accomplished is thanks to you.

REEL VULNERABILITY

Introduction

UNMAKING VULNERABILITY

In the first season of the Baltimore cop drama *The Wire* (HBO, 2002–2008), police officer Kima Greggs recalls her experience as a rookie cop. "You're in your radio car alone, working your post. Most women aren't getting out of that car—not without side partners showing up. They're intimidated, physically." Kima's description of being "straight-out-of-the-academy-type scared" accurately captures the uncomfortable cocktail of fear and pain that has been at the heart of cinematic depictions of women's difference.The calculation Kima ascribes to "most women" is the advice patriarchal culture gives all women: don't get out of the car; don't jog by yourself; don't walk outside after dark. In response to the cultural imperatives that ask women to stay scared in order to avoid injury, Kima offers a surprising solution. "I wasn't about to *stay* scared. You know, you get your ass kicked once or twice, you realize it's not the end of the world, right? Most of the women, they don't want to believe that. Most of the men, too—they don't even want to go there." Kima's bracing insight—that certain kinds of pain *don't* end the world—remains something that we, as feminists and film critics, haven't wanted to know.

This book argues that our ideas about vulnerability reside in bodies, but they also shape perception. Why do we think of women's and children's bodies as especially vulnerable? Doing so has enabled important antiviolence and antirape work, but the discourses that construct vulnerability also work to reify whiteness, infantilize women, and hide a more widespread vulnerability. Traditionally, vulnerability has been constructed onscreen in a way that valorizes patriarchy, or at least hides its ideologies. If women think of themselves as especially vulnerable, they will be more compliant to a system that claims to protect them. We must name the thing in order to see and then dismantle it. But it is also my contention that popular culture is richer, more nuanced, and more full of progressive possibilities than we sometimes know or acknowledge, particularly in big-budget middlebrow films like *G.I. Jane* and *Saving Private Ryan* that are often assumed to parrot dominant ideologies. I trace the cinematic construction of vulnerability onscreen, arguing that two competing models of vulnerability—sentimental and resistant—structure the way we think about men, about women, and about our shared vulnerability. The readings that follow, of westerns, war films, and other fictions of the body in danger or pain, reveal the logics of paternalism, erasure, and replacement that are at the heart of our social belief in women's special vulnerability. Patriarchy has made women's bodies the site of political, social, and physical violence and policing, but the assumption that women need special protection also enables our continued compliance. This book asks what happens when pain doesn't rob the woman onscreen of her subjectivity. Women take a step toward being seen as people, not merely as humans rather than objects, but as diverse and complex—in other words, as fully human.

Defining Vulnerability

The first printed use of the word "vulnerable"—"susceptible of receiving wounds or physical injury"—occurs in the final act of Shakespeare's *Macbeth* (1605). Macbeth, having murdered his way through much of the cast list (in person or by proxy), taunts Macduff during their final battle: "Thou losest labour. As easy mayst thou the intrenchant air with thy keen sword impress as make me bleed. Let fall thy blade on vulnerable crests; I bear a charmed life, which must not yield to one of woman born."[1] This play, so fixated on the physical properties of blood, ends with a debate about Macbeth's own blood. Shakespeare uses the word "vulnerable" to signify several different anxieties. When Macbeth claims that his is not a "vulnerable crest," he speaks on one hand of his lineage, his house—represented by the crest that depicts his family coat of arms. In this context, the term "vulnerable" implies that Macbeth's claim to the throne is shaky, politically and ethically indefensible. On the other hand, the line literally refers to the crest's placement on Macbeth's shield. When Macbeth challenges Macduff to "let thy blade fall" on *other* crests, he means those other claimants to Scotland's crown, but the spectacle onstage is of two human bodies, fighting to the death. A literal blade waits to fall on Macbeth, and, depending upon how a director stages the play, the final act depicts a human man made increasingly vulnerable in every sense: emotionally, politically, and physically. Because, of course, Macbeth is wrong—his crest, his chest, and his body *are* vulnerable.

This first recorded use of the term "vulnerable" is a male insistence on power, immediately followed by violence; the play's murdered children and "unnatural" women are not the last bodies we see onstage. Macduff is able to kill Macbeth and fulfill the witches' prophecy because he was born by cesarean section, not "natural" childbirth ("Macduff was from his mother's womb untimely ripped"). Even in this earliest use of the term, anxieties about the body's vulnerability cluster around an image of the womb—here replaced with the other "wound" in Macduff's mother's body, the unseen incision through which Macduff was "untimely ripped." Macduff, not of woman born, has made Macbeth's body vulnerable. In this play, obsessed with the imagery of wombs and wounds and the primeval magic that drives men to murder, Shakespeare, looking for a word to describe the radical fragility of flesh and blood and bone, coins the term "vulnerable."

The root of the word is the Latin *vulna,* which means "wound." The term is used in a variety of ways—economic, geopolitical, emotional—but this book focuses on the term at its most visceral, when it describes the fragility of our bodies, and the terror, confusion, and fellow-feeling that can come from our perception of our shared embodiment. I refer both to the physical fact that a thin layer of skin separates the inside of our bodies from the outside world and also to what Raymond Williams has described as complex "structures of feeling," in this case those that define our *sense* of ourselves as vulnerable.[2] It is these structures of feeling that I argue work differently than we sometimes imagine they do. "Vulnerability" in this sense usually means a system of beliefs, images, and narratives that imply a capacity to be harmed. Generally, the word has also implied a powerlessness or victimization that I aim to strip from our understanding of the term, especially in regard to images of the female body. To this end, I argue that contemporary popular culture portrays three kinds of vulnerable bodies onscreen: the traditionally vulnerable female body, the female character overcoming vulnerability through masculinized aggression, and a third body that I will label "resistant vulnerability."

The most commonly listed synonyms for "vulnerability" are "susceptibility," "weakness," "defenselessness," "openness," "exposure," and "liability." I am interested in the tension between terms like "weak" and "defenseless" and words like "openness" and "exposure" because I believe this tension is at the root of our culture's fraught, ambivalent relationship to the idea of vulnerability. The traditional model of vulnerability, which I call "sentimental vulnerability," sees women as especially vulnerable to pain and injury, and reads pain and injury as debilitating to the female subject.[3] Our culture, politics, and academic criticism remain troublingly invested in a story of female fragility, a story based on a few key assumptions: women, children, and nonmasculine men are the victims of male violence, female injury demands society's retribution, and pain renders the victim of violence helpless. These assumptions are not limited to war reportage and television news—in fact, they're operative in most film and television genres that take violence and injury as a central spectacle: crime dramas, war films, rape-and-revenge narratives. These expectations rely, emotionally, on sentimental vulnerability. This traditional model asks us as viewers to reserve our greatest sympathy for the suffering *female* body. To give just one example from 1980s narrative film, *Full Metal Jacket* makes its ideological point about the horror of war by focusing its camera on the intimate, protracted death of a Vietnamese female sniper. The film intends to disrupt its audience's complacency about military violence, but it does so by tapping into very traditional assumptions about vulnerability. We're meant to *feel* the sniper's suffering more acutely because she's female. Similarly, *Boys Don't Cry* (1999) uses Brandon Teena's exposure and rape at the hands of working-class men to gender vulnerability female. The camera's protracted, unsettling focus on Hilary

Swank's naked body during moments of sexual violence uses the viewer's sudden, explicit awareness of that body's *femaleness* to heighten audience investment in the character, whom the film had previously resisted gendering. The film gets its power as a critique of homophobic violence by leveraging what I argue is a very traditional notion of vulnerability—once we register the body as female, we feel protective toward it.

Common antonyms for "vulnerability" are equally revealing: "invincibility" and "resistance." Images of women fighting back through masculinized aggression take two forms: rape-revenge heroines in films from *I Spit on Your Grave* (1978) to *The Girl with the Dragon Tattoo* (2011), and the objectified figures of fantasy in films like *Lara Croft, Tomb Raider* (2001) and *Sucker Punch* (2011). The rape-revenge heroine, as pleasurable as her revenge might be for the audience, still participates in traditional models of vulnerability because her body is seen, by herself and the audience, as always on the edge of violation. I sense that the fantasy figures trouble us because they imagine the first antonym as a response to the problem of vulnerability: invincibility. And this seems like a dodge, a lie, a betrayal of what we know as feminists about the ethical cost of violence. For this reason, I am more interested in the second antonym—resistance. The combination of these ideas—the openness and susceptibility associated with vulnerability and the counterintuitive frisson of resistance—embodies what I call "resistant vulnerability." A different set of films and television shows—*G.I. Jane, Battlestar Galactica, Saving Private Ryan*—destroys the assumptions made by *Full Metal Jacket* and *Boys Don't Cry* as well as the rape-revenge heroines and the figures of fantasy. Instead, it offers us images of vulnerable men that demand our sympathy, abused women who don't want our pity, and images of the body in pain that don't register as powerless. Resistant vulnerability works in two ways. It proves that vulnerability needn't be gendered female, and it suggests that we alter our basic assumption that a suffering body is vulnerable and needs our pity and protection.

Unlike the sentimental constructions of vulnerability at work in *Boys Don't Cry,* a film like *G.I. Jane* (1997) offers specific narrative and visual strategies to code audience response to Demi Moore's tough naval officer, asking viewers to reconsider their attitudes toward violence against women. Thus *G.I. Jane* assuages audience anxiety about women's increasing presence in the armed services by training its audience to read the abused female body as a step toward equality. This book is in no way a celebration of aggression or a dismissal of violence, and the shift to resistant vulnerability does not ask that we ignore pain. Instead, it demands a greater awareness of the stakes in the stories we tell ourselves about violence. The culture industry teaches viewers that women's bodies are fragile, and academia often teaches scholars to fear divorcing pity from pain. But doing so is necessary if we wish to understand the shifting gendered imagery that current popular culture produces.

Fighting like a Girl: *Buffy the Vampire Slayer* and the Problem of the Feminine

Vulnerability has been a fact and a fantasy in popular culture as well as in the everyday lives of women. *Buffy the Vampire Slayer* (1997–2003), the cult television program created by Joss Whedon, used the opening frames of its pilot episode to exploit, mock, and finally subvert genre conventions that silence or marginalize women. Before a human figure appears onscreen a long Steadicam tracking shot, evocative of the opening frames of *The Shining* (Stanley Kubrick, 1980), destablizes the viewer's point of view. This camerawork has long been cemented in viewers' understanding as the harbinger of horror. As Carol Clover demonstrates, we are trained to read this shot as the killer's point of view and to feel a certain complicity in the violence that is sure to follow, destroying whatever creature it stalks.[4] For Whedon's camera to slide eerily over the empty halls and classrooms of the show's primary setting, Sunnydale High, creates the quickening in the pulse that registers the body's vulnerability to impending injury.

This camerawork is unsettling because it registers an absence, and that absence feels to the viewer like danger. But before that danger manifests itself onscreen, the scene shifts our perception of where the danger hides. The tracking shot enters the school's science lab, showing the viewer a series of objects that represent human attempts to understand, measure, and categorize life: an animal skeleton, a microscope, a human skull encased in glass. The camera frames a window, which is smashed from the outside by a hand that invades the space of the lab. These genre signifiers, which seem familiar, demand a series of emotional and cognitive shifts from the viewer. Breaking glass promises danger and the arrival of a threat onto the scene, an assumption solidified by the dark hair and black leather jacket of the man who enters through the window. But once a young woman crawls through the window behind him, blond and dressed in a Catholic schoolgirl's uniform, our vulnerability sensors switch, quickly and completely. We perceive her as vulnerable, both to the man's attempts to coerce her and to the undefined presence signified by the opening tracking shot. This is the language of horror as a genre, and on the one hand Whedon is taking advantage of the fluid identification central to its ideological project. As contemporary television viewers, we are remarkably adept at shifting allegiances quickly; however, this sequence doesn't just demand that the viewer shift from sadistic identification with him to masochistic identification with her, but that we adjust our basic sense of who and what is vulnerable.

Their conversation once inside sounds like the hackneyed patter on any number of after-school specials and reality TV shows, but following its rhythms and elisions shows how deftly it skewers viewer assumptions about gender. She's hesitant, obedient, asking if he's "sure this is a good idea," while he's assertive and dismissive: "It's a great idea—now come on!" When he suggests that they go out on the roof of the gym, her response increases the viewer's sense of her vulnerability, but also reveals how this vulnerability is constituted by a patriarchal culture's denial of the female voice: "I . . . I . . . I . . . I don't want to go up there." Her reluctance to name herself "I" and the danger she seems to fear stem from the same source. As she glances nervously around the empty hall, reading shadows as possible hiding places of danger, her perception of danger and ours diverge. For the viewer, the male companion begins to register equally as a threat, especially given how eager she seems to please him. True to genre form, he dismisses her fear, snapping, "It's nothing," when she claims to have heard something. He leans around the corner to "check," but the mocking tone of his "Helloooo?" indicates contempt for her perceived weakness. The camera stays behind him, slightly to the right of her literal viewpoint, signaling the unseen presence of that other perspective that opened the scene. He turns back toward the camera, telling her "there's nobody here." She steps into the frame in front of him. "Are you sure?" she asks, timidly. "Yes," he huffs in exasperation, "I'm sure." She turns toward him, and in the space where the camera obscures her face from view, her generic blond prettiness transforms into vaguely reptilian monstrosity, protruding fangs labeling her one of the show's titular vampires. She quickly dispatches her male companion, who, framed as a potential aggressor, is definitively rewritten as a victim.

Once the opening credits have aired, the blond vampire is replaced by Buffy (Sarah Michelle Gellar), the "slayer"—the one human girl endowed with the quasi-mythical ability to fight the vampires and demons that populate the show's California town of Sunnydale. Whedon's audio commentary on the episode calls this moment "genre-busting," where the girl who had always been the victim of this kind of narrative becomes the hero. The slight physical resemblance between Gellar and Julie Benz, who plays the blond vampire, Darla, is a visual trick that finesses Whedon's point, since the opening sequence does not feature the show's hero, Buffy. But their resemblance is also part of Whedon's ideological point: one pretty blond girl is not interchangeable with another. On its face, the teaser sequence merely reverses audience expectations in order to hook the viewer, a narrative joke that works because audiences understand and anticipate the semantics of the horror genre even if they've never read Clover or Rick Altman.[5] But the Steadicam trains, or perhaps tricks, us into sensing another presence—that uncanny "other" that lurks in the shadows, unseen by Whedon's camera, understood later in the series as an ineffable "evil" that marks Sunnydale High School's physical location on top of the "hell mouth." *Buffy*'s teaser sequence prefigures the combination of irony and affect that has made the show a cultural phenomenon and an influential text for feminist scholars of film and media. It also lays bare many of the assumptions about audiences, bodies, and feeling that this book investigates. The scene succeeds in creating tension because audiences know what the floating, stalking tracking shot usually signifies—this kind of audience sophistication is crucial to the resistant vulnerability I identify in part II. Further, the scene relies on our assumption that a slight, blond woman is an embodiment of vulnerability; it (first) figures the male body as far less vulnerable than the female body and, indeed, as a potential instigator of sexual violence. *Buffy,* both the series and the titular character, offers us a way to interrogate the assumptions about danger and pain that animate both popular culture and the scholarship that analyzes it.

"Resistant vulnerability" combines two terms usually defined as antonyms because, at its heart, the shift to resistant vulnerability depends on counterintuitive images—narratives that we think we understand turned on their heads or familiar images put in patterns that push the existing cultural script away from traditional investments in female fragility. *Buffy,* with its knowing dialogue and metafilmic narratives, is full of such counterintuitive moves. Looking at a series of vulnerability slippages, when the show begins self-consciously to construct itself around and against its viewer's assumptions about the female body, helps to set up the terms important to understanding and defining vulnerability. In the show's third season, the arrival of Faith, also a slayer, complicates Buffy's position. The tension between the working-class, brunette, "bad" slayer Faith and dutiful, blond, middle-class, "good" slayer Buffy provides the third season's arc, and in the fourth-season episode "Who Are You?" the two slayers temporarily switch bodies. This body-swapping trope allows the show to ask whether the self resides in the body or elsewhere, questions that, not surprisingly, coalesce around the issue most central to American culture's investment in female vulnerability: sex. After the body-switch occurs, Faith (in Buffy's body) stands, newly bathed, in front of a bathroom mirror examining Buffy's face. In this scene the signifiers of Buffy's status—her makeup, well-coifed hair, and stylish clothes—have been stripped away, leaving Sarah Michelle Gellar an interesting opportunity to unpack the signifiers of her stardom as "Buffy" by playing Eliza Dushku's performance as "Faith." Reappropriating the signifiers by which a patriarchal culture denigrates women as shallow and fashion-obsessed and making them neutral markers of its heroine's personhood is one of the show's most transgressive elements. But this moment in front of the mirror asks uncomfortable questions about whether these markers are actually neutral. The stationary camera positions the frame of the television screen literally as a mirror, which reflects Gellar's small shoulders and delicate limbs with unusual clarity.

She practices saying "You can't do that! It's *wrong*" in the mirror, twisting her features so that Gellar's face, usually the object of the camera's desiring gaze, looks slightly grotesque. The dialogue operates as a sarcastic act of ventriloquism; Faith resents Buffy's strict policing of the slayer power. But in the embodiment onscreen of Gellar-playing-Faith-playing-Buffy, it also gains a frisson of transgressive spectacle for the *Buffy* viewer. Although full of ironic quips and fan-boy in-jokes, the show is usually in deadly earnest about its heroine and her ethical quest, so there is an element of rebel pleasure in seeing it satirized by Sarah Michelle Gellar herself, whose on-set disagreements with series auteur Joss Whedon were by this time well documented.

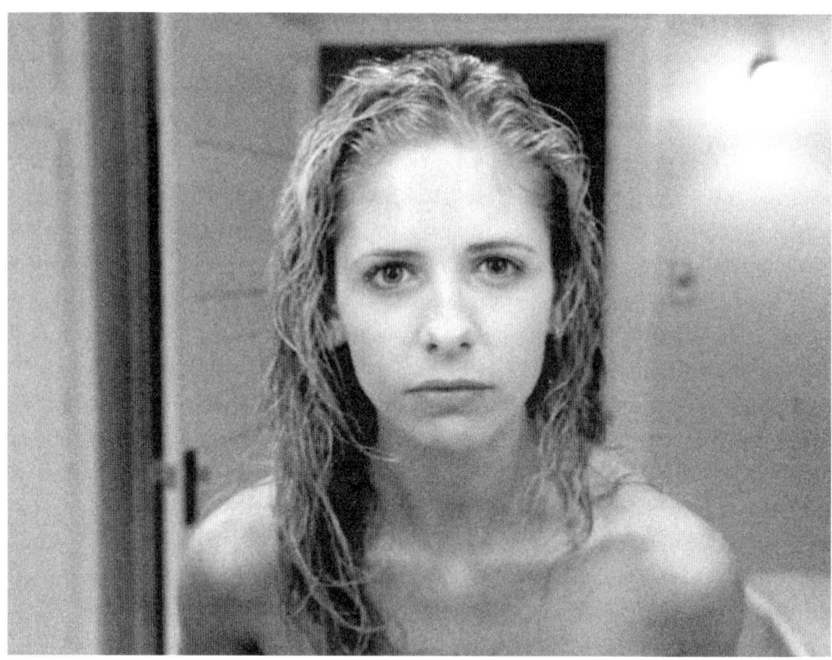

Figure 1 Faith in Buffy's body

Figure 2 Faith examines Buffy's face

But spectral identification with Faith leads to a more destabilizing scene later in the episode, when Faith uses Buffy's body to bed Buffy's boyfriend Riley. A series of disorienting jump cuts shows Faith/Buffy's body in bed beneath Riley. He whispers, "I love you," and she begins to struggle: "Get off. No. No, no—get off me!" She exits the bed and stands naked beside it, asking Riley, "Who are you? What do you want from her?" Gellar's voice stumbles on "her"—drawing attention to the visual disconnect that this episode simultaneously demands from Riley within the show's narrative and the viewer outside of it. While we, unlike Riley, know that the person who has exited his bed is Faith, not Buffy, the evidence presented by our senses disputes it. And once Faith/Buffy is penetrated by Riley, she seems unmoored from her "self." The episode gets its title not, as we first imagine it will, from the confusion over who Buffy and Faith are—the "who are you?" at issue is who *he* is. Thus the logic of substitution by which we are made vulnerable to one another, in sex, in violence, and, in this case, in the very substance of our individual subjectivity, becomes the answer to the episode's question.

Buffy's status as fantasy television allows it to ask these questions literally, by imagining a world where a 100-pound teenager bests opponents who should outmatch her in physical fights and where literal body-swapping stands for the more quotidian means by which the war films and westerns I consider in the following chapters will construct and deconstruct vulnerability onscreen. Iris Marion Young, seeking to bridge the gap between existential phenomenology and feminist theory, picks apart the tendency in girls and women to take up less space than is physically available to them and to restrict the free motion of their bodies in sports and other physical activities. Young posits that "throwing like a girl" comes from a fear of injury that trains girls to perceive themselves as weaker and more physically fragile than they actually are. In Young's research, the differences in physical strength between biological men and biological women are less important to this dynamic than the self-policing that comes from "experienc[ing] our bodies as a fragile encumbrance." If patriarchy teaches women to perceive of their bodies as delicate—and Young's research shows that the "more a girl assumes her status as feminine, the more she takes herself to be fragile and immobile"—then perhaps *Buffy* is less a fantasy about supernatural "slayer power" than it is an attempt to imagine a world where women understand themselves as powerful.[6]

Film Studies, Postfeminism, and Masochistic Bodies

Scores of critics have analyzed the tough women, female avengers, and final girls who have populated the cultural imaginary in the past twenty years, but there is ongoing scholarly discomfort with the potentially regressive politics of these images.[7] Caroline Heldman has coined the term "fighting fuck toy" (FFT) to describe the "hyper-sexualized women protagonists who are able to "kick ass" (and kill) with the best of them—and look good doing it."[8] Heldman names *Elektra* (2005), *Catwoman* (2004), and *Sucker Punch* (2011) as examples of this phenomenon, which for her is about capitulation to patriarchal looking positions, even as "the FFT appears empowered." Yet, as I will demonstrate, an equally robust set of images—Buffy, *Battlestar Galactica*'s Starbuck, *Deadwood*'s Trixie—challenges the fighting fuck toy's capitulation to the established order. On the masthead of the *Fighting Fuck Toy Blog,* a cartoon image of a buxom, handgun-wielding woman shouts, "Sexism is over." While this is a pithy, ironic distillation of what many label "postfeminist" culture, I can't help thinking that culture's reification of the fighting woman is a more complicated phenomenon than the label "postfeminism" suggests. Uncovering the politics of these images is difficult because the very things that scholars criticize in the "fighting fuck toy" image are also the things patriarchal culture has used to denigrate women—interest in fashion, physicality associated with traditional femininity. The FFT is what we get when popular culture changes its codes about women fighting—women *causing* injury—but not about women *being* injured. Part of the *Buffy* teaser's transgressive punch comes from the idea that something lurks under the blond woman's schoolgirl looks and her halting, self-abnegating speech patterns: a monster, a killer, or a hero. Clover has been rightly influential to a generation of feminist scholars as well as to auteurs like Whedon, and her analysis of the "female victim-hero" offers an important model for understanding the female body in genres that would slash, kill, or exploit it. But Clover's final girl has to be unmade by pain in order to be reborn as a killer, an avenger, and an icon.

In working to uncover the narratives at work in popular culture after the Cold War, I've found that the shifting spectacle of the body's vulnerability is at once a touchstone and a locus of anxiety. Anxieties about the body's vulnerability haunt horror as a genre and also inform scholarship on films and television shows that focus on murder, rape, or other forms of injury. Much of the scholarship on these cultural products takes vulnerability as a given, though recent work by Judith Butler and Laura Kipnis has begun to create a language for how culture constructs vulnerability.[9] Butler's use of the term "precarious" provides an important starting point for this investigation, especially when we remember that the opposite of "precarious" is "safe." Butler defines vulnerability, at base, as a breach of boundaries—of the nation, of the body—but also as a state of radical dependence on others. An important part of her theorization of what she calls "corporeal vulnerability" is its frisson of fear. This fear is central to what I call "sentimental vulnerability"; and often, in ways this project attempts to complicate, that fear is sexual. The threat of rape, and the relation of that threat to other forms of physical violence, are absolutely central to the way we think about men's bodies, women's bodies, and the gulf in our perceptions between the two. I argue that popular films and television in the 1990s begin to undermine assumptions about female vulnerability by severing the link between vulnerability and powerlessness that earlier forms of cultural production had trained audiences to expect. There are scores of scholarly investigations of men proving they can be emotionally vulnerable and women proving they can be physically strong, but this book goes *beyond* that narrative by identifying the various forms of vulnerability, sentimental and resistant, that posit vulnerability as a shared human experience. My readings of *G.I. Jane, Saving Private Ryan, Battlestar Galactica,* and *Deadwood* challenge the way film theorists and feminist cultural critics have continued to conflate suffering and vulnerability with the image of the female body. For Butler, vulnerability reveals our commonality—we each have bodies that leak, bleed, and spill. But vulnerability also marks our difference. Female bodies are perceived to be more vulnerable than male bodies; children's bodies more vulnerable than adult bodies.

For thinkers like Kipnis, Sarah Projansky,[10] and David Greven, gender remains a crucial facet of vulnerability's construction in culture and onscreen. Not surprisingly, Kipnis's chapter on vulnerability deals with rape and the threat of rape, and the ongoing hold that both have on our cultural imaginary. Although Kipnis's interest is in the ways that feminist critics like Andrea Dworkin and Naomi Wolf remain invested in framing women as victims, the connection between the concept of women's vulnerability and the threat of rape remains stubbornly hard to sever. Projansky's critique of rape narratives in popular culture analyzes this connection but doesn't explicitly challenge it; she identifies two kinds of narratives about the "relationship between rape and women's vulnerability . . . those that depict women's vulnerability as leading to rape and those that depict the rape of an independent woman as making her vulnerable,"[11] figuring vulnerability as female and placing it on the opposite side of a binary with the term "independence." The solution these films provide, then, to the problem of vulnerability is *dependence,* on men, on a patriarchal culture of protection, and (as Projansky notes) on the heterosexual family. Greven's *Manhood in Hollywood from Bush to Bush* (2009) provides one of the most interesting recent investigations of the male body onscreen, arguing that our current critical language for understanding male suffering is insufficient. I share Greven's frustration with the language of masochism to describe this suffering, and his analysis of the abject body that contemporary theory "refuses to recognize" is crucial to my sense that a logic of erasure is at work in the way we represent and theorize vulnerability.[12] While Greven's analysis focuses on representations of the queer body, I see a similar logic at work in the representation of bodies coded as normative in films like *Saving Private Ryan* (1998) and *The Men* (1950). Discussions like Projansky's and Greven's usually take place in different parts of the scholarly conversation, but I argue that they are part of a single dynamic in popular culture and in scholarly inquiry. At a theoretical level, scholars acknowledge that gender is performative and that all bodies are vulnerable to injury, but the image of the woman onscreen remains a problem. Theorized as such by feminist film theory, she continues to stride across movie screens, causing viewers and scholars alike to stop in their tracks at the sight of her body in danger or in pain.

A growing number of scholars see female representation onscreen turning in the late 1990s toward "postfeminist" imagery. The June 29, 1998, cover of *Time* magazine featured a photograph of *Ally McBeal* (Fox, 1997–2002) actress Calista Flockhart alongside images of Susan B. Anthony, Betty Friedan, and Gloria Steinem under the blaring headline "Is Feminism Dead?" Scholars often use this cultural artifact to signal a turning point in culture away from the action heroines of the Carter/Reagan/Bush years toward the "postfeminist" era of Bridget Jones and Carrie Bradshaw. Most critics who use this example assume that *Time* is right to see Ally McBeal as representative of 1998 as a cultural moment. But what would it look like to trace a different cultural history? Is it possible that *Time* chose Ally McBeal to grace its cover alongside feminist pioneers like Anthony and Steinem so that the story it tells can be about feminism's decline into postfeminism? This narrative, while it has real explanatory power for the decade following the 1980s backlash against feminist politics, cannot account for characters such as Demi Moore's G.I. Jane. Surely Flockhart's Ally was not the most interesting pop-cultural icon of 1998. While Ally's miniskirts and pigeon-toed stance framed a Harvard-educated lawyer as an insecure girl-woman, Demi Moore's shaved head and muscular body on *G.I. Jane*'s promotional materials offered a very different vision of female stardom. And if we're going to focus on the fantasy of female perfection of a revered male auteur, why focus on David E. Kelley's Ally and not Joss Whedon's Buffy, who wisecracked her way into the cultural consciousness in the same years that Ally came to represent the culture's ambivalence about feminism?

Yvonne Tasker and Diane Negra's introduction to their 2007 collection on postfeminism defines the term as an alternative to the "backlash" formulation popularized by Susan Faludi and others. I share their sense that the relationship between feminism, popular culture, and politics is complex and fluid, but challenge the assumption that the cultural landscape is quite as dire as they suggest. Tasker and Negra frame figures like Buffy as "emblematic and problematic icon[s] of female empowerment within postfeminist culture."[13] Indeed, the way that *Buffy* keeps tough, curvy Faith secondary to bird-boned, blond protagonist Buffy seems like a classic postfeminist move. But, as Alyssa Rosenberg argues in her tribute to *Deadwood*'s former prostitute Trixie, places where characters we admire seem to fail, or present themselves in ways that trouble us, are merely honest depictions of the way ideology operates: "[Trixie]'s empowered, but the show doesn't fall prey to the trap that strong female characters created by men often do—that women's liberation is purely a matter of will, not circumstance."[14] Scholars of postfeminism rightly critique culture for imagining a fantasy where sexism is over, but, as Rosenberg reminds us, we as scholars often fall into a similar trap—to crave female characters who are stripped of the vestiges of "femininity" that signal the way our subjectivities have been formed by patriarchy. Whedon takes precisely the things that have been used to denigrate women and turns them into markers of power, positioning the girl, usually seen as dumb or disposable, as the hero. What I call "resistant vulnerability" is very different from the "postfeminist" cultural discourses that claim (erroneously) that feminism is no longer necessary and that its antiviolence work is complete.

Since the moment Laura Mulvey labeled the camera's gaze an assault, film criticism—like culture—has equated vulnerability with femaleness, despite important work done in the past fifteen years to separate the figure of woman from the status of victim.[15] Psychoanalytic film theory's interest in the camera's gaze and our identification has focused attention on the sadism or masochism of violence onscreen; most of this scholarship has assumed that the bleeding, bruised body is vulnerable, victimized, and passive, that our only identification with such a body is masochistic. The opening frames of Quentin Tarantino's *Kill Bill* (2003) feature the sound of a woman's labored breathing, her gasps, sharp intakes of breath, and guttural cries indicating pain or danger. The sounds continue, unexplained, as the film's opening credits appear in white letters on a black screen, until the frame abruptly cuts to a black-and-white close-up of Uma Thurman's face, covered in bruises and blood. A male voice asks, "Do you find me sadistic?" This emotionless voice competes for the viewer's attention with her breathing, which is louder than his words, as if this is her point of view though not her literal perspective. A white handkerchief identifies this voice as belonging to "Bill," who goes on to answer his own question: "No, kiddo. At this moment, this is me at my most masochistic." To hear Bill's claim of masochism, the viewer must listen through not only the sounds of "kiddo's" suffering but also the sound of bullets being loaded into the chamber of a pistol. She whispers, "Bill, it's your baby," as we hear the sound of a shot and blood explodes behind her head on the floor. Tarantino's explicit play with the dynamics of sadism and masochism in this scene's dialogue functions as a sly joke on the discourses of masochism used to discuss male suffering onscreen. "Kiddo" lies on the floor, pregnant and bleeding, while Bill stands, unseen by the camera's gaze, claiming the masochistic identification with her that the viewer is too disoriented to fully register. Tarantino—like Whedon, constantly riffing on both generic and scholarly discourses around film and spectatorship—returns here to *Macbeth*'s bloody bodies and compromised wombs.

Tarantino's Bill, marked for death by the film's title, alludes to a history of cinematic male suffering when he labels himself a masochist. As evidenced by the box-office success of the *Rocky, Die Hard,* and *Lethal Weapon* franchises, mainstream American cinema in the 1980s and early 1990s seemed obsessed with masculine white men in pain. But, more often than not, these images merely reasserted male prowess, as cultural-studies analyses of hard bodies and male masochism have shown.[16] The spectacle of watching Mel Gibson's Martin Riggs tortured in *Lethal Weapon* is pleasurable for the switch from suffering to action when Riggs drags up his broken body and fights back, saving both Danny Glover and Glover's gorgeous teenage daughter, whom the bad guys have tied up in her underwear. The film codes vulnerability female so explicitly that there's no question it's the half-naked girl who needs protection, not the white cop covered in his own blood. This seemingly transgressive spectacle—a strong man suffering—actually works to reinforce traditional notions of masculinity and vulnerability.[17] Searching for a way to understand the popular culture of the twenty years after the end of the Cold War, criticism has argued itself to a standstill. Pop-cultural depictions of male masochism are now more ironic or knowing than in the heyday of Gibson's career as a leading man, but the language we use to describe these male and female bodies has not changed much.[18] However, in the chapters that follow, I argue that war films' and cop dramas' embrace of dominant power structures actually *depends* on a fairly radical revision of what it means to be vulnerable. The texts I study question the very meaning of vulnerability by eliciting a new audience response: they undermine our emotional sense of how feminization, victimhood, masculinity, and control stand in relation to one another.[19]

Clover's compelling analysis of the "female victim-hero" offers an important step toward understanding identification with the suffering body that looks beyond the discourse of masochism, but her focus on a specific and often-marginalized genre concentrates her argument on the adolescent male spectator and the "politics of displacement" on which his identification rests. In Clover's analysis, vulnerability remains female.[20] Adolescent boys' identification with that vulnerability might, indeed, be subversive, but Clover's final girl still relies on traditional models of female vulnerability for audience identification and sympathy. Recognizing resistant vulnerability and the demands it places on our perception opens this conversation to possibilities for identification with the injured body beyond masochism, and bodies that master pain instead of being made helpless by it. This gives us a way to react to the suffering body beyond pity and lets us see feminist images of the female body where we least expect to find them. Thus the tough women this project analyzes owe a great deal to the final girl. They carry her, however, outside of the specific genres to which 1970s and 1980s film relegated her.

The readings that follow show how texts like *G.I. Jane* and *Deadwood* shift audiences' cultural assumptions about the meaning of the body in pain, changing it from a site of abjection to a site of agency.[21] Most of the recent scholarly work on postfeminist culture and neoliberal subjectivity assumes that popular culture celebrates individuality above all else, but in my view twenty-first-century popular culture is full of narratives that are deeply skeptical of individualism. Specifically, television shows, structured as expanding narratives that unspool over time and extend into all kinds of paratexts, train viewers to value collective subjectivity over individuality. This book takes up the challenge posed by Greven and Lisa Coulthard[22] to imagine new ways of analyzing violence onscreen and joins Butler and Kipnis in theorizing how and why we perceive of our bodies as vulnerable—to injury, to death, and to one another. The emergence of a resistant vulnerability in the popular culture of the 1990s shows an inchoate awareness that vulnerability need not always be coded white and female. To understand it this way both infantilizes women and hides the patriarchal structures that would contain them.

Whiteness and Racial Erasure

The process of constructing vulnerability in popular culture gets its power by being invisible. In the early stages of this research, I planned chapters on the African American female body and discourses of nonwhite vulnerability. What I did not yet realize is how central vulnerability has been to the construction of white womanhood and how stubborn the association of whiteness with vulnerability remains. Indeed, the removal of the black female body from the story U.S. culture tells itself about women's special vulnerability is one of the ways that dominant culture has secured its power. I argue that popular culture consistently and relentlessly imagines vulnerability as female, and that other bodies—usually male, often nonwhite—are moved offscreen. But we don't *just* construct vulnerability as female; we construct it as white and female.[23] How is it that twentieth-century American culture has taught women, particularly privileged, white women, to understand themselves as especially vulnerable? As Butler argues, global privilege has created in the American consciousness the dangerous, unacknowledged belief that certain lives are more vulnerable, valuable, and grieveable than others. But in addition, American popular culture's impulse to figure the human experience as universal tricks us into thinking that brief acknowledgment of nonwhite vulnerability justifies returning again to the image of the sweet blond girl.[24]

Buffy's season-five episode "Fool for Love" shows the narrative and iconographic displacement of the nonwhite female body that happens even on this self-aware, feminist show. The episode opens with one of the few times Buffy doesn't best her opponent. She fights a vampire with her usual physical and verbal panache until she suddenly loses the upper hand and the vampire penetrates her with her own stake. The episode's plot details Buffy's fear and confusion over this sudden reminder of her body's vulnerability, and she seeks out Spike, a charismatic vampire, to tell her the story of how previous slayers lost their final battles. Spike has killed two previous slayers, one in China during the Boxer Rebellion and one in New York City in 1977. The episode's structure intercuts Buffy and Spike's emotionally charged conversation with flashbacks of Spike's transition from effete nineteenth-century poet to Sid Vicious–emulating vampire and his murder of the two slayers. At the level of the show's season-long arc—Buffy must face her ambivalence about her power and the violence it enables her to wreak—Buffy and Spike's conversation is the most important part of the episode. But on the visual level, the short flashbacks to Spike's murder of the past slayers enacts the replacement of the African American female body with the white female body as both vulnerable and heroic.

Spike's memory of the second slayer he killed finds him on a subway car in New York City, fighting an African American slayer, Nikki (April Wheedon-Washington), who is costumed and coifed to resemble Pam Grier in blaxploitation films of the 1970s. Scriptwriter Doug Petrie calls the episode "my fan-boy dream of doing a 70s cop movie in New York City," but when Petrie describes Nikki as "the *Shaft* of slayers," he reveals more than just a fan-boy interest in the way that black female power is coded socially and politically onscreen.[25] Because while Buffy understands her vulnerability to injury and death through the stories Spike tells her about the other slayers, the *Buffy* viewer understands them through the cinematic markers of the two genres that influence the show: Hong Kong action cinema and blaxploitation. The flashback structure that outlines Spike's death as a human and his rebirth as a vampire—a trope of "becoming" to which the show obsessively returns—has consequences that Petrie and Whedon may not intend. Since Spike narrates these events to Buffy in the show's present, the flashbacks are necessarily from his point of view. Nikki is a powerful onscreen presence, but as viewers we are asked to share Spike's exuberance at the memory of their fight and Buffy's disgust at it, never to identify with Nikki herself. The show transitions to Spike and Nikki's final battle, cued by Spike's dialogue, which explicitly associates Nikki with Buffy: "The first [slayer] was all business, but the second—she had a touch of your style." Here Spike links the memory of Nikki's transgressive power to Buffy's own, but the viewer cannot help noticing that Nikki has a touch of *Spike*'s style, right down to the black leather duster that costumes Spike throughout the series and here adorns Nikki. After he's killed Nikki, Spike returns to her body to retrieve the coat, which audiences have learned to read as a signifier of his sexual appeal and power. On one hand, this detail about the coat's origin is surprising and transgressive—a man wearing a woman's coat becomes the ultimate marker of "cool" masculinity. But it also acknowledges that bad-boy white masculinity gets its edge from a cultural association with blackness, just as Buffy secures her status (within the show as slayer and for the audience as protagonist) with Nikki's removal from the screen. This episode dramatizes in miniature the ways that American culture has constructed white female vulnerability as a way of erasing the vulnerability of nonwhite women's bodies.[26] Two women die onscreen in the episode—Nikki and the unnamed Chinese slayer—but the bodily vulnerability the show highlights is Buffy's, and, by the end of the episode, Spike's own. As will so often be the case in the readings that follow, there is one story this episode tells with its dialogue—Buffy faces her attraction to the slayer power's darkness—and another, more transgressive story it tells visually: the African American slayer's murdered and abandoned body is the locus of her becoming, and his.

This book traces the discourses of sentimental and resistant vulnerabilities from the 1950s to the present. Drawing from war films, torture narratives, and sci-fi shows, it outlines the way we understand vulnerability through seeing the body—watching it bleed and tremble as if made newly aware of its susceptibility to pain and injury. Every film and television show I consider in this book can be considered either a western or a war narrative, since it is in these genres that popular culture remains most invested in a gendered vulnerability. Part I traces the two important shifts—one in acting style and one in the conventions for depicting onscreen violence—that enable resistant vulnerability to emerge in the 1990s. In part II, I investigate resistant vulnerability, which challenges but does not completely replace the assumptions that enable sentimental vulnerability to persist. Part III traces resistant vulnerability's move from the silver to the small screen post-9/11, challenging the critical commonplace that post-9/11 culture represents either a backlash or a politically ambivalent "postfeminism."

War, the West, and the Cinematic Language of Vulnerability

If we think about the production of vulnerability onscreen as a narrative, the story begins after World War II when filmmakers challenging the authority of the Production Code censors begin to work through more explicit representations of male vulnerability and female agency. The narrative continues post-Vietnam in the war films of the 1970s and 1980s as squib technology enables a more "realistic" portrayal of violence and we can see a new ideology that emerges around the American soldier as a psychological casualty of war. Representations of physical vulnerability onscreen vary historically, but I have chosen the moments after the cultural upheavals of World War II and Vietnam because they help establish the formal and ideological conventions that prepare the viewer for resistant vulnerability. *The Furies* and *The Men* (both released in 1950) illustrate the logic of replacement that codes vulnerability white and female offering two iconic stars, Barbara Stanwyck and Marlon Brando, as early examples of resistant vulnerability. Looking at acting styles in *The Furies* and *The Men* shows that the gradual replacement of Delsartian acting, focusing on training the voice and the body, by Stanislavskian Method acting, focusing on emotional and psychological work, led to a certain kind of embodied acting becoming associated with the masculinity of actors like Brando. Similarly, war films dealing with U.S. involvement in Vietnam from 1978 to 1988 exemplify an important shift in the cinematic codes used to signal vulnerability in mainstream American film that comes with the explicit depiction of onscreen violence. Robert De Niro's performance in *The Deer Hunter,* Vincent D'Onofrio's in *Full Metal Jacket,* and Sean Penn's in *Casualties of War* allow us to see the lineage that connects Brando's wounded WWII veteran in *The Men* to the vulnerable male bodies in *Saving Private Ryan* and *Boys Don't Cry.* Part I traces that lineage alongside the one that connects Barbara Stanwyck in *The Furies,* wielding scissors as a weapon to fight those who would dispossess her, to Uma Thurman in *Kill Bill,* slicing her samauri sword through the premises of the rape-revenge film. These readings in part I set the stage for the emergence of resistant vulnerability after the Cold War, which I analyze in part II.

Resistant Vulnerability at the End of the Twentieth Century

After the end of the Cold War, representations of vulnerability shift, asking us to rethink our reactions to the spectacle of the female body in pain. In the late 1980s and early 1990s, tough female icons in films such as *Aliens* (1986) and *Terminator 2*

(1991) emerged faster than cultural ideas about vulnerability changed. This phenomenon creates a problem for both audiences and film scholars, who are forced to rely on theories of spectatorship and feminist engagement that cannot fully account for the triumphant, bleeding women and vulnerable, penetrable men who are increasingly central to American culture in the 1990s. My readings of *G.I. Jane* and *Saving Private Ryan* detail the complex emotional work these films demand of their viewers, asking us to rethink our investments in gendered vulnerability. Part II pairs readings of these war films with readings of *Boys Don't Cry* and *The Laramie Project* (2002), which show the landscape of the American West reimagined as the locus of queer vulnerability.

The early 1990s was also the first period in which a considerable number of women had grown up since the passage of Title IX in 1972, which guarantees gender equity in the funding of sports in public high schools and universities. A generation of women that grew up playing organized sports also meant a critical mass of women familiar with the playing-though-the-pain ethos so iconic to the American cultural conception of boyhood but, before Title IX, not part of what it meant to be a girl. Therefore, it is no surprise that two of this book's clearest examples of resistant vulnerability, *G.I. Jane*'s Jordan O'Neil (Demi Moore) and *Battlestar Galactica*'s Starbuck (Katee Sackhoff), are fictions in a military setting—a "training" scenario where commanding officers and drill sergeants function narratively like coaches. The structure of the U.S. military was in transition during this period, which makes the representation of the military in war films and action narratives especially important. As women fought for entrance into all-male military bastions such as the Citadel and as military technology seemed poised to displace the hard-bodied Special Forces soldier of 1980s cinema, these genre fictions were one of the places where anxieties about these changes were addressed.

Of course, women and girls participating in the sort of character-development-through-pain that feminists have rightly spent decades critiquing as part of the destructive effects of patriarchy is not an unambivalent good. Similarly, though this new model of vulnerability has real potential to change the cultural assumptions about gender that keep women from serving in combat positions in the military, the implications of this discourse are uncertain. As decades of important antiviolence political work have shown, divorcing suffering from pity is a dangerous enterprise. But it is, I argue, a potentially useful and necessary one. Fetishizing female suffering and vulnerability has mired culture in reductive ways of understanding women. It has, moreover, worked as a cover story for a more widespread vulnerability—of men's bodies as well as women's, adults' as well as children's.

Television Narratives and the Myth of the Individual

Representations of vulnerability operate differently in the 1990s than they do after 9/11. After notions of vulnerability shift in the 1990s, on post-9/11 television, competing models of vulnerability—and cultural ambivalence about what they mean—*dismantle* the edifice of heroic individuality that visual media has relied upon to tell its story about culture. The conventional wisdom about culture post-9/11 is that it produces an America willing to embrace Jack Bauer, to reelect George W. Bush; part III uncovers a powerful counternarrative that emerges on television. The revision of vulnerability going on in the 1990s refracts and transforms into a challenge to the idea of the individual; my readings of *24, Battlestar Galactica,* and *Deadwood* question not only gendering of vulnerability but the very nature of the human. Characters such as Starbuck and *Deadwood*'s Trixie (Paula Malcomson) dismantle our cultural assumptions about female fragility. More importantly, perhaps, these shows reveal that our investment in the special vulnerability of the female body—as both academics and consumers of popular culture—has political consequences as well as academic ones. Thus part III focuses on shows that use the political debate about torture to reframe vulnerability as a problem of individual subjectivity. Post-9/11 television encourages us to ask a certain question, to feel that we are on familiar ground. Will Jack Bauer find the nuclear warhead before the day is over? Are *Battlestar Galactica*'s Cylons machines or humans? Ultimately, these shows teach us that these are the wrong questions to ask and that the questions we desperately want answered are not the ones we should be asking. The television of the past ten years is starting to work through in narrative what we won't allow ourselves to think about in politics—the disruption of individual subjectivity. Shows like *Deadwood* dismantle the cult of the individual that has structured our understanding of spectatorship, clearing the way for the Starbucks, the Buffys, and the Calamity Janes that will populate our television terror dreams.[27]

PART I

THE CINEMATIC CONSTRUCTION OF VULNERABILITY

The Furies, The Men, *and the Method*

CINEMATIC LANGUAGES OF VULNERABILITY

The Furies (Anthony Mann) and *The Men* (Fred Zinnemann), both released in 1950, mark an important moment in the construction of gendered vulnerability onscreen. The complex negotiation of genre conventions and gender representation in each film helps to define the cinematic languages of vulnerability that post–Cold War popular culture will critique and dismantle. Both of these films show the process by which acting onscreen becomes "naturalized" and therefore invisible. Method acting seems to dissolve the barrier between the body of the actor and the art of performance, and the seeming authenticity of the resulting emotions onscreen enables sentimental vulnerability. Tracing the cinematic precedents for the transgressive women of contemporary film and television shows that an iconic female character like Uma Thurman's Beatrix Kiddo does not emerge solely from Quentin Tarantino's pastiched artistic imagination any more than HBO's tolerance for violence and profanity on the small screen wholly created Robin Weigert's Calamity Jane. Thus *Kill Bill* and *Deadwood* owe a complicated debt to iconic female figures in an earlier era of cinematic representation. Barbara Stanwyck's performance as Vance Jeffords in *The Furies* is a fascinating early example of what I will define as resistant vulnerability, though Stanwyck is certainly not alone in creating iconic images of female power during this period in film history. We can see in both of these films an early trace of the counterintuitive images that resistant vulnerability will depend upon: not fragile but triumphant women and not victorious but penetrable men.

This process happens most viscerally when bodies are captured on film in motion, enacting a certain set of codes that audiences are trained to read as indicators of vulnerability. Three facets of *The Furies* and *The Men* help to establish these codes: a protagonist who transgresses gender norms, a logic of racial substitution where the white protagonist replaces the vulnerable nonwhite body, and the narratives of homecoming that are central to each film's plot. Although each film resists strict genre identification, *The Furies* operates as a western and *The Men* as a dour, aggressively realist drama about injured veterans. Both genres have thematic similarities to the American captivity narrative tradition in which racial otherness is a threat and traditional gender roles must be reinscribed in order to purge the sexual, religious, and cultural threat posed by civilization's confrontation with a "savage" other.[1] These films share the captivity narrative's interest in gender and race, but instead of the logic of extermination—the captivity narrative's solution to the problem of racial difference[2]—these films propose a logic of substitution. In each case, a noble, family-oriented Latino character dies in order to midwife the white protagonist's rebirth. Thus Vance is reborn as a female avenger in *The Furies,* and Marlon Brando's Bud is reborn as a husband in *The Men.*

In order to understand the logic of racial substitution in these films, we must unpack the complex ways that gender operates in these genres. In a 1957 interview, *Furies* director Anthony Mann opined on women in westerns:

> [Borden Chase and I] always throw a woman into the story, because without a woman, a western wouldn't work. Even though she isn't necessary, everyone appears to be convinced that you cannot do without a woman. But as soon as you get to fighting against the Indians, or to the chase scenes, or when the heroes discover the traitor, then the woman gets in your way. So then you have to come up with a clever trick to send her somewhere so she won't be in your way, and you won't need to film her. It's sad to say, but women do not have much importance in westerns . . . On the other hand, maybe someone will make a western some day with a woman as the main character.[3]

Mann, who had begun his film career as a director of B-movie film noirs and cemented his reputation as a director of westerns in the 1950s, reveals here several levels of assumption about genre, about action, and about gendered bodies onscreen. He understands "fighting against the Indians" as a male activity undertaken in defense of absent women and suggests that the spectacle of the chase depends upon a form of physical prowess and control unavailable to the female body. Certainly the set pieces Mann describes—fighting, chasing, and discovering treachery—in which "the woman gets in your way" are at the heart of the western as a genre. These tense and pleasurable spectacles are also the most central to the genre's construction of vulnerability onscreen. Mann's insistence that the female character must be hustled offscreen in these moments belies her centrality to the forms of violence, flight, and betrayal in this genre. Westerns rely upon but remove women, figuring them as symbols of a more widespread vulnerability. But Mann's point also illustrates the logics of erasure and replacement in U.S. culture's depiction of femininity. Most strikingly, perhaps, Mann seems unaware that he himself directed a western with a female protagonist in 1950. Perhaps Mann does not consider *The Furies* a western; Robin Wood labels it "part western, part woman's melodrama, part excursion into Freudian psychoanalytic material."[4] Wood is right about the film's hybridity, but these categories are not as separate as he seems to assume. The western is always part melodrama and part investigation of the characters' and the culture's murky unconscious, more implicated in the melodrama's emotional excess than Mann likes to acknowledge.[5] Certainly, the returning-veteran films of the postwar years—*The Best Years of Our Lives* (1946), *The Men* (1950), *White Christmas* (1954), *Sayonara* (1957)—acknowledge their debt to the romance plots and contested domestic spaces of the woman's film.

In 1950, Stanwyck was a four-time Academy Award nominee, and Brando was at the start of a promising career, having just completed a two-year run as Stanley Kowalski in the debut production of *A Streetcar Named Desire* on Broadway opposite Jessica Tandy. Brando's emergence into film stardom in *The Men,* a position his performance as Stanley in the 1951 film version of *Streetcar* (Elia Kazan) would solidify, figures the iconic man of the new decade as a darker, more troubled figure than his prewar screen counterparts. Meanwhile, *The Furies* (1950), with its lurid violence and sadomasochistic desire, finds Stanwyck and Mann creating out of the archetype of the western heroine the blueprint for the female transgressive power that I will call "resistant vulnerability." These two films, disparate as their ideological strategies appear, show that popular culture nearly always defines vulnerability by replacing one body with another—thus the child Debbie in *The Searchers* stands in for the bodies of her murdered mother and sister, and the dying female sniper in *Full Metal Jacket* replaces the bodies of the dead American soldiers. This logic of replacement works differently in the two films; *The Furies* conflates the oppression of its ethnic minorities with the subjugation of its female protagonist, while *The Men* replaces the idealized nonwhite body with the specific kind of white masculinity valorized by Method acting.

Like the domestic novel tradition and the "woman's" films of the 1930s and 1940s,[6] *The Men* and *The Furies,* despite their generic and tonal distinctions, construct vulnerability around distinct conceptions of "home." While the characters of *The Furies* refer to their contested home as an "empire," *The Men* provides a deeply ambivalent portrait of postwar suburbia and its inability to provide a home to the returning veteran. *The Men*'s bitter, alienated protagonist exemplifies an emerging style of masculinity marked by Brando's identification with countercultural politics, fluid sexuality, and notions of acting as a craft. Brando, of course, was an early and prominent example of the Method acting taught at the Actors Studio. The debate in film studies about the politics of the Method falls into predictable lines, with some arguing that the Method poses a real challenge to gender norms and others suggesting that it "enforces the passive habits of viewing associated with realism and with bourgeois ideology in general."[7] Of course, this is a commonplace debate in cultural studies of popular film; however, Method acting, like continuity editing and linear narrative—which have also been accused of reinscribing patriarchal power dynamics—is a "realist" artistic strategy but also, as we will see in the next chapter, a vehicle for some fairly transgressive investigations of male vulnerability.

Method Acting and Film Realism

The Men shows how resistant male vulnerability is written into the DNA of Method-acting masculinity, particularly as practiced by Brando and inheritors of his style like Robert De Niro, Sean Penn, and Vincent D'Onofrio, whose performances in Vietnam films of the 1970s and 1980s I investigate in the next chapter. "The Method" is a system of actor preparation popularized in the United States by Lee Strasberg and associated with the Actors Studio, founded in 1947 by Elia Kazan, Cheryl Crawford, and Robert Lewis, where Strasberg taught in the 1950s.[8] Based on Konstantin Stanislavski's "System," codified in his trilogy *The Actor Prepares, Building a Character,* and *Creating a Role,* the Method encourages actors to use the raw material of their own memories and experiences to create psychologically plausible characters on stage or screen.[9] Through a series of exercises and work inventing a background for the character, Method actors attempt to disappear into their characters using a process Strasberg labels "affective memory."[10] While performances like Stanwyck's get their power from clear, declarative readings of dialogue and the deployment of iconic imagery, the Method's reliance on the hidden emotional work of actor preparation and its preference for deflection are exemplified by Brando's buried face and mumbled dialogue in his first hospital scene in *The Men.*

Method acting has enjoyed a long run as the primary acting style taught in American theater departments, and its attention to realist detail and elevation of emotional authenticity have made its conventions the primary markers of realism in U.S. film.[11] Arbiters of middlebrow taste like the Academy Awards and film critics from Pauline Kael to Roger Ebert have celebrated Method performances so consistently that the majority of film and television audiences seem to conflate "good" acting with the specific markers of the Method—a combination of nuance and raw emotionalism that American audiences are trained to understand as "real." In addition to codifying a set of visual and vocal performance strategies, the rise of Method acting in postwar America also helped to solidify acting as a profession and a craft, as an artistic form in its own right. Braudy argues that "post-war ambiguity about the actor's authority [is] rooted in the fragility of male self-definition,"[12] and, from its earliest moments, the Method has been associated with male actors and codes of masculinity, despite the importance of female actors like Uta Hagen and Cheryl Crawford to the Method's development and dissemination. As we will see in chapter 4's investigation of queer vulnerability in 1990s American film, the Method becomes so effectively sutured to our sense of vulnerability onscreen that female actors most associated with the Method (such as two-time Academy Award winner Hilary Swank) win acclaim for "masculine" performances that depend on very traditional notions of gendered vulnerability. Meanwhile, the performances of female actors like Demi Moore, Linda Hamilton, and Sigourney Weaver, which do not attract the same critical praise as Swank's, offer the 1980s' and 1990s' most radical revisions of female vulnerability. Barbara Stanwyck's transgressions of gendered vulnerability could be rewarded in the 1930s and 1940s, but by the time the Method takes over the Academy in the 1950s, Stanwyck's performance style is no longer an available model of "good" acting. Having been nominated for Best Actress in a leading role by the Academy four times between 1930 and 1949, after her nomination for *Sorry, Wrong Number,* Stanwyck is never nominated again.[13]

The Method style embodied by Brando was merely the clearest example of a long historical trend toward greater "naturalism" in actors' performances, as James Naremore and others have shown.[14] This movement toward naturalism over a codified set of gestures, working from the inside out instead of the outside in, is most famously associated with Konstantin Stanislavski and his Method. Naremore associates the older tradition ("pantomime" tradition) with François Delsarte, saying that in the last quarter of the nineteenth century the Delsarte System was "so deeply embedded in the culture that a good many actors could be described as Delsartean whether or not they ever studied him."[15] The "cultured" style of diction, pronunciation, and carriage taught by Delsarte's system remained influential long after Stanislavski's Method replaced it as the primary model of acting as a craft.[16] Naremore challenges the dismissal of "stagey" acting and the celebration of naturalistic acting, pointing out that "[Stanislavski's] own 'theory' had been little more than a distillation of commonplaces that governed Western theater since the seventeenth century, combined with strictures against pantomime and a series of training aids adapted from behaviorist psychology."[17] But to describe the semiotic, Delsartian model as "bad" and the psychological, Stanislavskian model as "good" is merely to place value judgments on a historically specific set of codes. If we watch these codes change, we can see how cinema constructs male vulnerability onscreen post–World War II and how it becomes sutured to faces like Brando's and De Niro's. But while the Method comes to be associated most intensely with male actors and a specific kind of rough-hewn masculinity, the Method performance was not the vehicle for signifying female strength onscreen.

When Mann speaks of shuffling the female character offscreen at moments of conflict or heightened emotion, he assumes a sentimental vulnerability in which men perform violence in defense of offscreen women. But his own 1950 film provides a bracing example of resistant vulnerability in Vance, who wields the weapons, drives the plot, and refuses to be driven offscreen. Analyzing both Brando's and Stanwyck's performances—Brando at the beginning of his film career and Stanwyck in the middle of hers—and investigating the visual and narrative structures of these underanalyzed films reveals the early construction of vulnerability onscreen at two levels: the narrative structures of these films trade in sentimental vulnerability, while their iconographies suggest something more complicated. At both levels—narrative and iconographic—these films rely on strategies of displacement that will become the language popular culture uses to talk about vulnerability. Both films structure their narratives and their emotional arcs around the search for home—its boundaries, its currency, and the possibility of ever returning to it. Whether that home is *The Furies*'s cattle ranch in the American Southwest or the domestic space and national family from which *The Men*'s injured veterans are exiled, the films work out the tension of banishment through the death of an idealized, sacrificial Latino character. In terms of the vulnerability juncture, contra Mann's suggestion that "the woman gets in your way" when your characters "fight against the Indians," nonwhite characters function as conduits and proxies for the relationship between violence and gendered vulnerability. This troubling dynamic is not unique to these films nor to this historical moment; U.S. film history has been and remains a repository of the stories the dominant culture tells itself about race and gender. These stories vary historically, but these films are narratives of displacement—from a family home and from the land in *The Furies* and, for the orphaned Bud, former football hero and reluctant husband, from both postwar society and from the alternative space of male bonds.

These films and their radically different treatments of the star body raise questions about what constructions of vulnerability owe to the Method. Though Naremore reminds us that "all forms of actorly behavior have formal, artistic purposes and ideological determinants," he also acknowledges that association of naturalistic, Method performances with whiteness and masculinity: "Though it is true that movies have helped to foster a restrained, intimate style, it is wrong to assume that 'good' film acting always conforms to the low-level ostensiveness of ordinary conversation. As a general rule, Hollywood has required that supporting players, ethnic minorities, and women be more animated or broadly expressive than white male leads."[18] Debates about acting style are important to an investigation of vulnerability because they question audience access to the body and emotions of the performer and the extent to which we are invited in to (or denied access to) identification with the image onscreen. In contrast to Marianne Conroy, who sees Method acting in Cold War America as a precursor to postmodernism in its style-mixing and fracturing of highbrow and lowbrow tastes, I see the Method and the visual and vocal strategies it enshrines as both defensively "realist" and the central technique through which American popular culture will construct vulnerability onscreen in the second half of the twentieth century.

The Furies: Female Resistant Vulnerability

Despite its transgressive female protagonist and prescient focus on border disputes, *The Furies* has received surprisingly little scholarly attention. In a welcome departure from this critical neglect, Howard Hampton uses *The Furies* to frame the argument of his book *Born in Flames,* tracing a trajectory from *The Furies* to twenty-first-century examples of extreme violence such as *Kill Bill* and *Sin City* (2005). Hampton's criticisms of these movies' stylized, metafilmic excess—he calls their characters examples of "aestheticized cartoon narcissism" and their narratives "processed, third-hand vestiges of the real"[19]—allow him to praise the nearly primal engagement of *The Furies* with sex, violence, and the land. But I want to trace a different trajectory from *The Furies* to our current cultural obsession with violent spectacle. I see in *The Furies* not a more authentic deployment of violence and female rage but an early and rousing model of female response to pain onscreen, one that will develop into a new form of female heroism in late-twentieth-century U.S. cinema.[20] *The Furies* models both the logic of replacement at the center of sentimental vulnerability *and* the transgressive female power I will call "resistant vulnerability" when we encounter it in the 1990s. It's precisely the things that mar the film's artistic and ideological unity that interest me—its counterintuitive sympathy for the Latino "squatters," its eleventh-hour attempt to redeem its characters, and Stanwyck's strange, indomitable performance.

Mann's film is based on the popular 1948 novel *The Furies,* written by Niven Busch, who co-wrote the film's screenplay with Charles Schnee. Busch dedicated the novel to "My mother, Christine F. Busch, who has always wanted me to write a book about a nice woman—but who will, I am afraid, be disappointed once more." It is not difficult to imagine what definition of "nice" Busch means in this tongue-in-cheek dedication—the kind of woman who doesn't stab her future stepmother with a pair of scissors or defy social and sexual conventions as Vance does. Vance, with her masculine name and seemingly male will to power, announces in the film's opening scene her refusal to live by the rules that govern "nice" women. Set in the New Mexico Territory in the 1870s, the film opens on TC Jeffords's cattle ranch, The Furies. The film's first scene juxtaposes Vance with her brother, Clay, whose upcoming wedding is the ostensible reason for their father's return.

Wearing her mother's gown, Vance caresses a pair of scissors lying on the vanity from which she has taken her mother's earrings, which Clay warns will anger TC: "You know he's been particular about keeping her room the same as before she died." Clay catalogs their mother's possessions and the domestic space that serves as a gilded cage: "Mother had everything. Calling cards for a woman whose nearest neighbor was miles off. Jewels for a woman who never looked at herself in a mirror. Sunshades for a woman who never left this room." Clay sees these things as markers of a life that's not the one his mother lived, while Vance sees the jewels as markers of the position she wishes to claim as mistress of The Furies. They are, in Naremore's term, expressive objects,[21] and, along with the scissors that she caresses absently during Clay's speech, they mark both her similarity to and difference from the woman whose room Vance and Clay have invaded. Unlike her mother, Vance does look in the mirror and does leave the room, but not before arraying herself in the gown and jewels of TC's romantic partner. The scissors on the mother's vanity table represent the female domestic work of altering clothes and trimming hats, but in Vance's hands they are repurposed as a weapon. She strokes their long blades as Clay, looking at his mother's portrait, says, "I'm only surprised he hasn't hung a sign on this. 'Wifely property of TC Jeffords.'" The film subtly shifts the markers of femininity from their traditional ornamental function (represented by the dead Mrs. Jeffords's portrait) to markers of financial and social power when the jewels adorn Vance.

Vance's repurposing of the scissors is merely one example of this dynamic, especially when we consider Stanwyck's performance, which is at odds with the narrative's treatment of the character. This disconnect stems from Stanwyck's physicality and vocal cadences, separating Vance from the narrative of female fragility that the film's plot might otherwise suggest. One is tempted to imagine a Method-style backstory study of the character—Freudian dynamic with her father, masochistic desire for her lover, the lynching of her childhood friend—but Stanwyck's performance resists any suggestion that Vance is damaged by these circumstances. What might at first seem to the twenty-first-century viewer a lack of psychological complexity in the performance can be understood instead as a refusal to use the traditional markers of female vulnerability to situations (domestic violence, romantic disappointment, a beloved's murder) that might usually be seen as destructive to female subjectivity. Here, the pre-Method style becomes a vehicle for challenging and suggesting alternatives to a sentimental vulnerability that would see Vance as emotionally or psychologically fragile. We can see the iconic (as opposed to psychologically realist) performance Stanwyck adopts for Vance in the scene where TC returns to The Furies. After an absence of some months, TC returns to find Vance dressed in her dead mother's gown and gives her a diamond necklace. "To go with her earrings," he quips, positing the necklace as the completion of the matched set that will "brand" Vance as both heiress to The Furies and a romantic object for him. Taunting Clay, who has been gifted the pearls Vance rejected, Vance holds the diamonds up to her throat—not draped, as the necklace might lie if it were fastened, but across her throat in a straight line.[22] In this moment, Vance looks in the mirror at the diamonds and declares "I like being TC's daughter" in Stanwyck's famous tone—husky, confident, with volume rising slightly toward the end of the line but with pitch lowering. This line reading—typical of Stanwyck's vocal performance in other films as well—differs from the upward lilt at the end of a sentence, a verbal tic of many post-1970s ingenues. The shift in actor training from a focus on voice and physical movement to psychological and emotional work that took place in the mid-twentieth century accounts, in part, for this distinction. Stanwyck's is merely one example among many of the clear, declarative vocal style that late-twentieth-century audiences no longer associate with female stars. Stanwyck's verbal confidence and mastery, as opposed to the deference and fragility associated with the upward lilt, are mirrored by her facial expression in the scene, a triumphant half-smile. Stanwyck's eyes are slightly smaller than is typical for ingénues in post-1970s Hollywood; along with her thick eyebrows, high cheekbones, and strong jaw, they create a visual spectacle that the viewer is trained to read as strength and defiance.

Although the bond between TC and Vance in this early scene unsettles the viewer with its incestuous undertones, Stanwyck's performance reveals none of the tension around the issues of land ownership, race, and class that will animate the film's central conflict between father and daughter. The diamond collar that marks her as "his" is at this point in the film inextricable from her own claim to the land, and Stanwyck's smile in this scene shows an unapologetic embrace of

Figure 3 Vance with her father's jewels

class privilege and whiteness. That privilege, and Vance's power within the film's narrative, become more complicated as TC's two rivals for her affection, Juan Herrera and Rip Darrow, try and fail to stake their own claims to the land and to Vance's body. The Production Code Administration (PCA) of the Motion Picture Association of America (MPAA) appeared to intuit something of the film's transgressive power. However, as we will see throughout this study, when faced with female power, patriarchal culture polices female desire more often than it comprehends or challenges the more genuinely subversive elements of the film and Stanwyck's portrayal of Vance. The relationship between desire and power is complicated in the film, operating under the competing models of masochism and capitalism, but in both cases, the censors police surface desire while leaving deeper connections between desire and power intact and unnoticed. In a PCA file riddled with complaints about the film's "brazenly lustful kiss[es]" and an obsession with the "open-mouth kiss" as a cinematic marker of an "illicit sex relationship," the censors seem only mildly concerned with the sadomasochistic tenor of the central romantic relationship between Vance and Rip. And they appear unconcerned about the incest narrative clear enough in the film to be noticed by the *Los Angeles Daily News*, which describes the relationship between Vance and TC as "somewhat incestuous."[23] In a May 18, 1949, letter to Hal Wallis, Joseph Breen demands script changes to alter the sadomasochistic dynamic that he rightly describes as central to the film's romantic coupling: "The repeated routine of Rip physically assaulting Vance before becoming romantic with her seems to us on the brutal and lustful side, and, it seems to us, could even be interpreted as possibly suggesting a bit of sadism."[24] Given the heat with which Breen and his office complain about the open-mouthed kisses that had Wallis and his production at tongue-in-cheek war with the PCA,[25] his hedging indicates something beyond his stated objections. It "seems" to Breen that the "routine between Vance and Rip in which he hits her and then kisses her" *could* be interpreted as *suggesting* sadism. Breen misses entirely that this dynamic cannot merely be excised from the film's script because the interconnection between violence and sex—indeed, between violence and the formation of the white, landed, nuclear family—gives the film its narrative drive. This relationship to violence reveals Vance as less a precursor to Tarantino's Beatrix Kiddo than an early model of the 1980s male action hero, whose masochistic displays of bodily endurance have been of such interest to film studies.[26]

The PCA's few qualms about the film's onscreen violence center on Vance's scissor-flinging attack on Flo, the interloper seeking to marry TC for his money, but the way the film handles the violence between Rip and Vance can show us something important about the growth of Vance's power and its dependence on her counterintuitive response to Rip's assault. After Rip ignores Vance's invitation to call at The Furies—and to sample a cake Vance has made, in direct contradiction to her usual disdain for pursuits marked as "feminine"—she rides into town in a fury and confronts him at his saloon, the Legal Tender. The blocking and camerawork of this sequence, as well as the performances—particularly Stanwyck's—reveal the film's interest in separating Rip's violence from the display of female fear or suffering that would traditionally attend it. Looking at the mirrored encounter between Vance and Rip later in the film allows us to see the ways it highlights Vance's movement toward both visibility and the financial and verbal power usually coded as male.

This first scene's camerawork keeps the viewer at a distance from the violence of Rip's assault on Vance and hides her face throughout most of the attack. Thus we only see Vance's face when it is composed and only hear her voice when it appears confident. Vulnerability's construction onscreen depends heavily on the face, but Mann withholds close-ups of Stanwyck's face during this sequence. When Vance enters Rip's office, the camera captures them in a deep-focus long shot, facing one another. "How clever of you," he says, "smart as a whip." Without further warning, he slaps her twice, then grabs her shoulder, which leads to a long struggle from which Mann's camera keeps its distance. He flings her onto a couch at the front of the frame, where she sits with her back to the camera. Throughout this sequence, her face has been at least partially obscured, which draws the viewer's attention to her flailing limbs and to his face, which expresses a mixture of frustration, anger, and mockery. When she charges toward him again, he pushes her face into a bowl of water, declaring, "Act like a child and I'll have to treat you like one."

If her father treats her like a lover, this suitor treats her like a child, punishing her "tantrums" physically and "rewarding" her for submission to his edicts. After she's dried her face, Vance picks up the cake she's baked him, her sly smile implying that she will smash it in his face. He catches the cake, and they engage in one of the "lustful" kisses the PCA found so objectionable. While her failure to smash the cake appears to signify a loss on her part, her convention-defying presence in his saloon and the PCA-offending passion of her response to his advances imply that the kiss was what she was after from the start.

The interconnection between violence and sex is not new, nor should the assumption that women are children to be punished and rewarded by men surprise viewers familiar with the film and advertising cultures of the 1940s and 1950s. The most transgressive elements of this, though, are the clarity of Vance's masochistic desire and the ways that this scene (set in the "Legal Tender") makes violence and desire inextricable from the use of currency. The film's opening crawl promises that *The Furies* will tell the story of "men who rule their lands like feudal lords," and, indeed, the film centers its investigation of the transition from feudal practices to a new economy around the body of its female protagonist and the male characters who are her lovers, antagonists, and proxies. While the three central male characters are *simultaneously* Vance's lovers, antagonists, and proxies, Rip's claim on her affections most explicitly links money and love to the violence that will be its price. The different kinds of currency favored by father, suitor, and friend map onto the relationships Vance shares with each, and each is tied to a very different conception of land ownership. TC's preference for paying bills with his self-named IOUs rather than currency mirrors his ego-driven claim to The Furies and his anger at the Latino population contesting his rule; TC wants the Herreras gone because the squatters constitute a "cloud on the title" to The Furies. Meanwhile, Rip's attempts to use the banking system to wrest from TC a contested piece of The Furies—the "Darrow Strip"—mirror his reliance on "legal tender." Juan's relationships to the land, systems of exchange, and Vance herself are the most organic of the three men's, which signals the film's investment in the legitimacy of his claim to the land but also its troubling use of Juan as a model of "authenticity" without allowing him to become a genuine alternative to either TC or Rip. Though the film certainly deviates from the captivity-narrative tradition by asking its audience to invest emotionally in the Herreras' claim to The Furies, it shies away from the novel's full engagement with the politics of interracial love. In Busch's narrative, Vance marries Juan; when TC hangs Juan, he widows his daughter. The film, never quite willing to validate Juan's claim to the land, cannot suppress the darker embedded narrative that the Herreras' presence on The Furies invokes.

If the viewer were under any illusion about the film's distrust of money, she needs only turn to the scene that most explicitly connects hard cash to the value of Vance's body as a commodity. When Rip finally agrees to call at The Furies,

TC offers Rip a choice of fifty thousand dollars in cash or Vance's hand. Rip takes the money; the fifty thousand dollars that will be her dowry if she chooses a man of whom TC approves, here the price of Vance's dignity, also buys her final freedom from the constraints of female fragility and its conventional treatment in Hollywood film. When Rip accuses Vance of not being "ready to marry—me or anyone else—because you're married already, to The Furies," her back is to the camera. As in the scene in the Legal Tender, when Vance is off balance, we don't see Stanwyck's expression. TC approaches, and, with her back still to the viewer, she declares, "TC, we've been taken like a couple of suckling pigs. He hit me, and no one else ever did before. He made me cry, and no one else ever did before," which prompts TC to say, "Welcome home." If we take only the film's dialogue and narrative arc into consideration, this moment highlights Vance's vulnerability. She's taken a risk pursuing Rip against TC's wishes, a romantic humiliation made more potent for its bald assumption that Vance, for all her independence, remains a commodity to be traded by men. But Stanwyck's performance in the scene offers an intriguing possibility for the ways that vulnerability—here both economic and social—need not be understood as either final or debilitating. TC's offer of "home" comes after he's forced her to voice the sadomasochistic tenor of her desire for Rip. But as we will see in the second half of the film, the next time Rip hits her, it doesn't make her cry.

In the second half of the film, once Vance and Rip are on the same side of a plan to ruin TC and claim the title to The Furies, the sadomasochistic dynamic of the relationship remains, but Vance's power within it has increased substantially. Now wearing the diamonds that marked her as TC's daughter around her neck, Vance commands both the camera and Rip. They face one another, and a series of over-the-shoulder medium two-shots shows the viewer each of their faces in turn. "You'd like to hit me right now, wouldn't you?" she asks with a glint in her eye. The camera flashes briefly to his face: "I would." "Go right ahead." As he slaps her, the camera remains on her face, which doesn't change from a self-satisfied smile. "Now you'd like to kiss me, wouldn't you?" "Yes, I would," he says softly. She approaches, sliding her arms around his waist. "What's in it for me?" she murmurs as she leans in to kiss him. Here, the camera is on her face for the entire scene except for one medium two-shot of his face early on. It's she who controls the kiss, she who breaks away. For all of the PCA angst about "brazenly lustful kiss[es]," the censors seem not to comprehend the truly radical element of the Vance/Rip interaction. As she realizes she can absorb a blow and not lose power, her ability to best her father financially, emotionally, and legally increases. The myth of female frailty is here *exposed* as myth. And the "furies" of the film's title comes to signify more than the name of the Jeffords ranch; it represents a chaotic and specifically female power unleashed by violence, embodied by two female avengers: Vance and Señora Herrera, Juan's mother.

Keener than a Knife, Quieter than a Gun

The film's first potentially fatal attack comes at the moment when Mann seems close to acknowledging the incestuous spark at the base of Vance's relationship with her father. TC's engagement to Flo ignites the first round of violence in a rapidly escalating war between Vance and TC and also strips Vance of the position of privilege the film had previously afforded her. Vance's newly precarious position lays bare the logic of both racism and misogyny undergirding this "border empire" and sets up the film's violent second act. Vance attacks her father's fiancée with a pair of scissors, disfiguring her and slashing, figuratively, through the safe space of the screen and the image of the heterosexual couple as the head of the family unit.[27] Busch's novel focalizes the confrontation between Vance and Flo through Vance, and the dialogue between the women more explicitly references the incestuous undertones of the Vance/TC relationship. Flo suggests that she might love TC, "though in a different way" than Vance. "In the words 'in a different way' Vance recognized the pulse of something new . . . With a fierce effect she lashed out at this new, dangerous thing." As she does in Mann's film, Flo represents a threat to Vance's power, but "this new, dangerous thing" is, in Busch's dialogue, explicitly romantic and sexual. Flo hints that there might be "a woman who can do more for him even than you." Answering Vance's confusion, Flo admits, "We might as well understand each other. I mean a woman who can go to bed with him." This exchange prompts Vance to reach for the scissors, which Flo wrests from her grip. Vance lies in wait until Flo is asleep and then stabs her, having chosen the scissors because they are "a perfect weapon, keener than a knife, quieter than a gun. Ever since she had held them that afternoon she had remembered and loved their smooth, balanced weight in her hand." Mann's film distills these scenes so that the work done by Busch's dialogue and descriptive language is accomplished visually.[28]

The confrontation takes place in the dead Mrs. Jeffords's bedroom, a space that the film's first scene had framed as a domestic prison. Here, it is refigured as a seat of female power over which Vance and Flo must struggle, symbolized by the scissors that wait on the dressing table. TC enters the bedchamber and interrupts a tense confrontation between Vance and Flo about the love and money they both desire from him. Once TC appears at the door, Mann's camera stays on him, withholding any view of Vance as TC and Flo reveal their plans to wed and bring in a man to "take the load of running The Furies from [Vance]." The way this scene is shot and edited, along with Stanwyck's performance, conflates the two forms of displacement at issue in the scene—the eviction of the Herreras and Vance's ouster as manager of the Furies. Her chin starts to shake, and her eyes fill; the camera holds its medium close-up on her so that when Flo says blithely that the Herreras will be evicted, her look of pain and terror signifies the Herreras' dispossession and her own, as if they are inseparable. Vance looks slightly off frame left and delivers her one piece of dialogue in response to these family-shifting revelations: "I've your promise the Herreras aren't to be touched." In theory, TC is the "you" to whom Vance addresses this charge, and we assume that her eye contact is directed at him. But the unusual framing of the camera in this sequence doesn't give us the eyeline match we expect, conflating TC and Flo's physical position in the same way that Stanwyck's delivery of the line sutures the pain of her own estrangement from the land to the Herreras' fate. Where we expect the eyeline match, Mann's camera cuts to a disorienting shot of the mirror behind Vance.

The shot forms a visual triptych, with the reflection of TC holding Flo on the right side of the frame, the reflection of Vance's back, with her hand reaching for the scissors, in the middle of the frame, and the side of Vance's body in front of the mirror in the left side of the frame. The future husband and wife hover in the mirror's reflection, whole, while Vance herself is split, her body standing upright while her hand searches for the "smooth, balanced weight" of the weapon. Flo says, condescendingly, "Remember, my dear, there will always be room for you at the Furies," and Vance strikes, hurling the scissors at Flo. But since this sequence alternates between medium close-ups of Vance and medium two-shots of the couple, when Vance flings the scissors, we don't at first know her target. The film makes far more explicit than the novel that it's the couple itself—the image of their hands joined—at which Vance lashes out. This visual strategy complicates Vance's motivation in the scene; she sees Flo as both interloper and rival, but the camera's refusal to separate TC and Flo in the frame implies that the nuclear family itself is a threat to the kind of primal power and rage that motivate Vance's violence.

If her previous power had rested on TC's approval, Vance's freedom here demands their total estrangement. Cradling the bleeding Flo, TC snarls at Vance, "If she dies, I'll kill you." But Flo doesn't die, and TC doesn't kill Vance, he kills Juan, whose dispossession the film has equated with hers. The camera follows Vance walking slowly, expressionless, down the stairs until she runs out the doors of The Furies toward the Herreras'. Though this is not the only time Mann's camera will follow Vance away from a scene of violence, Vance's flight from The Furies marks her first step away from the social and class privilege of her father's name; she is now displaced from the land in the same way the Herreras are. The abrupt reversal of Vance's fortunes clarifies a daughter's position in relation to the land—it depends upon her father's approval. The film attempts to equate this precarious position with the position of the nonwhite people whom European colonialism displaced, illustrating the logic of substitution the film will use to understand vulnerability in its second half: Juan's body for Vance's. Vance's violence against Flo leads to this exile, and the scene at the Herreras' is the only time we really see the film using sentimental understandings of vulnerability to characterize Vance.

Constructing Frames—Deep Focus and Racial Replacement

Vance's flight prompts TC to pursue her, hoping to avenge Flo's injury and finally evict the Herreras from The Furies. As TC and his men approach, Vance stands behind Juan, and he has to tell her there is "no need for fear"—the first time in the film we've seen Vance figured as someone who needs protection. After promising that Vance and the Herreras may leave unharmed, TC threatens to hang Juan for stealing a horse from The Furies. This confrontation is shot in deep focus, with Vance and Juan side by side deep into the frame and Señora Herrera in the bottom left corner of the frame, her grief-ravaged face in close-up. This frame composition mirrors the narrative's approach to the Herreras and the border disputes they represent. TC thinks that his possession of the title to The Furies justifies his violence toward its residents and deputizes him to lynch Juan in retaliation against Vance. Juan and Vance are technically the focus of this exchange—they are speaking, and it is Juan's body and Vance's pride that are at issue in the dispute. But while the viewer's eye is directed to these two, and Stanwyck's steely facial expression, Señora Herrera and her haunted eyes will not leave the frame. Juan's death erases him from the film's frame, but Mann's film engages in a more troubling erasure when we consider Juan's status in Busch's novel. The final cut of the film excises explicit reference to a romantic relationship between Juan and Vance; in the novel, they wed after Vance's flight from the scene of her crime. In Busch's narrative, where a significant amount of time passes between Vance's attack on Flo and TC's hanging of Juan, Vance imagines a courtroom where she is called to account for her crime and the people who would "stand up and shout, 'Lynch her!'"[29] Busch's use of the term "lynch" perversely reworks the history of racial terrorism against nonwhite people, imaginatively replacing the bodies of nonwhite men with Vance herself (and her vulnerability to the legal system). But, of course, Vance is not lynched in either the novel or the film; in both versions, Juan's death at the hands of TC and his lynch mob pays for Vance's crime but also for his romantic association with a white woman—a relationship the film refuses to really acknowledge.

Rather than see Vance humble herself in front of TC, Juan sacrifices himself in a moment Jim Kitses rightly identifies as racist caricature.[30] As Juan comes forward to fulfill his function in the film's racist system of signification, Mann's camera captures an inverted version of the previous three-shot. Now, Juan stands nearly beside his mother in the front of the frame, with Vance visible in the back of the shot, framed between them, replacing them in both the film's narrative and in its visual composition as the victim of this act of capitalist and racist violence. As Juan walks forward stoically to meet his fate at the hands of the white rancher's lynch mob, a grinning ranch hand poised to place the noose around his neck, the camera follows Vance on her horse as she rides away from the scene, promising vengeance against TC. The camera remains on her as she turns back to look, but only Juan's mother's cries signal his death. Since his body is offscreen at the time of the hanging, the emotions of the bystanders signify vulnerability onscreen. The sentimentalizing work of a close-up on the face is done by Señora Herrera, not Vance. In the moment of the hanging, Vance is doubly replaced by the Herreras—replaced on the scaffold by Juan and as mourner by Señora Herrera. But from this moment

Figure 4 Señora Herrera, Vance, and Juan

onward in the film, Vance herself will appear as the party injured by this crime, and her revenge against TC will be monetary.

Throughout, *The Furies* associates female figures—particularly Vance and Señora Herrera—with extremity, violence, and nonnormative sexuality. After Juan's death, Vance and Rip ally to ruin TC, but with their victory complete and TC's "own legal tender" on fire in the street, Vance forgives him. Here, at the film's end, the narrative refuses to punish Vance for her violations of feminine virtue—not even with permanent estrangement from either the patriarchal seat or the affection of the patriarch himself. While Vance seems to grow in determination and stature after Juan's death, TC seems diminished. Late in the film, staring moodily into the fire, TC admits, "I've been cold ever since that dawn I hung him." Juan has been dead, and unmentioned by any character onscreen, for half an hour of running time and months within the film's diegesis. While the film's dialogue never names the "him" to whom TC refers, the viewer understands this moment as a crucial shift in our perception of the character, laying the groundwork for his eventual redemption. This is Walter Huston's final film performance, and in this scene he mimics onscreen the form of emotional recall that Stanislavski's Method labels affective memory.[31] TC is physically cold as he stands before the fire, and that sense memory triggers the return of an earlier time he was cold—the morning he hanged Juan. Juan is no longer a person—a figure onscreen with whom TC, Vance, and the viewer has to grapple. Instead,

Figure 5 Juan steps forward

he's a trigger for white male remorse. Robin Wood calls the final reconciliation between TC and Vance unmotivated, problematic. But the logic of racial replacement that governs the film requires this reconciliation. Juan's sacrifice purges *both* Vance's crime against Flo and TC's crime against Juan, which has been reconfigured as a violation of Vance herself. Thus the race and border issues that open the film are subordinated to the question of vulnerability—which bodies are vulnerable, and in which bodies the film asks us to invest. Because while the film's removal of the Vance/Juan romance dulls the novel's critique of racism, the film's ending foregrounds race and gender in ways that the novel's ending does not. In Busch's novel, Juan's mother is killed before his lynching, in a raid on the squatters ordered by Vance herself, and the Herrera revenge on TC is meted out by male relatives. In the film, Señora Herrera, having replaced Vance as mourner, here replaces her as avenging angel. By allowing Señora Herrera to shoot TC at the end of the narrative, Mann's film very explicitly associates TC's death with primal female power, and with grief and vengeance, and with a violence that affects the author of a crime, not its proxy. Both the film's narrative and its gorgeously constructed frames posit Señora Herrera less as Vance's mirror than as TC's own wilder, freer double. And Señora Herrera's rifle, along with her laugh, trilling on the soundtrack as TC dies, proves you can't buy your way out of the problem of displacement and dispossession, not with TCs and not with legal tender. The Furies will have their price.

The Men: Method Acting and Male Vulnerability

The price of dispossession is paid in a different currency in *The Men,* one of scores of prestige films about returning veterans released by the major Hollywood studios following World War II. Leo Braudy sees a focus on "male weakness and frailty" in these returning-veteran films; indeed, the trope of male dislocation, both physical and emotional, remains an important facet of male vulnerability as I describe it in 1990s popular culture.[32] *The Best Years of Our Lives* (1946) is the film most often analyzed in this regard, but *The Men,* containing Marlon Brando's first screen performance and featuring paraplegics from a VA hospital in the roles of paralyzed veterans, makes this film an ideal site for an investigation of Method acting's reality claims. The film also allows us to see the actorly strategies and cinematic techniques that form the blueprint for male vulnerability onscreen in the second half of the twentieth century. The relationship between Method acting and male vulnerability is complex, but, while resistant vulnerability in women onscreen usually involves a refusal of the emotionalism associated with the Method, for male actors, the verbal and physical smoothness and mastery of the Delsartian model give way to a Method emotionalism that highlights male vulnerability. Most scholars interested in Brando's star image and in Method acting's influence on the film industry in the 1950s mention *The Men* only in passing and focus their attention on Kazan's *A Streetcar Named Desire* or *On the Waterfront* (1954). Focusing on *Streetcar* allows critics to see Brando's performance style in contrast to the more theatrical style of his Blanches (Jessica Tandy on Broadway, Vivien Leigh on film). Meanwhile, focusing on *Waterfront* allows critics to understand Brando's style of masculinity as an allegorical representation of Kazan himself in relation to the House Un-American Activities Committee (HUAC), before which he famously named names in 1952. Both *Waterfront* and *High Noon* (1952) are often read as allegories of the entertainment industry's confrontation with the HUAC, *Waterfront* justifying Kazan's testimony and *High Noon* celebrating industry resistance to the blacklist. *High Noon* and *The Men* were both penned by Carl Foreman and directed by Fred Zinnemann, a collaboration that was interrupted by Foreman's blacklisting after his refusal to name alleged members of the Communist Party to the HUAC.[33]

Looking at *The Men* can show us the Method codified on film as a series of conventions that signify vulnerability onscreen. This film contrasts Brando's Method performance not only with fellow actors modeling an older style but with actual paraplegics. If the Method offered actors a system to simulate reality onscreen—what we might call technologies of the real—*The Men* visually contrasts these technologies with "actual" reality, ultimately positing the Method performance as *more* authentic than reality.[34] Thus the nonactors' performances as Bud's fellow patients (which it is tempting to describe as at times wooden or amateurish) provide a counterpoint to Brando's actor-as-professional performance. By identifying the emotional, psychologically realist performance as genuine, Method acting contributed to a model of masculinity emerging in the postwar period that favored "authenticity" over invulnerability. *The Men* is an important and underanalyzed part of Brando's emergence as the model of an emerging style of masculinity in the 1950s and of the story scholars tell about Method acting and its relationship to the Cold War. This film shows us—in ways that *Streetcar* and *Waterfront* do not—how clearly this new masculinity forms in relation to women and nonwhite men, and how deeply indebted the masculine style of Brando, Montgomery Clift, and James Dean is to notions of the body's vulnerability. Both *Streetcar* and *Waterfront* allegorize Brando's new masculinities in the context of shifting social relations—between men and women, worker and union, the common man and the rising bourgeoisie. But *The Men* does this work most explicitly at the level of the body as a proxy for the male characters' value to the postwar nation—its failures, its malleability, and its status as a symbol. In terms of the film's plot, this means that Brando's Bud must be exiled from the male domestic space of the hospital ward, a space where "the men" recognize their expendability to a society that doesn't want to be reminded of war's costs. Although the fear of what the veteran brings home with him will be a primary trope of the Vietnam War films of the 1970s and 1980s, the seeds are planted in this film, which reveals an anxiety not only about whether the men can perform (sexually, romantically, socially) but also about whether the returned veteran brings home a diseased or dangerous masculinity. And in both this exile and this drama of expendability, paraplegic actor Arthur Jurado, who plays Angel, becomes the body worthy of emulation. As we will see in an analysis of the film's two central training montages, Bud's body comes to mirror Angel's and thus becomes the body worthy of reintegration into society—capable of functioning as a new model of masculinity. In the same way that Vance's body replaced Juan's onscreen after his death, Bud's body replaces Angel's. Thus, in what we begin to see as American cinema's consistent way of dealing with the spectacle of vulnerability, a nonwhite body is taken offstage and replaced with the new star body, here represented as white and male.

What Kristin Hatch calls the "turning point in the representation of the male body" in *Streetcar* actually has its genesis in *The Men,* where it's not (as it is in *Streetcar*) the two women's bodies against and around which Brando's virile, vulnerable masculinity gets defined, but the bodies of the other men, with his fiancée's body usually offscreen.[35] This definition of masculinity happens at the level of both the film's narrative and its iconographies. Scholarly fascination with *Streetcar*—understandable given the film's powerhouse performance by Brando and its tense, dog-whistle investigation of heterosexuality's allure and bankruptcy—coalesces around the way Kazan's camera treats Brando. Hatch suggests that *Streetcar*'s camera reverses Laura Mulvey's looking positions by "making Brando a feminine object of the gaze without offering a compensatory image of female beauty."[36] This alleged feminization of Brando influences critical discussion of *On the Waterfront* as well, with critics such as Paul Ryan identifying a "vulnerability" in the "touching softness" of Brando's performance as Terry Malloy. Critics circle around a similar set of words to define Brando's physicality, facial expressions, and performance style—"sensitive," "vulnerable"—terms that seem to indicate either feminization (the term Michael Schuyler prefers) or "sexual ambiguity."[37] Hatch labels this blend of hypermasculinity and vulnerability the "disruptive body," arguing that Brando's allure onscreen is caused by the "tension between his muscular build and his beautiful face."[38] As we saw in *The Furies,* the face is often the locus of cinematic constructions of vulnerability, so the tension between muscles and face becomes the paradigm for resistant vulnerability in male actors.

With the power of Brando's muscular body mitigated by his character's paralysis, *The Men* draws our attention instead to the details of Brando's performance and the visual and narrative strategies the film uses to propose the wounded veteran as "new" man. The question of whether "[Brando]'s position as the object of female desire undermines his masculinity," as Hatch suggests it does in *Streetcar,* becomes more complicated in Brando's performance as Bud, since the film structures its central romantic drama around the question of whether his injury compromises his position as object of female desire. For example, in one of the film's opening scenes, Dr. Brock (Everett Sloane) explains paraplegia to an anxious audience of wives, mothers, and girlfriends, including a surprisingly frank discussion about the possibility of a paraplegic's sexual functioning. But for most of the film's running time, Brando and Teresa Wright seem to be starring in separate, parallel films; Bud and Ellen share fewer than twenty minutes of screen time in an eighty-five-minute film.

Scholars like Braudy and Hatch see this "new" masculinity—most often discussed around stars like Brando, Clift, and Dean—as a rejection of old norms of masculinity. We can see this battleground drawn around the confines of the hospital ward that viewers tour along with Dr. Brock in one of the opening scenes of *The Men.* Dr. Brock approaches the beds in turn, speaking to each man, haranguing one, encouraging another. Each patient has gelled and coifed hair and answers in the confident patter associated with WWII-era radio announcers. "What do you want me to do, walk? I had enough of that in the infantry," one quips. "Everyone's a comedian around here," Brock mock-sighs; this image of the American soldier as jovial and confident even when injured forms an important baseline from which Brando's character and performance will deviate. Leaving his conversation with "jokester" Leo (Richard Erdman), Brock circles the bed, and the camera pulls back to reveal Angel, addressed by Brock as "Tarzan," shirtless, unlike the other men. The camera lingers on his defined muscles and handsome face as Brock massages his shoulders and encourages him about the bank loan for which he's applying to buy a house. Angel, we learn, is a model patient, Brock's greatest hope for the success of his tough-love treatments. The film signals Angel's status as good patient through Brock's clear affection and regard for him, cemented through its contrast with the viewer's introduction to Bud, whom we've only seen previously in a pre-credits montage.

The camera fades out on Leo's grinning face and in on Brando's, his hair mussed, his eyes fixed defiantly on Brock, spitting out his lines in his distinctive mumbling voice. "I'm just a bad patient, that's all. I'm sorry I'm spoiling your record," he says, scowling. Bud's rejection of Brock's "rules" for the ward enacts the unruliness that his paralyzed body cannot signify. Braudy argues that the "search for the new text and the new character" in the 1950s depended on "invigorating what was difficult if not impossible to assimilate: the individual, the inarticulate, the mad."[39] These are precisely the things that *The Furies* tried but failed to purge, represented by Señora Herrera. But here, the sacrificial Latino character works as a representative of the normative but still new style of masculinity that Bud tries, with varying degrees of success, to imitate. Angel's work ethic and emotional resilience in the face of injury mark him as both an ideal patient and a grown man—one still capable of being his family's patriarch. Bud's resistance to the ethic of self-knowledge and hard work Brock tries to instill in his patients is at once a plot device in the film's redemption arc and the first in a series of performances by which Brando will craft a star persona at odds with the style of masculinity modeled by the male stars of the 1940s.

Brando's rejection of midcentury masculinity was often framed by the 1950s press as "childish," a "failure to live up to the standards of adult masculinity,"[40] and in the first half of the film, Zinnemann consistently contrasts Bud's intransigence to other patients' success in the gendered project of adulthood. When Ellen succeeds in visiting Bud, who has told her not to come, he yells and then cries, covering his face with his arm. The other men return from the celebration of the marriage of one of the nurses to one of the patients, and Zinnemann's camera shows them in long shot, lit, laughing, with Ellen and Bud in shadow in the foreground of the frame, a moody counterpoint to the rowdy shouts of the other men and the legacy of chin-up humor in the face of suffering that Brando's performance leaves behind. Finally, Bud lets Ellen embrace him as he lies on the bed, his lip quivering just above her head. "Sure I want us to be happy, honey, but I don't know. I don't know," he says. Brando sounds genuinely plaintive, and the happy scene of his newly wedded fellow veteran appears as both an impossibility for Bud and a trap, since the "false hope" of regaining function in the lower half of the body has been identified by Brock as a danger to be avoided by the patients.

Scholars who study the Method and its relationship to Cold War–era U.S. culture are forced to complicate the assumption that the theatrical style's replacement by Method acting represents the triumph of the "real" over the stilted and the artificial. Bruce McConachie suggests: "Triumphalist accounts of the spread of 'the Method' in post–World War II America generally explain its success as the victory of natural truths over benighted allusions about acting."[41] If the Method trains actors to use the raw material of their own memories to create "real" characters onstage or onscreen, *The Men*'s use of paraplegic veterans for many of the supporting roles casts the Method's twin goals of professionalism and "authenticity" into greater relief. In fact, the publicity around the film at the time of its release touted

Brando's status as a near unknown as a further mark of the film's realism. Ted Anderson, the injured veteran who served as the prototype for Brando's character and as a technical adviser on the film, argued:

> Some have commented that they thought the leading part should have been played by a better-known or more polished actor than Marlon Brando. I cannot agree with this opinion. Too much polish in Brando's role would have stuck out like a sore thumb among the non-professional paraplegic actors . . . A Tyrone Power or Burt Lancaster in the main portrayal would have destroyed much of the realism; audiences would be constantly aware that they were acting the wheelchair role. With Brando, unfamiliar on the screen, audiences are apt to forget that he isn't paralyzed. As a matter of fact, it will be difficult for the public to dissociate the actors from the paraplegics, because Jack Webb and Richard Erdman, both unfamiliar screen faces, turn in excellent acting performances.[42]

Of course, what Anderson labels a positive lack of "polish" in Brando's performance is the studied Method formula of naturalistic facial expressions and vocal performance, while the style Anderson fears as "too much polish" is the older theatrical style championed by actors and directors such as Tyrone Guthrie and Michael Redgrave who lamented the ascendance of Method acting in the 1950s.[43] Dr. Brock was modeled on Ernest Bors, the neurologist at the Birmingham Veterans Administration Hospital in Van Nuys, California, where Brando prepared for the role. Patients from the hospital played most of the men in the ward; the most prominent of these in the film was Arthur Jurado. Jack Webb as Norm and Richard Erdman as Leo join Brando and Sloane as the only other professional actors in the hospital-ward scenes.

Many critics have suggested that "through its casting and performance, *Streetcar* staged a struggle between acting styles that enabled Method acting to become visible as a distinctive style."[44] This reading almost invariably aligns Brando's brooding, emotionally wrought performance as Stanley with the white ethnic working-class identity that separates the character from the dying aristocracy represented by Blanche and given theatrical and filmic life by the more "theatrical" or "finished" performances of Tandy and Leigh as Blanche. Much of the drama of the film's first half comes from Bud's decision to accept Brock's help and try to build up his strength. This decision, the film's narrative suggests, rises from his hope that he might yet wed Ellen. His transformation occurs onscreen in two training montages—one with Angel and one after Angel's death. In these montages, we see Brando becoming Brando, inventing the vulnerable masculinity that will make him famous as Stanley in the film version of *Streetcar*.

In the first training montage, Bud does assisted sit-ups in his hospital bed, clad in a long-sleeved pajama top, buttoned tightly to the neck. The camera remains stationary while he sits up again and again, the motion ending each time with his blank face and dead eyes in close-up, never making eye contact with the camera. He lifts weights while lying on his back in bed. Near the end of the montage, Bud sits on his bed, struggling to pull apart a chest expander, grimacing. The camera pulls back to a medium two-shot that reveals Angel next to him, shirtless, grinning and doing endless repetitions on a similar device with ease. This sequence, full of odd visual jokes and scored with a jovial track that encourages us to laugh at this discrepancy, figures Bud's Method moodiness as a joke, Angel's seemingly uncomplicated masculinity the goal. They cycle through a series of exercises, Angel eventually clad in the tight white T-shirt that will become Brando's signature in the popular press in the mid-1950s, performing each task faster and better than the struggling but improving Bud. The film's narrative contrasts model patient Angel, who works hard to recover and once again provide for his mother and siblings, with Bud, for whom the physical and emotional processes of recovery seem darker and more complicated. Visually, Angel is a model as well, his muscled torso providing the masculine body that Brando as Bud will come to inhabit.

Here, racial replacement enables the replacement of one model of masculinity—Angel's authority-respecting, family-oriented optimism—with another, more vulnerable model. But that replacement means that the white male star body will come to occupy the space in the frame and in the film's conception of masculinity previously dominated by Angel. Angel's death from meningitis at almost exactly

Figure 6 Angel coaches Bud

the film's midway point clears the stage for Brando to emerge as the new model of masculinity, but also serves as a chilling reminder that the problem of corporeal vulnerability is not a joke or a game. *The Men*'s earnest pursuit of the real and its early attempts to locate male vulnerability in the complex masculinity of injured war veterans tells only part of the story about society's failures to truly envision a kind of masculinity scholars so often label "new." Zinnemann's production notes housed at the Margaret Herrick Library tell a different, darker story about U.S. culture's inability to integrate this new masculinity into the gendered norms that were struggling to reassert themselves in the decades following World War II. On a sheet titled *"This is a sort of Roll of Honor,"* Zinnemann's notes describing the veterans who worked on the film indicate that of the three men who served as technical advisers—Ted Anderson, Herbie Wolf, and Pat Grissom—only Grissom lived to see the end of the Cold War. Zinnemann's last entry on Grissom reads: "last saw him in 1989." Zinnemann's last entry on Anderson reads: "suicide later?"; his last notation on Wolf reads: "suicide later."[45] The character death that serves as catalyst for Bud's emergence as the new model patient and prototypical body is here presented as a result of Angel's physical wounds, not any psychological toll, from which his character had always seemed immune. But though Bud will now mirror Angel's diligence and declare that "I'm going to be married standing up," the film's focus on the wounds of war shifts from Bud's paralyzed lower limbs to Brando's signature tortured psyche.

In the second montage scene, Bud alone cycles through the same series of weights, ropes, and ball-throwing exercises, only this time the long-sleeved shirts are gone and his shirtless torso has replaced Angel's, his muscles are revealed, and in parts of the montage, he wears the tight white T-shirt as he performs the exercises with the same speed and confidence Angel had. At the end of this montage, edited in the same three- to four-second shots and set to the same cheery score, Bud and Ellen ride together in a car now rigged so that Bud can drive. We see them at the construction site of a new house, see Bud learning to bowl. Rather than just revealing the construction of the male body onscreen, these images codify the construction of the very bourgeois identity that cultural-studies critics accuse popular culture of mindlessly reinforcing. The trappings of middle-class identity are only available to Bud after his body has replaced Angel's as the authentic and hardworking body, and the montage does not end until he is at the altar with Ellen, trying to stand. Bud can only imperfectly embody the suburban middle-class ideal; he can drive a car and buy a house, but the vision of American prosperity and the returning veteran's place in it has been too compromised for Bud's journey toward a position as husband to proceed without cost.

The Technologies of Vulnerability

Bud's physical transformation into a hard-bodied model patient and his marriage to Ellen are not the end of the story the film tells about middle-class America and

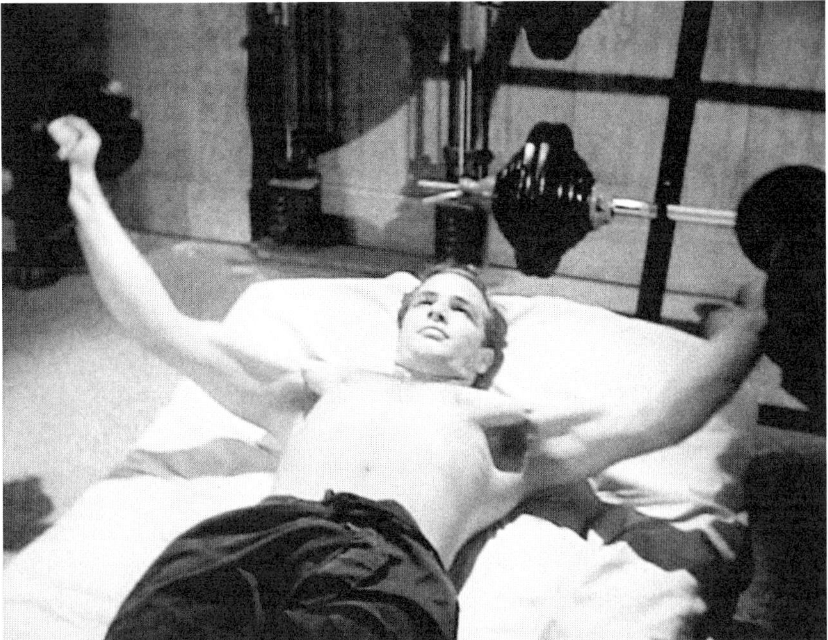

Figure 7 Bud commits to training

the plight of the returning veteran. After their wedding, Ellen tries to interest Bud in the details of the drapes and the lamps with which she has decorated their suburban home. When Bud opens their family album, she brightly announces, "They say no home's complete without one." But the picture of the nuclear family that "they" say completes the home might not be possible for these characters, and unanswered questions about Bud's sexual potency infect every frame of this scene. Seeing pictures of himself as a football star in the album, along with the squeaking wheels of his chair and the champagne that spills on the carpet, prompts a confrontation where we see the Stanley Kowalski side of Bud. He violently grabs Ellen's arm and bullies her into saying she is sorry she married him. Bud leaves the family home and returns to the ward, where he joins the men in a darkened room watching a boxing match. The men sit, looking at a screen that we never see, the camera alternating between shots of Bud staring at the television and the men staring at him—spectacle of the boxing ring mirroring the spectacle of the failed wedding night. Finally, Bud grabs a crutch and smashes the windows of the room, the first of a series of violent outbursts that will lead to his exile from the ward.

Discharged from the ward after a drunk-driving incident, Bud drives away from the hospital, toward Ellen and the domestic space of postwar suburbia; the camera captures his face in a close-up that gets tighter, his eyes moody and unreadable. Arriving at her parents' home, he wheels up the brick walkway until he hits the steps. She comes out to greet him, he accepts her help up the steps, and the camera stays in long shot as they enter the door. Although the scene's dialogue encourages viewers to hope that their relationship will be repaired and the nuclear family restored, this is an awfully ambivalent scene of homecoming. Staging the confrontation between Bud and Ellen on their wedding night and fading to the end credits at precisely the moment when Ellen welcomes Bud into the suburban family home elides the question of the paraplegic's sexual functioning with which the film introduced the hospital ward. It also closes the film having exiled Bud from the ward, the only real home the film identifies for him. Is this a radical acceptance of vulnerable masculinity, or a reactionary lament for its loss? Ellen and Bud's figures retreating farther back into the frame refuse to tell us, and Zinnemann's camera won't show us their faces.

The position of dependence in which *The Men* leaves its central character allows us space to wonder how we might define the technologies of vulnerability and how we see them gendered. I would here like to propose a set of terms that will guide the rest of this study and allow us to see how constructions of vulnerability change in the aftermath of Vietnam and the Cold War. Invulnerability onscreen is thus associated with what we have seen in Stanwyck's performance in *The Furies:* her particular style of female beauty (small eyes and strong features) and her distinctive performance style (upturned chin; vocal cadence that starts loud and high, moving to lower and deeper; clear, sharp enunciation of dialogue). Meanwhile, *The Men* constructs vulnerability onscreen through the details we have seen in Brando's physicality and performance: large eyes, wide, mobile mouth, and soft vocal cadences, originally aligned with the sacrificial Latino character in each film, eventually attaching themselves to Brando. In Brando, who is allowed overt displays of emotionalism denied the Latino characters, vulnerability is constructed both by his relaxed facial muscles, downturned eyes, and mumbled dialogue and in his outbursts of emotion after the wedding and in the ward. As Naremore reminds us:

> The Method was articulated in terms of "essences," but audiences looked at surfaces; for them, the much-talked-about new technique was associated with behavioral tics and a star image. Thus, while the Actors' Studio valued emotional freedom and individuality, it soon elevated Brando's work to an ideal. In subsequent years, a good many aspiring male actors approached the Studio like the shrine, hoping to make their performances more "real"; in practice, however, they often imitated the early Brando, who became godfather to several generations of players.[46]

In *The Men,* Brando puts a crack in the edifice of invulnerable masculinity. In the following chapter, we will see Robert De Niro, Sean Penn, and Vincent D'Onofrio drive a wedge into the crack, and in the third chapter we will see Steven Spielberg split it open.

Victimized, Violent, and Damned

IDENTIFICATION AND RADICAL VULNERABILITY IN *THE DEER HUNTER*, *FULL METAL JACKET*, AND *CASUALTIES OF WAR*

By the time Brian De Palma released *Casualties of War* in 1989, the image of the American soldier was cast by popular culture as neither invulnerable nor heroic. Twenty years of Vietnam films from *The Green Berets* (1968) to *Platoon* (1986) had created a new genre; as early as 1980, Peter McInerney argued in *Film Quarterly* that there existed a "Vietnam genre" that traditionally portrayed "the Vietvet as devil or saint, but each insisted he was damned."[1] If films like *The Men* could forsee a return to the suburban home and nuclear family, however ambivalent, by the end of the 1980s such a return seemed the stuff of fantasy or farce. The intense Method focus Marlon Brando had used to signify male vulnerability in *The Men* and the increasingly graphic violence available onscreen after the end of the Hollywood Production Code creates a new model of emerging male vulnerability in the Vietnam films produced and released between the end of U.S. involvement in Vietnam and the end of the Cold War. These films reveal a fascination with but also an anxiety about vulnerable bodies. Scholars have responded to this anxiety as if it reflects the politics of the war film as a genre. Charles Foran, for example, reads the 1979 Academy Award Best Picture matchup between *The Deer Hunter* and *Coming Home* as indicative of the still-unfinished battle about Vietnam's legacy in the American cultural imagination.[2] This is a commonplace of the scholarship on representations of the Vietnam War—that the political and cultural battles that coalesced on U.S. campuses during the war and on theater screens thereafter are never really over. These questions of politics and aesthetics depend upon how a given film constructs a few of the central questions of violence onscreen: What are the costs of violence? At whose door can its devastations be laid? Whose gendered body pays its price? All of these questions have to do with the truth-claims that various Vietnam films set for themselves, or the ones the audience sets as it sinks into the theater seats, or the ones critics bring as they pick up their pens and confront the uncomfortable place into which any war film puts the politically progressive film viewer.

Looking at three Vietnam films from the 1970s and 1980s—*The Deer Hunter* (1978), *Full Metal Jacket* (1987), and *Casualties of War* (1989)—we can see what happens when the Method-acting vulnerability established by Brando and other actors of his generation confronts the politics of gendered violence in the Vietnam War film. All three of these films contrast competent, "hard" masculinity with "soft" male characters. *The Deer Hunter* kills or maims these "soft" characters, Nick (Christopher Walken) and Steven (John Savage), and shifts its focus to Robert De Niro's Michael. *Full Metal Jacket* turns Steve / Nick into one character, Private Pyle, whose embodiment by Vincent D'Onofrio in his star-making role puts Method-acting vulnerability into direct contrast with more distancing performance models. Finally, *Casualties of War* makes this character the hero by casting sitcom star Michael J. Fox as PFC Eriksson and posits the masculinity usually at the center of the war film as depraved and grotesque. All three of these films triangulate male suffering through female figures—victimized Vietnamese women or American women left behind. Looking at them can show us how the cinema of the 1970s and 1980s helps to create distinctly gendered models of vulnerability that hijack audience identification and sympathy. In each film, the figure that represents an interim model of masculinity—perhaps best embodied in *The Deer Hunter*'s doomed, haunted Nick—expresses the film's own ambivalence about the extremes of "hard" and "soft" masculinity. This ambivalence gets voiced most clearly in uncertainty about how and where to focalize the experience of the soldier in war.

The uneasy politics of identification in each of these films depends on audience desire to identify with power while simultaneously sympathizing with vulnerability. In each case, the relationship between identification and vulnerability hinges on audience response to the representation of women. *The Deer Hunter* replaces Meryl Streep's Linda with Steven and Nick as the figures who most clearly represent the audience's investment in vulnerability. *Full Metal Jacket* employs a dual strategy, replacing the dead Pyle with a girl sniper as the locus of audience identification and sympathy. *Casualties of War* gives us the vulnerable male as a point-of-view character but then must use the body of a Vietnamese woman as a conduit for its anxieties about the vulnerability of that body. Of the three films, *Casualties* makes this move most explicitly and foregrounds the sexualized violence that is its instrument, asking "the question of whether the qualities of a good sergeant are also those of a good rapist."[3] Rarely is rape depicted both as a weapon of war and as a defining feature of manhood as explicitly as in these films. Thus the U.S. soldier, an intensely ambivalent figure in these films—victimized, violent, and damned—emerges as both rapist and victim, an image of masculinity that will continue to obsess popular culture into the twenty-first century.

The Deer Hunter: Class and the Costs of Masculinity

The Deer Hunter won Best Picture at the Fifty-First Academy Awards, edging out *Coming Home,* the other Vietnam-themed prestige picture of 1978. But *Coming Home* dominated the acting awards, with lead-acting wins for both Jon Voight and Jane Fonda. Of *The Deer Hunter*'s acting nominations—De Niro (Lead Actor), Meryl

Streep (Supporting Actress), and Christopher Walken (Supporting Actor)—only Walken won an Oscar, beating Bruce Dern as *Coming Home*'s jingoistic, traumatized returning vet. In each case, the Academy rewarded the gentle, meditative performance (Voight's Luke Martin and Walken's Nick) instead of the more truculent, traditionally masculine one (De Niro's Michael and Dern's Bob Hyde). This preference prefigures a trend in the scholarship dealing with *The Deer Hunter* in which scholars recognize the film's lyric force but balk at the style of masculinity that gives the narrative its power. And indeed, the film's goodwill with critics did not last long—critics and scholars since 1979 have accused the film of racism and misogyny, while others have insisted that it is a complex, class-based critique of U.S. involvement in Vietnam.[4] Still others have suggested that the multivalent readings the film makes available complicate critical attempts to discern its ideology.[5]

I want to suggest that the puzzle of the film's politics hinges on its intense, insistent emotion, notable even by the standard of the war film, a genre with a well-documented tradition of heightened stakes and maudlin excess. But while the film's detractors dismiss this emotionalism as easy or sentimental, when taken as a measure of the film's gender politics, it is both radical and complicated. Critical evaluations of the film seem to depend, in part, on what scholars make of De Niro's passionate, puzzling performance as Michael Vronsky. De Niro's name looms large over the antlers in the 1978 poster for the film. The critical and commercial success of *Taxi Driver* (Martin Scorsese) in 1976 and his turn as the young Vito Corleone in *The Godfather, Part II* (Francis Ford Coppola) in 1974 made De Niro the most recognizable of the actors in the film. But despite De Niro's importance to the film's marketing, the film itself lurches dramatically between different cinematic points of view, denying the viewer a stable source of identification with Michael at precisely the moments our perspective seems most sutured to his.[6] For all of the critical insistence that the shattered point of view of the Russian roulette sequence represents a tonal shift from the rest of the film, the long sequence in Clairton, Pennsylvania, that takes up a third of the film's running time insists on viewing the male characters as a group, not as individuals, and the viewer would be forgiven for assuming that the bridegroom, Steven, also bound for Vietnam the following day, is the film's protagonist. After all, Steven's coming separation from the male group through marriage forms the drama of this first act. While most scholarly studies take Michael's position as protagonist as a given, director Michael Cimino's refusal to settle on a single protagonist until well into the film shows how deeply ambivalent the film remains about the style of masculinity it ostensibly celebrates.

Most defenses of the film suggest that it is not fundamentally about Vietnam and that the sequences set in Da Nang or in Saigon are merely nightmare visions of the American psyche or visual placeholders for the universal horrors of war.[7] Peter Lehman, rightly skeptical of Cimino's own attempts to label the film apolitical, argues instead that *The Deer Hunter* posits Vietnam as essentially unrepresentable, either in speech by the characters in the film or by the American filmmaker in the war's aftermath.[8] Sylvia Chong insists that we *can* take Vietnam as the film's subject and still see its racial politics as a function of something more complicated than mere xenophobia. Through the visual style she calls "the oriental obscene," the film "creates an intimate relationship between the American and the Vietnamese soldiers that might not be supposed from a narratological or political viewpoint."[9] The intense fracturing and retrenchment of racial and gender categories when vulnerability is constructed onscreen mimics the "circulation" Chong posits in violence from Asian to non-Asian bodies. In order to see how this process operates, and how clearly it depends on audience identification with both power and vulnerability, I focus on two scenes that form the basis of critical debate about the film: the Russian roulette sequence in the middle of the film and the singing of "God Bless America" at its end. I also consider two moments scholars rarely mention: a scene of domestic violence on the home front and the moment when Michael's male caretaking appears to break down.

The War Is Already Home

Working-class Clairton, with its bars, steel mill, and Russian Orthodox cathedral, serves as a visual and emotional counterpoint to the Vietnam sequences in the film, but critics disagree about the exact nature of this dyad. Many have seen the two as fundamentally opposed spaces, noting the differences in camerawork and editing as well as mise-en-scène.[10] But understanding the film's structure and its odd pacing demands our recognition that the violence, disorientation, and loss of the Vietnam sequences have their seed in the opening Clairton sequence. Robin Wood understands the film's structure as a movement from "plentitude" to "impoverishment," but, convincing as this argument is in terms of the film's elegiac tone, the early Clairton scenes do much to complicate the picture of prewar life as an idyll.[11] After introducing the male camaraderie of the steel mill and John's bar, Cimino's camera introduces the viewer to Linda, a fresh-faced bridesmaid in pink organza rushing to prepare a tray of food, which she takes upstairs to her father. He sits slumped next to a window that lets in the late-morning light, and the camera pulls back from him as he mutters, "Go to fucking hell. I'll give every car in the town a flat tire, every goddamn one." As the camera pulls back to a longer shot and his figure grows smaller in the frame, we see that what originally appeared to be the camera's focus—Linda's father looking out the window—is a reflection in the mirror on the vanity table. This double framing means that when Cimino's camera follows Linda as she enters the room to try to help her father stand, we see him on the right-hand side of the window. The slight confusion caused by this violation of the 180-degree rule shows that the disorientation critics have ascribed to the Vietnam sections of the film actually begins in Clairton. The film's opening sequences established cars—particularly Michael's Coupe de Ville—as a visual representative of both the American dream and the promise of the open road. Linda's father's fantasy of doing violence to the whole town by flattening the tires of the cars provides a chilling contrast to Nick's claim that Michael's car makes him feel "safe."

The space of her father's house provides no such safety to Linda, who helps her father off the floor as he shouts about the "ocean of flat tires." Once upright, he calls her a "fucking bitch" and strikes her across the face, sending her sprawling to the floor. "All bitches," he growls, as the camera stays focused on Linda standing up and wiping blood from her mouth as she tries to soothe him. "Daddy, no—it's me," she says as he stands and hits her again. Unable to enact his fantasy of power over the town and its means of both production and escape, he must settle for doing violence to Linda. This violence matters because it shows that violence belongs to the domestic space as well as the Vietnam landscape and also because it physically marks Streep's Linda.[12] She appears bruised in the rest of the scenes in this first section, making her the clearest physical representation of violence's impact on the vulnerable body. If the bitter vet in the dance hall, unable to describe "over there" except to say "Fuck it," is Vietnam's hollow remainder, Linda is its harbinger—in the Russian roulette sequence, we will see Nick and Michael struck a series of savage blows to the face that mark them in the same way. The fact that her father doesn't seem to recognize Linda foreshadows as well Nick's fatal misrecognition of Michael in the film's last act.

While Nick and Michael, the two candidates for Linda's affections, are portrayed as kinds of men different from her father, Nick's reaction to Linda's bruised face is framed by the camera as a disturbing mirror of the scene in her childhood home. As the male friends and the other bridesmaids tease each other around Michael's car at the front of the double-wide trailer Nick and Michael share, Linda comes alone around the back, carrying a suitcase. Nick runs down to meet her, but his concerned queries—"Linda, what's the matter?"—shift as she evades him and runs for the trailer's door. The camera stays stationary, and Nick grabs her several times, saying he wants to ask her something. The camera cuts abruptly to inside the trailer, where Nick and Linda are visible through a living room window, their dialogue muffled but still audible. "Hey, wait a minute, God damn it," Nick says. "You don't walk away from me. What the hell is that on your face?" Belatedly, the viewer realizes that this inside-the-trailer perspective is Michael's view as he stands in the living room packing for the hunting trip the men will take before the wedding. The camera withholds the shot of Michael that establishes point of view until midway through Linda and Nick's conversation, once Nick's tone has softened and he promises Linda that she can use the trailer while he and Michael are gone. But the hunt Michael prepares for, while it appears to valorize Michael's role as leader and endorse his "one shot" ethic of the hunt, never quite establishes the baseline model of masculinity that Cimino wants to idealize. While the film's title—a nod to James Fenimore Cooper's 1841 novel *The Deerslayer*—and its marketing highlight the importance of the deer hunting sequences, their embrace of Michael's model of masculinity fits uneasily with the film's deep ambivalence about the viability of this model. Walken's performance as Nick grants extra narrative importance to the alternative kind of masculinity he represents, but the film can't afford to really invest in these alternative models. Robin Wood makes a convincing case that we can see Nick, not Michael, as the film's truest protagonist.[13] However, protagonists dueling for the narrative's focus matter less than the film's refusal to cement audience identification with a singular protagonist until more than halfway through. And it is in this regard that Walken's presence and performance in the film have been underanalyzed.[14] Many critics note the character's narrative and ideological importance, but I argue that looking at the details of his performance alongside De Niro's can show the ways the film constructs vulnerability as a function of femininity and a catalyst for audience identification.

The film's anxiety about the more vulnerable models of masculinity with which it flirts becomes explicit after the wedding, when Michael sprints from the dance hall and strips off his clothes, pursued by Nick. Michael lies on an empty, moonlit basketball court, and after Nick theatrically drops his tuxedo jacket over Michael's lap, they sit back to back discussing whether or not they'll ever come back from Vietnam. "You know something?" Nick asks. "The whole thing is right here. I love this fuckin' place. I know that sounds crazy, but if anything happens, Mike, don't leave—don't leave me over there. You got—you gotta . . . Just don't leave me. You gotta promise me that, Mike."[15] As Michael gazes earnestly toward his friend and makes the promise, it is also a contract with the audience, and the captivity-narrative search for Nick that structures the second half of the film will also become a search for the more vulnerable masculinity he modeled, to which Michael himself has little or no access. From the moment Michael runs naked down the streets of Clairton, the film seems to give the audience what it wants—identification with Michael's mastery, his clear position as leader, and his ability to harness violence in protection of more vulnerable men. But just at that moment, identification with Michael breaks down because the relevant dyad isn't Clairton/Vietnam but the *Deerslayer* masculinity represented by Michael in opposition to the new, more vulnerable masculinity embodied by Nick.

"Forget him, Nick"

Nick, after securing Michael's promise not to leave him "over there," won't let Michael leave Steven behind in the film's centerpiece, where Michael, Nick, and Steven are held prisoner in Vietnam and forced to play Russian roulette. Steven is the often-disregarded part of this triangle, but the Michael/Steven/Nick triangle comes in the Vietnam section to replace Clairton's Michael/Linda/Nick homosocial triangulation.[16] John Savage has certainly not had the subsequent career of either De Niro or Walken, but Steven is an integral part of the harrowing sequence that causes so much of the vitriol directed at the film. While it is tempting to suggest that Steven comes to stand in for the female, and that the trauma of the roulette game appears from his perspective (emotionally if not visually), the horror of the body's vulnerability does not repeat the Clairton scenes' strict gendering. Chong and others have argued that the visual style of the Vietnam sequences is fundamentally different from that of the Clairton sequences, and that "the Russian roulette scenes in *The Deer Hunter* cannot be understood through a lens that strictly separates reality from illusion."[17] In his crucial reevaluation of the film in 1986, Wood identifies the problem of realism as one of the key factors in dismissals of the film as racist and reactionary.[18] The ethics of representation and the perceived responsibility of "realist" film are the actual subject of this debate about *The Deer Hunter*'s racial politics and its purported jingoism. Wood reminds us that our understanding of "realism" on film remains historically contingent: "Even a cursory glance back over the past hundred years will show that yesterday's realism is today's stylization. Our notions of the realistic are very much dependent upon our familiarity with, and acceptance of, current conventions of representation—our ability to decode *automatically*."[19] Just as the shift in acting styles I traced in the previous chapter engrains the Method as both "good" and "real," the visual strategies that coalesce around the Vietnam War films of the 1970s and 1980s train audiences to associate vulnerability with the feminine while unmooring—in ways that are often radical and disturbing—our sense of identification with masculine power and mastery. And it's in this sense that Cimino's refusal to let us identify wholly with Michael in the Russian roulette sequence matters.

The roulette scene is structured in three parts. First, two South Vietnamese soldiers are forced to "play" while Michael, Steven, and Nick listen below, trapped in a cage half-submerged in water. Next, Steven becomes the victim of the game as Michael coaches him. Finally, Michael and Nick are forced to play and eventually mount an escape. During the first part of the scene, Steven alone gives in to the horror of the spectacle that the characters can see through the slats of the hut's wooden floor above them. Throughout most of the sequence, Steven's terror comes from sound, not sight. The viewer's position never aligns clearly with any of the captives'. Although Cimino's camera returns obsessively to the caged men below the hut, these shots alternate with shots of the roulette game taking place above, where the viewer's literal point of view remains unclear.[20] The roulette game's tension comes from the uncertainty—which viewers share with the characters onscreen—about whether pulling the trigger will release a bullet or the soft, dull click of the hammer hitting an empty chamber. The first part of the sequence makes Steven the locus of vulnerability onscreen; while everyone else above and below the floor of the hut remains devoid of any emotion but anger, Steven screams, hyperventilates, and needs to be comforted by Michael, who cradles him and repeats a litany of promises he can't keep: "I'm here, I'm here . . . Take it easy, Stevie, it's gonna be okay." Steven's lack of control over his body's boundaries and functions serves here to establish him as a victim of the action above, and ultimately to align him with the Vietnamese prisoner who is the first to die in the sequence.

Chong identifies Russian roulette as a psychic reworking of the famous "Saigon Execution" photograph, but it also throws the vulnerability of the body into unusually stark focus. Male vulnerability in war films is usually a function of the body's penetration by bullets or shrapnel. In the reworking of warfare as Russian roulette, the time between injury and death—the in-between space that we will see *Full Metal Jacket* and *Casualties of War* exploit to maximum emotional effect—usually the space where the body's vulnerability comes into greatest relief, is absent. The body is not penetrated except by a single bullet that kills instantly. The crying, screaming, and labored breathing that in other war films are the result of gunshot wounds here happen *prior* to a violation of the body's boundaries. And in this scene we see those markers projected onto Steven, relocated from injury to fear. In the second roulette game, Steven and Michael face each other at the table, and Michael's litany of encouragement becomes training in how to survive the game: "You can do it, Stevie." As Steven cries, seemingly unable to pick up the gun and mimic Michael's own mastery of his emotions, Michael barks, "Stevie, look at me! Do it! Do it!" When Steven eventually puts the gun to his temple and pulls the trigger, he follows Michael's orders, not the untranslated shouts of their Vietnamese captors. The viewer's point of view appears more stable in this sequence than in the previous one, but no less fraught with tension. In one respect, these moments suture audience identification to Steven—with him, we learn to trust Michael. But as Michael takes control of the game, he also begins to control the scene's point of view. When the guards drag Steven below, to "the pit" as punishment for delivering only a glancing shot to his own temple, the camera stays in the hut with Michael. Back in the cage below the hut, Michael turns his nurturing attentions to Nick: "Nicky, listen—it's up to us now. It's me and you." When Nick asks about Steven, Michael says to "forget him," that he "ain't gonna make it," which prompts Nick to accuse Michael of playing God. This exchange, which appears out of character for Michael, given the lengths to which he goes later in the film to save Steven, establishes the limited ability of cinematic point of view to reveal the "truth" about war or about the costs of vulnerability.

When Michael and Nick face each other in the final roulette game, Michael sits in the position at the table that Steven had occupied, but figuratively Nick comes to stand in for Steven as the most visible representative of vulnerability. While more stoic than Steven, he, too, eventually balks at the game and begins obeying Michael's orders, not those of their captors. As Michael shouts, "It's gonna be alright, Nicky! Go ahead, shoot! Shoot, Nicky!" the viewer, along with Nick, must trust that Michael's ruse to get more bullets in the gun will pay off. Michael's insistent coaching in these scenes establishes him as powerful, but the logic of the roulette game also compromises that power. He comforts and encourages the other men, but his literal role in the scene is to translate the shouts of the captors ("Shoot!") and to move the burden of agency off of Nick, Steven, and their captors and onto himself. And once the film has established Michael's effectiveness in this role, when he and Nick kill their captors and escape with Steven, Cimino's camera denies us identification with Michael's mastery. Once he delivers Steven safely to passing South Vietnamese troops, the camera loses Michael in a crowd of Vietnamese civilians evacuating down the road, not to find him again until Nick stumbles upon him in the Saigon roulette den.

"God Bless America"

Cimino uses the fall of Saigon to stage a more intimate rescue as Michael returns to fulfill the promise he made to Nick on the basketball court in Clairton. Upon finding Nick playing Russian roulette for pay and addicted to opium, Michael attempts to reach his blank-eyed friend with the same combination of nurture and command he'd used so effectively in the first Russian roulette sequence. But this time, his orders do not carry the same force of translation. His questions now are tentative, demanding recognition instead of action. "Nick, are you alright? Nick, it's me . . . Nicholas, what's the matter? Do you know it's me?" Michael asks. "Tell me 'It's Mike.'" "It's Mike," Nick repeats woodenly, but his misrecognition of Michael seems as complete as Linda's father's of her back in Clairton. As Michael and Nick sit facing one another in the final roulette game, the scene is a mirrored image of the last time they sat across the roulette table. This time, Nick sits on the right side of the frame, Michael on the left, and Michael pleads, "*Don't* do it." Michael's orders caused Nick to pull the trigger the first time they played this game, and the film suggests, of course, that Nick never really left that hut. But this roulette scene inescapably suggests that Michael put him there, and that Michael's style of masculinity represents a thing from which Nick cannot return. "Is this what you want?" Michael asks softly as he places the gun to his own temple—"I love you, Nick." Walken's impassive face shows the hint of a smile that marks his lack of recognition. But this second dull click seems to have awakened something, and Nick appears to recognize Michael. "You remember the trees, Nicky?" Michael asks. "The mountains—you remember all that?" Michael's reliance on this emotional trigger—Nick's memories of the deer hunt—says something about the film's own reliance on the deer-hunting sequences to cement audience affiliation with the masculinity Michael represents. But the idea of "home," and of America, that he tries to call up in this desperate moment doesn't provide Nick a way out, or a way home. Chong argues that "Nick's suicide complicates the critique that *The Deer Hunter* is a mirror that narcissistically reflects American identity and values and that ignores Vietnamese subjectivity . . . Even if we were to 'rectify' the representational politics of *The Deer Hunter* by restoring Americans to the role of aggressor and the Vietnamese to that of victim (as it 'really' was), we cannot escape the permutational logic that flows from the primal scene of violence."[21] Nor can Nick escape the violence that has its first shadow in the film in Clairton, where Michael takes Nick's body home.

Dismissed as jingoistic, defended as ironic, and analyzed as ambiguous, the final funeral sequence mirrors the film's own ambivalence about the kinds of masculinity represented by Michael and Nick.[22] After the funeral, the remaining members of the wedding party gather at John's bar. They chatter nervously as they arrange chairs around a table and gather the coffee mugs, plates, and beer glasses to observe this final ritual. Though he stands out visually, in his military dress uniform, Michael cannot stage-manage the community's collective grief. While Cimino seems to want to see the second deer hunt as the place where Michael's changed relationship to his masculinity becomes manifest, Michael cannot become the catalyst for the group's farewell to Nick. While at each of the other crucial junctures in the film it has been Michael's voice that others have followed, here it is John's voice, coming from the kitchen where he scrambles eggs for the group, humming the bars of "God Bless America" that the others pick up. Nor is Michael the translator, as he had been in the first roulette game. Meryl Streep's voice makes the song truly legible; her voice gives shape and definition to the words that become the script to this final ritual. Linda's voice remains dominant in the first verse of the song until it falters and the voices of the men rise softly to a B-flat on the final "home," which returns the song musically to the place where Linda began it. In the world to which the Vietnam veteran returns, Michael is no longer the catalyst or the translator. Although the final freeze frame of the group around the table, raising their glasses to Nick, captures Michael and Linda locked in the eye contact they'd been denied throughout the scene, the bittersweet tone of the image implies that Linda, and we, will be left only with the kind of masculinity Michael represents, not the fluid, liminal masculinity that died in Vietnam.

Full Metal Jacket: Gendering Vulnerability Female

The Deer Hunter's earnestness and emotional heat make it representative not only of a certain style of late-1970s American filmmaking but also of a kind of narrative sprawl, employing languid pacing and operatic imagery in contrast to the precision and emotional starkness of Stanley Kubrick, who released his own Vietnam War film, *Full Metal Jacket*, in 1987. Critics at the time of *The Deer Hunter*'s release were often frustrated with the film's refusal to signify in any politically legible way, and much of the scholarly work on the film reflects this frustration. *Full Metal Jacket* sidesteps at least some of this debate, given Kubrick's reputation for icy theoreticism and the film's satirical tone. But the film's gender politics—like its attitude toward the military machine it ostensibly satirizes—are more complicated than they first appear.[23]

Alone among the films I analyze in this chapter, *Full Metal Jacket* is often called "cold"—so often that James Naremore uses the term "aesthetics of the grotesque" to describe moments that elicit "shock, disgust, horror, obscene amusement, and perhaps even sadistic pleasure" and their "bearing on Kubrick's so-called coolness."[24] The film's coldness, usually considered a function of its formal elements and of Kubrick's famous demands that actors denaturalize their performances,[25] also depends upon Kubrick's point-of-view strategy, thwarting our attempts to identify with the ostensible protagonist. Most scholars take at face value Joker's (Matthew Modine) position as point-of-view character, likely because his voice-over posits him as such and the second half of the film bears it out. But the destabilizing effect of the first half comes, I suggest, from its unstable point of view. We can see this instability in raw moments of slippage where the radical vulnerability of the "soft" male or female body is the site of audience identification. Michael Pursell defends Kubrick's distance from his characters as an antipatriarchal move, arguing that "to see these men as protagonists in their own drama [would require us] to stop seeing them as victims of the roles and values dinned into them by [drill instructor] Hartman."[26] But Pursell's formulation here reveals the difficulty that both audiences and critics have seeing characters simultaneously as victims and protagonists. This film's radical potential lies not so much in its stripping bare of the boot-camp process of dehumanization—a move familiar to the boot-camp genre—but in its attempts to complicate what the term "victim" means. I will focus on three of the film's most iconic scenes, arguing that Kubrick's filmic techniques validate the equation of vulnerability with the female body.

Identification with Mastery Onscreen

Full Metal Jacket engages more explicitly than most films of its genre with the counterintuitive pleasures of emotional violence, an effect heightened by Lee Ermey's satirical turn as the sadistic Sergeant Hartman.[27] But the question of where the viewer's sympathies are engaged in this early section depends on a reckoning with Hartman's linguistic authority and our cinematic training in identification with power.[28] Hartman's verbal brilliance creates a real audience exhilaration placed in tension with the audience impulse to identify with the recruits who are the objects of his gloriously histrionic rants.[29] A wide range of scholars have outlined the ways Hartman's "profane poetry" constructs masculinity as a radical excising of the feminine, though tantalizing disagreements remain about whether this ends up as an embrace of misogynist masculinity or a devastating critique of it. I would merely point out that Hartman's position in the narrative as both ideological villain and primary generator of audience pleasure creates an effect similar to the one created by the film's ambivalent point of view throughout its first half.

In the scene that introduces the viewer to the characters, Hartman stalks around the Parris Island barracks insulting and renaming the recruits. After christening "Snowball," "Joker," and "Cowboy," Hartman approaches Leonard Lawrence (Vincent D'Onofrio), whose bulk and physical softness make him stand out among the other recruits. "I don't like the name Lawrence," Hartman shouts, "only faggots and sailors are called Lawrence! From now on you're Gomer Pyle." While enduring Hartman's litany of homophobic abuse, Pyle tries unsuccessfully to repress a nervous smile, which eventually leads to a violent confrontation with Hartman over Pyle's inability to "wipe that disgusting grin off [his] face." James Naremore suggests that the audience identifies with Private Pyle in this sequence, since he is the only onscreen character to laugh at Hartman's intensely, if uncomfortably, funny monologue. Naremore argues, "The chief irony of the sequence is that even though Pyle's reaction to Hartman seems slow-witted, it resembles the reaction most viewers are likely to have: a bewildered mingling of amusement, fear, and disgust . . . In contrast to the stony looks on the faces of the other recruits, Pyle's reaction is sensible and sane."[30] Pyle's facial expressions and bodily reactions mimic those of the film's viewers, but it's not the "sense" and "sanity" of his reaction that we're being asked to identify with. This opening sequence begins a long and uncomfortable audience identification with Pyle's vulnerability and incompetence. Because the boot-camp genre encourages us to sympathize with the recruits' fear and confusion, we identify with Pyle's vulnerability. But due to Kubrick's antihumanist impulses, we're also slightly disgusted by his failure—even though it's failure to perform a version of masculinity that the film suggests is problematic at best, monstrous at worst.

Vulnerability and the "Soft" Male Body

The least stylized moment in the boot-camp section, the squad's disciplinary attack on Private Pyle, establishes the film's equation of visible pain with nonmasculine vulnerability. Untangling the scene's literal or emotional point of view depends on the extent to which the recruits act as one "body," reflecting Hartman's will, or as discrete characters whose ethical judgment excites our interest and identification. Richard Rambuss suggests that by this point in the film, they are no longer individual characters in any meaningful way; he calls the attack scene a moment when "the corporate body learns this new work of self-regulation."[31] Pyle fails to perform adequately in basic training and hoards fattening, forbidden food. Already marked as vulnerable by his physical softness and his need to be taught basic skills by Joker, Pyle's suffering at the hands of his frustrated fellow recruits marks the film's first moments of realistic violence, absent the farcical tone established by Ermey's performance as Hartman. When Hartman punishes the whole squad for Pyle's overconsumption, the recruits retaliate. This scene's use of close-ups and diegetic sound—the moaning, crying, and screaming audiences associate with physical vulnerability—establishes two kinds of masculinity: Joker's masculine violence and Pyle's feminized vulnerability.

The intense nurturing Joker has shown to Pyle in the scenes leading up to this one, which has provided the one point of emotional connection between viewer and characters, complicates Joker's position, and the viewer's. Prior to the attack, we are treated to an eerily lit shot of Joker peering into the top bunk, where the camera reveals Pyle sleeping on his back, mouth slightly open, dressed in boxer shorts and an undershirt, which rides up to expose his belly. The recruits immobilize, gag, and beat Pyle for thirty excruciating seconds of screen time. Joker, initially reluctant to participate in this violence, eventually hits the sobbing Pyle six times with increasing viciousness.[32] Susan White calls this "the first moment of

[Joker's] moral collapse,"[33] but the frustration Kubrick has encouraged the viewer to feel with Pyle's incompetence and childishness complicates this collapse. Pyle's physical vulnerability in this scene enlists audience sympathy with him, but it also highlights the difference between Joker, who talks back when Hartman assaults him, and Pyle, who suffers and cries.[34] Vulnerability, figured as female, provides the leverage Kubrick uses to enlist his audience's disgust at military cruelty.[35] Yet, as viewers, we are invited to identify (partly) with the ambivalent Joker as an alternative to having to identify fully with the vulnerable and feminized Pyle.

Pyle's change after this scene, and the end of the "male mothering" that had encouraged audience identification with Joker, intensifies the film's ambivalence about the liminal masculinity Joker represents. And here the film's attempts to parse Joker's embrace of Hartman's discipline with his crowd-pleasing irony and self-awareness seems less ambivalent than incoherent. While it appears that Joker resists the military machine by talking back during boot camp and by affixing a peace symbol to his helmet alongside the "Born to Kill" he's scrawled across it, the film's first half remains so haunting because Pyle is the only character to actually resist the machine. Rambuss defines what appears to be blankness or absence in D'Onofrio's expression as "technologization"; for Rambuss, Pyle "functions as the sacrificial emblem upon which the costs of conformity to the machine are to be spectacularly tallied."[36] What Rambuss sees as a cost is for Thomas Doherty a harbinger of war's terror itself, unleashed: "No one fixes an actor's gaze like Kubrick—think of Jack Nicholson leering demonically in *The Shining*—and Leonard's face holds a terror more potent than anything awaiting the boys in Vietnam."[37] Doherty has called the character "Leonard" instead of "Pyle," a move unusual in the scholarship on this film, which often unintentionally reinforces the very dehumanization of characters scholars want to recuperate. In getting the viewer to think of this character as "Pyle" instead of "Leonard," Kubrick includes his viewer in the process of dehumanization that we're watching Joker, not Pyle, undergo. Before the squad's attack on Pyle, Joker still called Leonard by his given name. "That's it, Leonard," Joker says as he teaches Pyle to climb over an obstacle-course barrier. As they climb down together, we see "Lawrence" and "Davis" on the backs of their uniforms. Though the film teaches us to call Leonard Lawrence "Pyle," we never know any name for our ostensible point-of-view character other than "Joker." We have to look to the edges and the corners of the frame, past the point where Kubrick's camera directs us, to see "Lawrence," the name Pyle leaves behind, and "Davis," the name we never hear Joker called.

In the final scene of the boot-camp section, Joker will again try to label Pyle "Leonard," but his attempts will mirror Michael's effort to get Nick to remember his name. In these films, Nick and Pyle are military casualties because they represent a particular model of male vulnerability that is both created and destroyed by Vietnam. Pyle's death is, like Nick's, a moment when the supposed protagonist's role as masculine nurturer breaks down. *Full Metal Jacket* has not asked us to invest in Joker's role as caretaker to the same extent that *The Deer Hunter* asks us to invest in Michael, but once Joker withdrawals from that role, Pyle retreats into a cold-eyed remove from reality that has striking parallels to Nick's descent into opium addiction. On the recruits' "last night on the Island," the viewer walks with Joker through the ghostly silent barracks and enters the head to find Pyle sitting on a toilet, his unkempt body—and the "soft" masculinity it represents—at odds with the brisk efficiency with which he loads ammunition into his rifle's magazine. This scene aligns our perspective more clearly with Joker's than any other point in the film, as the light from his flashlight illuminates first Pyle's face, with its Kubrickian leer, then his hands as they load the live rounds.[38] "Leonard, if Hartman comes in here and catches us, we'll both be in a world of shit," Joker cautions.

While Cimino's framing of Nick's death in intense close-ups and two-shots and De Niro's emotional performance connected the audience to both the action and the relationship between the characters, Modine's line readings are oddly distancing. He slows down the pace of the dialogue, pausing slightly after each word to achieve the denaturalized affect. If Michael can speak of a "home" to which Nick knows he can't return, Joker has no such possibility to offer, only the hollow plea that the "world of shit" might be avoided if they evade detection by Hartman. "I *am* in a world of shit," Pyle insists, and begins a litany of training commands, the script by which Hartman made him into a marine. But this moment, which is usually understood as Pyle's complete capitulation to the military machine—his rebirth as nothing more than a weapon—is actually his moment of greatest resistance. He alone recognizes that the world of the marine *is* a world of shit, and he alone kills Hartman, that world's representative and creator. Kubrick's camera stylizes Hartman's death, the film's first, nearly to the point of caricature, but the dead body on the floor alters the emotional dynamic of the rest of the scene. Modine's performance becomes far more Method-realist as he says softly, "Easy, Leonard. Go easy, man." Here Joker mimics the viewer's response to the action as Pyle had in the opening barracks sequence, but even as the film seems to suture our perspective to his, Kubrick's famously cold camera won't let Pyle out of our sight. The last shot of the film's first half shows his body in repose, the bright red of his blood against the pristine white of the bathroom wall, the cost of resistance and the cost of war visually united.

Female Snipers and the Visual Language of Rape

The film's second half, set in Vietnam, shifts the locus of bodily vulnerability from the "soft" male body to the body of the female other. At the film's end, a hidden sniper picks off members of Joker's squad one by one until the remaining squad members find and kill the sniper, a young Vietnamese woman. Kubrick's representation of her drawn-out death equates physical vulnerability in its most palpable form with the female body. As the men gather around the mortally wounded woman, they argue over whether to shoot her or leave her to die slowly. Joker, the only soldier who recognizes her soft speech ("she's praying"), argues "we can't just leave her here," while cartoonishly masculine Animal Mother (Adam Baldwin) says, "Fuck her. Let her rot." Finally, Joker shoots her, both to put her out of her misery and to silence her. "Hardcore, man," the other men murmur, seeming to imply that Joker has killed the woman out of anger over his comrades' deaths, and that this act of violence has finally made him part of the ambivalent community of men whose ethical sensibilities have been shattered by the military-industrial complex.[39] But the film's actual moral calculus is both more complicated and less subversive: Joker kills the woman because he cannot stand watching and hearing her suffer. Here, as elsewhere, he functions as the viewer's stand-in. The viewer, through Joker, negotiates between models of masculinity under the pressures of war. Michael Klein finds audience identification with Joker in this moment potentially redemptive: "[When] the young woman is surrounded and shot by the marines who have managed to survive her attack, there is fear in her eyes and in the eyes of our figure of reference, Corporal Joker . . . The look in her eyes and in the eyes of Corporal Joker is the only glimmer of potential redemption in Kubrick's bleak and savage film."[40] But the vulnerability of the body in this sequence has been almost entirely divorced from Joker himself and projected onto the dying woman. Joker's confrontation with the sniper comically catalogs his failure to perform, but once she lies dying on the ground, the camera's approach toward her shifts dramatically. After several straight minutes of listening to her labored breathing, choked praying, and soft begging ("shoot me"), we want to hear the shot that kills her as much as Joker wants to fire it. As he shoots, the camera focuses on his face, not the dying woman. The vulnerable body in pain, established as female, has served its purpose—to reclaim Joker from the nihilism in which the film thinks it implicates him.[41] The audience's uneasy reaction to the sniper's death depends on the film's conservative visual strategies: it is especially horrifying to watch a woman suffer, because women (like Pyle) are more vulnerable than men. The film's antiwar power thus depends on a strictly gendered sentimental vulnerability.

It has become commonplace for scholars to read the sniper's death as a figurative rape. Rambuss suggests, "While the ethical valences of Joker's action are uncertain, perhaps even undecideable (what began as a desire for revenge ends with a mercy killing that feels like murder), the scene itself is visually composed so as to evoke a gang rape."[42] Meanwhile, Susan White connects the "gang rape" discourse to the violence against Pyle: "[The men] stand over the woman's body as though this were a gang rape, as they had stood over Pyle when they hit him, and as they had stood over their dead comrades, and as they had figuratively surrounded the $5 whore."[43] Timothy Corrigan suggests that "by the [film's] conclusion, the narrative-media eyes of Joker no longer witness the military action but . . . become the killing technology whose final glory is the death and metaphorical rape of the young girl sniper."[44] Critics use the word "rape" to describe this scene because of the camera's insistence on the sniper's vulnerability. As we will see in *Casualties of War* and in the chapters that follow, rape as an act—or as a weapon of war—bears a great deal of symbolic meaning in terms of our cultural construction of vulnerability. Each of these Vietnam films asks what it would mean if we tried to do some of that symbolic work through violence against the male body. But the example of *Casualties of War*, particularly, shows that popular culture will have to wait until the 1990s to really answer that question.

Casualties of War: Female Suffering and Whiteness as Redemption

If Cimino offers Russian roulette as a metaphor for Vietnam and Kubrick offers the destruction of Private Pyle's subjectivity, De Palma's central metaphor is rape. While John Newsinger rightly argues that *Casualties of War* posits rape "as something that happens to men as victimizers rather than to women as victims,"[45] the film's narrative and visual strategies—which equate the position of woman with the status of victim—gender physical vulnerability female even more explicitly and more aggressively than either of the other two films. By the time the Vietnam War film reaches the end of the Reagan era, male caretaking of other men becomes a training in rape, and male caretaking of women is either a trap or a joke. In a particularly full-throated defense of the film,[46] David Greven argues that "De Palma's film offers an unflinching critique of American force as figured by the phallus/penis—it critiques the symbolic (phallic) power of American force by exposing this power's investment in the literal biological organ (penis) that figures it. *Casualties* casts the penis not as nostalgic icon but as weapon of destruction and death." Greven is right to suggest that in this film the kind of masculinity that was treated with ambivalence in the two previous films is revealed as grotesque and perverse. But the film's reliance on Eriksson as a clear point-of-view character mitigates the force of this critique, since it refuses to force its audience into identification or complicity with the violent male characters who represent U.S. exploitation of the Vietnamese. The film's much-derided framing device establishes Eriksson as the film's narrator, and De Palma's casting of 1980s television star Michael J. Fox gives audiences an easy entry into the nightmare-world of the film's Vietnam. Viewers are lulled into a false sense of safety when introduced to Eriksson's sergeant, Meserve, played by a forceful Sean Penn.[47] Eriksson, ill suited to combat, displays a feckless incompetence in the film's early scenes that allows Meserve to emerge as a protector of weaker men. Meserve saves Eriksson, who is trapped in a partially collapsed tunnel, and Eriksson's one act of military competence in the scene—shooting an enemy soldier who is concealed in a tree—happens only after he begins to mimic Meserve. Fox must literally repeat Penn's dialogue—"Yeah, motherfucker!"—in order to adequately handle his weapon.[48] Thus far, *Casualties* seems to follow *The Deer Hunter* and *Full Metal Jacket* in encouraging the viewer to invest in the rough male nurturing that the more aggressively masculine character shows toward a weaker, more vulnerable man. Alone among these films, *Casualties*, sometimes dismissed as heavy-handed and sentimental, dares to really criticize the brothers-in-arms ethos of the war film as a genre.

Once the squad sets out on a patrol that will keep them away from the base for several days, the film begins to expose the camaraderie between the men as a sinister form of complicity with group violence and sexual exploitation. Meserve—unhinged by his friend Brownie's grisly death in the first section of the film—informs the squad that they will "requisition" a Vietnamese woman for some "portable R & R." Eriksson's open dissent from this plan and the more passive resistance of Private Diaz (John Leguizamo) keep them at a distance from both Oahn (Thuy Thu Le) and the other men in the squad, who at first offer their "prisoner" a warped version of the kind of care they offer one another. When Oahn coughs, Corporal Clark (Don Harvey) puts his hands on her shoulders, asking "You all right? You're all right, aren't you? Come here, I'm not gonna hurt you." De Palma intercuts Diaz and Eriksson's first hushed conversation agreeing that they don't want to "mess with" the girl with these entreaties, to which Oahn reacts with fear. Meserve gently removes her gag and gives her aspirin, pouring water into her mouth from his own canteen. The abrupt tonal shifts in De Palma's representation of Meserve and Clark disorient the viewer, who is placed in a position similar to Eriksson's own—so long as a fiction of normalcy remains intact, Meserve's caretaking of both Oahn and Eriksson can continue. But this brief respite from the verbal and physical violence just under the surface of Penn's performance as Meserve depends on Eriksson's silence and consent. Once Eriksson openly defies Meserve, Meserve labels Oahn "a VC whore." Meserve, Clark, and Hatcher abandon any pretense of caretaking, forcing Oahn to carry their rucksacks, and also reject the premise—usually sacrosanct in the war film genre—that even a dissenting member of the group is part of the whole. If Oahn is now a "VC whore," Eriksson is a "queer" and a "VC sympathizer."

Eriksson's one real ally in the squad, Diaz, cannot resist the pressure of expulsion from the squad's protective and coercive embrace. Though still marked by the film as a resistant participant in Oahn's rape and murder, Diaz leaves Eriksson as the only squad member to openly challenge Meserve. By the time of the rape, we have learned to distance ourselves as viewers from the sexualized taunting that would mark Eriksson as either female or "queer" for refusing to rape Oahn. But De Palma's camera participates in a feminizing of Eriksson throughout the film that places the viewer in a tense and counterintuitive relationship to Meserve's explicit attempts to question his masculinity. The majority of the rape sequence is filmed in a slightly canted long shot; Eriksson has been sent away to stand watch, and this shot is visually coded as his perspective. Michael J. Fox's literal placement in the frame suggests that he refuses to watch the rape,[49] and this slight mismatch of cinematic point of view is discussed by David Greven as "masochistic male looking, indicative . . . of the fragility, vulnerability, and powerlessness of the male eye."[50] Greven reads this scene as a figurative rape of Diaz: "[When he] complies in the rape of Oahn, we see his delicately beautiful body in undress from behind; from this posterior perspective, he looks as fragile and defenseless as Oahn. De Palma visually implies that, in being made to rape Oahn, the vulnerable and conscientious Diaz, another racially different character, is also being raped, by Meserve and the homosocial order he represents."[51] Diaz functions here, visually and narratively, as Eriksson's replacement. Up until this moment, he had been a site of audience identification, and while I agree with Greven that Diaz is positioned as a victim, his capitulation to Meserve's pressure signals the last moment that De Palma will allow audience identification with him. In this sense, the rape scene's camerawork allows us to stay with Eriksson, apart from any sense of complicity in sexual violence, but also from identification with Diaz's vulnerability. And in the morally stark universe De Palma constructs, once Diaz has committed this act, the film has very little use for him, since he is neither the leering figure of excessive male violence typified by Clark nor the model of thwarted male virtue represented by Eriksson. *Casualties of War* lacks the interim figure that was so central to *The Deer Hunter*'s and *Full Metal Jacket*'s ambivalent portrayals of masculinity. But here, instead of offering a liminal masculinity, Penn's performance as Meserve exposes the discomfort with which Hollywood film in the 1970s and 1980s figures male vulnerability.

The camera's view hides Oahn in the aftermath of the rape. Diaz sits in the back of a deep-focus shot inside the hooch, his face expressionless, while Clark, Hatcher (John C. Reilly), and Meserve sit in the rain in middle depth. "When was the last time you had a real woman, Sarge?" Clark asks. Meserve looks at the sky and says softly, "*She* was real. I think she was real." As Meserve walks toward the camera to inform Eriksson, "Diaz will relieve you at 2400," the camera cuts to an extreme close-up of Eriksson's rain-streaked and traumatized face, and the editing makes it unclear whether he's facing Meserve and the scene of the rape or whether he's facing away. We have seen the ways that Method acting creates a blueprint for both masculinity and vulnerability onscreen, but the moment when Penn mutters "I thought she was real" divorces vulnerability and masculinity, and the film becomes simultaneously more critical of male violence and less demanding of its audience, since it erases the frisson of complicity with racist and misogynist violence that the power of Penn's performance generates in the first half of the film.

Greven describes Penn's performance as "flamboyant theatricality," defending its excess as central to "the film's portrait of Meserve as a manhood in the process of decohesion."[52] Penn, the inheritor of De Niro's mantle as the most widely recognized icon of male Method acting, here exposes the "theatricality" always at the base of Method portrayals of masculinity in moments of crisis. In this film, Penn is an emblem of what I would label Method theatricality, here contrasted visually with the less intense performance style that Michael J. Fox imports from his television persona as Alex P. Keaton on *Family Ties* and from his film role as Marty McFly in *Back to the Future* (1985). Thus the work Marlon Brando begins in *The Men* here reaches its seemingly foregone conclusion—the Method breaks down at the moment masculinity is exposed as a training in rape. Greven suggests that *Casualties of War* "forces us to recognize that the homosocial vanquishes the normative men who protest it no less efficiently than it does its more apparent enemies, queer men, women, and racial others."[53] But this view, convincing as it is about the role of homosocial coercion in the film, ignores the ways that Eriksson's whiteness *does* protect him—in the expectations audiences bring to a film starring Michael J. Fox as well as in the film's narrative, where Eriksson fights to win justice for Oahn in a military court. As Susan Fraiman argues, "The result is that male America gets to see itself as the winsome hero of *Family Ties,* while Oahn, in addition to being physically abused, is deprived even of the right to struggle and speak on her own behalf."[54]

Back at the base camp, Eriksson confides in Rowan (Jack Gwaltney), and their conversation about Eriksson's failure to stop the rape and murder and his dilemma about reporting it is constantly, comically interrupted by a new "cherry," whose inability to find his own squad and his desire to obtain MRE pound cake mark him as the double of Eriksson in the film's opening scenes. The cherry—played by Darren E. Burrows, who would later gain television stardom of his own as budding filmmaker Ed on *Northern Exposure* (CBS, 1990–1995)—stammers that he'd better go find his own squad: "I feel like I'm doing something wrong. I'll see you guys later." As he turns to go, Eriksson grabs his jacket and pulls him around to deliver a tough-love speech meant to establish Eriksson's passage from being a cherry himself to being a teacher of inexperienced, more vulnerable men. "Hey!" he barks, "I don't think you *will* see us later if you don't stop bopping around here like it's a goddamn playground." But this moment doesn't quite work to establish Eriksson's changed relationship to his own masculine authority the way De Palma seems to intend. Burrows is several inches taller than Fox, so Eriksson has to look up at the cherry in the close two-shot. This visual framing combined with the Alex P. Keaton tenor of Fox's voice never quite mimics the gruff authority that makes Penn both magnetic and terrifying as Meserve. Eriksson, no longer the cherry, has been initiated into something the film is not quite ready to name or value. Fox has neither Penn's confidence nor his charisma, and Eriksson's performance of male nurturing is both incomplete and unconvincing. Though the film has worked hard to expose the darkness at the center of Meserve's masculinity, and to celebrate the more vulnerable, empathetic masculinity Eriksson represents, the plot posits Meserve as the more effective teacher in survival. Eriksson lives through his first contact with "the enemy," while Eriksson's pupil steps on a booby trap offscreen and is left dead on the side of the trail, bamboo spikes penetrating his body.

This shot mirrors De Palma's final shot of Oahn, and the nameless "cherry" comes to occupy the position as visual representative of vulnerability she previously held in the film.[55] If, as Fraiman suggests, "[Oahn's] brutalized and silenced body . . . mediate[s] both American men's savagery toward the Vietnamese and their fantasy of being forgiven for it,"[56] the replacement of her body with the dead boy's gives Eriksson the impetus he needs to press charges against Oahn's killers.

Figure 8 Oahn's body

Figure 9 The nameless "cherry"

But while De Palma's camera focused obsessively on Oahn's bleeding, broken body, the cherry's death happens offscreen. It is only his motionless, dead body that mirrors Oahn's, after the crying, screaming, and moaning that established the female body's vulnerability have been silenced. American popular culture will have to wait nearly ten years for Steven Spielberg's *Saving Private Ryan* to make characters like the cherry the film's protagonists.

PART II

RESISTANT VULNERABILITY AFTER THE COLD WAR

3

The Body at War

SEXUAL POLITICS AND RESISTANT VULNERABILITY IN *SAVING PRIVATE RYAN* AND *G.I. JANE*

In August 1991, *Vanity Fair* hit newsstands with a cover of a naked, pregnant Demi Moore, shot by famed celebrity photographer Annie Leibovitz. *Ghost* (Jerry Zucker, 1990) had made Moore a bankable star, and at the time of the shoot she was pregnant with her second child. In the cover photograph, Moore refuses to meet the gaze of Leibovitz's camera; she looks up and to the left as her left hand cradles her round stomach and her right hand covers her breast. Moore's gaze is determined, nearly defiant, and her short hair and the conspicuous diamonds on her ears and finger compete for control of the image. In a second Leibovitz-shot *Vanity Fair* cover a year later, the gender dissonance becomes more explicit, featuring a naked Moore with a man's pinstriped suit painted on her body.

Despite these bracing visuals, the articles that accompany the covers seem eager to contain the transgressive iconography of Leibovitz's photo spreads. "More Demi Moore," the 1991 cover proclaims, but the accompanying article reveals how fraught Moore's star image was quickly becoming in the early 1990s. The article quotes Denise DeClue, co-screenwriter of *About Last Night,* the 1986 film starring Moore: "Demi Moore has this accessible vulnerability that makes her attractive." In the same piece, then-husband Bruce Willis adds, "She's so open and honest and not afraid to be vulnerable."[1] The 1992 cover fronts an article titled "Demi's Birthday Suit" that channels the early 1990s cultural uncertainty about what Demi Moore's star image signified: Vixen or vulnerable wife? Hardheaded businesswoman or hard-bodied plaything? The article mentions *Indecent Proposal,* which Moore was in the process of filming: "Chatting eagerly about the movie—which, as ego trips go, has got to be the best thing since *Pretty Woman*—she seems to take for granted the extravagant compliment contained in the story line."[2] *Indecent Proposal*'s storyline involves Robert Redford's character offering Moore's character and her husband (Woody Harrelson) one million dollars for a night with her. Presumably, the only compliment author Jennet Conant considers better than Robert Redford buying you for a night is Richard Gere buying you for a week. But the discourse that has Moore taking the compliment for granted is indicative of her public image, solidifying in the early 1990s, as a woman who expects too much—too much power, too much money, too much control over her image and what it signifies. That the authors of both articles answer this implicit charge with descriptions of her "vulnerability" or speculations about how she can be reimagined as a sex worker reveals the female star's body as a site of much cultural tension.

The photo spread inside the 1992 magazine features more shots of Moore in the painted suit, images that have become the subject of debate among theorists trying to parse 1990s attitudes toward gender and sexuality. Judith Halberstam, in the introduction to *Female Masculinity,* argues that "Moore's body suit fails to suggest even a mild representation of female masculinity precisely because it so anxiously emphasizes the femaleness of Moore's body."[3] Presumably Halberstam here refers to Moore's prominent breasts and the almost languid line of her pose. But the composition of these images and Moore's posture, particularly the photo with Willis inside the magazine, is more unsettling to early-1990s notions of the female movie star than Halberstam admits. Moore sits, legs spread-eagled, on the side on the bed, arms akimbo—one hand on her thigh, the other on Willis's head as he sleeps, naked, the white sheet coming up to his waist. This gender reversal of the classic "male breadwinner leaving for work" shot is a sly commentary on the public obsession with the Moore-Willis marriage and the tension the media blamed on her career's ascendance over his. The popular-press interest in this tension built steadily between the 1992 *Vanity Fair* cover and the 1997 release of *G.I. Jane* (and the 1998 publication of *Female Masculinity*). Moore and Willis announced their separation in 1998 and their divorce in 2000, but the public fascination with Moore's body as spectacle did not end with their marriage.

I want to suggest that Moore's involvement in *G.I. Jane* is an attempt to publicly rehabilitate her career after the bad press surrounding *Striptease* (Andrew Bergman, 1996), public allegations that she terrorized her domestic staff, and rumors of trouble with Willis. Perhaps more importantly, *Jane* also represents her attempt to rewrite that famous body with another valence. At roughly the same time that Moore's star was waning, Tom Hanks had solidified his position as one of the most influential actors of his generation, transitioning from the man-child roles that made him a star in films like *Splash* (Ron Howard, 1984) and *Big* (Penny Marshall, 1988) to the more serious fare that won him back-to-back Academy Awards for Best Actor in 1994 (*Philadelphia*) and 1995 (*Forrest Gump*). In the mid- to late 1990s, both Moore and Hanks were in the process of reworking their star images, and it should come as no surprise that the body at war is the place where these reimaginings take shape. Moore's and Hank's films leading into *G.I. Jane* and *Saving Private Ryan* serve as focal points for a 1990s-specific investigation of the tough woman, the new man, and how each becomes a political statement when combined with the iconic imagery of the war film in an America then caught between nostalgia for the WWII era and confusion about the end of the Cold War era. What can these military fictions, produced as vehicles for two of the top-grossing and most culturally iconic stars of the 1990s, tell us about the constantly shifting dynamics of gender and violence? About their filmic and televisual depiction, but also their place in the actual cultural debate about women, men, and the costs of war?[4]

When *G.I. Jane*'s male protagonist lectures the film's heroine on the nature of pain—"Pain is your friend, your ally. It will keep you awake and angry"—he does more than upend audience expectations about the familiar image of a woman in pain. He creates an iconography unique to this moment in Hollywood cinema; on film, pain has not been women's ally. Rather, film has explored pain's power to unmake, in Elaine Scarry's term, typically representing the violated female body as a sign of women's limited autonomy. The film industry uses the violated body to critique war; film scholarship uses it to trace violent films' impact on cultural gender codes. War films have long shown audiences the spectacle of suffering, but the specific ways that the body's vulnerability operates in that spectacle remains underexamined. This chapter considers two famous bodies—Moore's and Hanks's—to see what replaces the more traditional focus of the war film on the vulnerable bodies of women and children left at home. In *Saving Private Ryan* (Steven Spielberg, 1998), the male body represents vulnerability: porous, penetrable, bleeding. In *G.I. Jane* (Ridley Scott, 1997) the vulnerability that threatens war efforts isn't the female body but rather men's reactions to the spectacle that body creates in the theater of war. Ridley Scott's credentials as a director of transgressive box-office hits from *Alien* (1979) and *Blade Runner* (1982) to *Thelma and Louise* (1991) were doubtless attractive to Moore when she chose him to direct *G.I. Jane.*[5] By uncovering the social fear and desire that drive the collective cultural fantasies at work in the film, we can see the political potential in the ways Scott and Moore retrain their audience to view a woman being beaten as a sign of triumph, not vulnerability. Steven Spielberg and Tom Hanks create a very different kind of cultural fantasy in *Saving Private Ryan,* one where we can acknowledge war's terrible cost and the vulnerability of male bodies, but where that fear need not destabilize our ideas about the gendered body. Surprisingly for such mainstream projects, both films ask audiences to invert their expectations about the ways we have conceived of the vulnerable body as female. If Hollywood is a mirror of our cultural preoccupations, then there are political consequences to the way *Saving Private Ryan* makes the *male* body vulnerable, even penetrable, without marking that vulnerability as female. *Ryan* also resists claiming that vulnerability as a site for national regeneration, as scholars such as Susan Jeffords have suggested war films and action films from the 1980s and early 1990s do. *Saving Private Ryan* does this by constantly focusing its camera on the intense physical suffering of its young soldiers. Where *Saving Private Ryan* keeps the abused body's vulnerability in place and flirts with switching the gender association of that vulnerability, *G.I. Jane* attacks the very association audiences are trained to make between the abused body and vulnerability. Instead of weak, Demi Moore's abused body registers as powerful.

The instability surrounding the gendered meanings of vulnerability these films posit threatens dominant cultural ideas about gender and war because it challenges two important assumptions. First is the assumption that society sends the strong (able-bodied men) to war in order to protect the weak or vulnerable (women, children, and nonmasculine men). This assumption allows the public to avoid the moral problem of war's cost in broken bodies by imagining vulnerability primarily in the bodies left at home. Second is the assumption that women are by definition vulnerable; subscribing to this view justifies an all-male combat force. Both positions depend on vulnerability being coded female. Granting that men are just as vulnerable as women to the gunshot wounds and bomb attacks that constitute much of modern warfare undermines the sacrificial logic of sending the men to battle. And if the female body is not, in fact, specially vulnerable, the justification for all-male combat forces erodes. *Saving Private Ryan* and *G.I. Jane* investigate the social costs of these assumptions, replacing these deeply ingrained understandings of vulnerability with a less gendered, more complex vulnerability. *Saving Private Ryan* thus complicates our understanding of male sacrifice, and *G.I. Jane* challenges society's ongoing physical paternalism toward women by shifting the way Moore's famous body registers onscreen.

G.I. Jane, as we will see, creates a new cultural coding that invites us to reject the idea that a bleeding body or a sexually threatened body is vulnerable, particularly when the body in question is a woman's. This presents the problem of vulnerability in war as a question of physical bodies, imagining that the debate about women in combat hinges on women's physical ability. But the film's rhetoric inevitably mirrors the political debate, which has always been structured around a different, thornier set of issues. The threat of rape in war, rehearsed tirelessly by those arguing against full integration, does not ultimately depend on the fiction that only women can be raped. Male bodies are vulnerable to rape, just as they are to gunshot wounds; the actual social fear driving this debate is that men cannot handle the image of female physical vulnerability that *viewing* rape registers. Echoing but also eliding the "physical strength" argument allows the film to sidestep the political consequences its production of vulnerability should have, as does its elision of its most crucial historical referent—the 1990s debate about the military's discriminatory Don't Ask/Don't Tell policy. President Bill Clinton signed DADT into law in 1993, and the contentious congressional hearings that led to its adoption made "unit cohesion" the centerpiece of the argument against homosexual service members being allowed to serve openly. Since this argument rests so explicitly on the *emotions* of the largely male combat force, the counterintuitive emotional response that both *Ryan* and *Jane* demand from their viewers has political consequences. These consequences matter increasingly as the late 1990s become an important cultural moment in shifting public opinion on both gender and sexuality in the armed forces.

Though anomalous examples exist in each historical period, war films from the 1940s through the 1980s form a baseline of cinematic precedent in their treatment of gender and vulnerability, relying on strategies of female victimization regardless of the film's politics. As this book's second chapter discusses, Vietnam War films made during the decades between Vietnam and the end of the Cold War such as *The Deer Hunter* (Michael Cimino, 1978), *Apocalypse Now* (Francis Ford Coppola, 1979), *Platoon* (Oliver Stone, 1986), *Full Metal Jacket* (Stanley Kubrick, 1986), and *Casualties of War* (Brian De Palma, 1989) provide audiences with an image of combat as dehumanizing and a new image of the American soldier as a psychological casualty of war.[6] But the Vietnam films also establish a visual baseline that genders physical vulnerability female even as it focuses attention on bodily suffering in a way that Production Code–era WWII films could not. WWII films dramatized soldiers dying and tied this suffering to a patriotic defense of women and children back home. The majority of Vietnam films produced during the 1970s and 1980s, however, take this formulation a step further, using the bodies of Vietnamese women and nonstoic men to gender physical vulnerability female.[7] This cinematic precedent produced a cultural shorthand that made female vulnerability seem inevitable in the genre.

The resistant vulnerability I see in *Saving Private Ryan* creates a different shorthand that views male bodies as vulnerable. Spielberg eventually retreats from this iconography, reasserting a stoic masculinity that inadequately resolves his film's tensions. Yet part of the film's emotional power for audiences rests in the difference between the film as spectacle—which undermines our assumptions about male vulnerability—and the film's storytelling structure, which writes women back into the script of an all-male military.

Opening the Body: *Saving Private Ryan* and Post–Cold War Masculinity

When *Saving Private Ryan* premiered in the summer of 1998, the press greeted the film, and Tom Hanks's performance as Captain John Miller, ecstatically. *Empire*'s tagline is typical of the tone that met the film's reverent treatment of World War II: "The most evocative battle scenes ever put to film. A powerful study of humanity in the face of madness. Steven Spielberg's *Saving Private Ryan* has been heralded as a masterpiece of historic cinema. [Writer] Ian Nathan meets Tom Hanks and the gallant men who endured sheer hell for the sake of absolute realism."[8] The moralizing tone of this pitch reveals the slippage between realist cinematic techniques and moral seriousness representative of this film's popular reception. At a time of considerable upheaval for the American military, *Saving Private Ryan* offered a retreat from the crucible of contemporary images of American masculinity embodied by President Clinton, soon to be impeached after having won a second term by defeating WWII veteran Bob Dole. With the exception of Ronald Reagan, Clinton was the first non-combat-veteran elected president in nearly fifty years. And Reagan had at least played a military man in the movies and had served in the Army Reserves. Clinton represented a very different style of masculinity, more in line with the "new," sensitive masculinity that Tom Hanks represented for most of the 1990s in films like *A League of Their Own* (1992), *Sleepless in Seattle* (1993), *Philadelphia* (1993), *Forrest Gump* (1994), and *Toy Story* (1995). That *Saving Private Ryan* offered Hanks—who had won his two mid-1990s Academy Awards for Best Actor playing a gay man dying of AIDS and a mentally handicapped savant—a chance to play John Wayne instead of Jimmy Stewart is the unspoken undercurrent to much of this coverage. If Hanks's role as Captain Miller shapes the 1990s image of the sensitive baby boomer into a more masculine mold, the film's young soldiers, played by mostly unknown actors, are the site of the new affect Spielberg creates in this film. The spectator's protective anxiety—so often projected onto women in war films—is here attached to the male body.

Film critic Neal Gabler pointed out at the time of *Saving Private Ryan*'s release that *Platoon, Apocalypse Now,* and *The Deer Hunter* are each as violent and uncompromising as *Ryan*, arguing that *Ryan*'s effect depends less on its aesthetics than on what audiences are invited to invest in it: "In effect, *Saving Private Ryan* has become the bloody, heartfelt cultural salve to the divisions and tumult that have riven this country throughout the postwar period. The text of this film may be warfare 1944; the subtext is unity 1998." This debate about the quantity of violence in the film matters less in my view than the affect attached to that violence, which I see as unique in a film of *Ryan*'s ideological conservatism. Turn-of-the-century America's fascination with WWII makes Spielberg's return to a sense of American triumphalism predictable,[9] but his use of vulnerability onscreen is considerably less conventional. The anti–Vietnam War films of the 1980s depend on a traditional model of gendered vulnerability, while *Saving Private Ryan* takes the camera's fascination with the destroyed body—for example, *Full Metal Jacket*'s focus on a dying female sniper—and trains it on men.

Spielberg's return to an older model of war film owes its success to the political context of the late 1990s. The small number of American combat deaths during the first Gulf War created an atmosphere in which the public was newly fascinated by cinematic portrayals of the American soldier's damaged body.[10] Anxieties about war's mechanization were met by large commercial projects like Spielberg's that again tied American militarism to the stoicism and bodily sacrifice that audiences are trained to associate with the WWII generation. I argue that *Saving Private Ryan* separates these concepts—stoicism and sacrifice—and makes the male body vulnerable, porous, and penetrable, focusing obsessively on this vulnerability in a way few films of its genre do. *Saving Private Ryan*'s visual strategies unsettle deeply ingrained social understandings of vulnerability, offering instead a vulnerability divorced from the female body. We might call these the new technologies of vulnerability, aided by both more sophisticated squib technologies than were available to 1940s and 1950s film directors and a more fraught affect established by 1970s and 1980s war films.[11]

The titular Private Ryan's vulnerability and absence ostensibly provide *Ryan*'s driving narrative force; in the film's central action Captain Miller and the squad search for Private Ryan, ordered home to his mother in Iowa after his brothers are killed in combat. But the film's third act uses Ryan's bland, reassuring solidity and physical wholeness to replace the destroyed bodies of the young squad of soldiers whose story has occupied most of the film's running time, and whose bodies are, in the film's patriotic finale, hidden from view. What many critics see as the film's unsettling effect can be more usefully labeled its unsettling affect, necessitating Spielberg's retreat from that affect in the film's sentimental final frames. This retreat is the site of the film's greatest interest to those invested in the war body and the politics of vulnerability. In order to reassert the stoic masculinity Spielberg's narrative demands, Hanks's Captain Miller must retain the screen's focus, and the broken bodies of the young soldiers whose deaths structure the narrative must be left behind, closing off the questions the film raised about male vulnerability. This formal strategy has political consequences, as audiences are encouraged to ignore the disconnect between the political causes of war and the cost in blood and broken bodies those wars demand, as well as the assumptions about vulnerability society uses to justify those costs.

If war films of the 1970s and 1980s take their cue from the cultural aftermath of Vietnam, with its pictorial legacy of bodies both in and out of caskets,[12] *Saving Private Ryan* responds to a very different moment in American military history. The end of the Cold War offered no cultural catharsis similar to World War II's V-E Day, and the major American military engagement in the years leading up to *Ryan*'s production was 1991's First Gulf War, won largely by U.S. airpower. John Hodgkins argues that this is *Ryan*'s most important political context and that Spielberg's goal is to "vanquish once and for all those doubts and fears that had been festering since Vietnam and return the U.S. soldier to his rightful place as a heroic icon."[13] Spielberg's intentions aside, I see in the film a fascinating remainder of Vietnam's iconography, most present in *Ryan*'s focus on the destroyed body. This confusion over the war body and its meaning in popular culture animates the late-1990s WWII craze—dubbed "World War II chic" by Richard Goldstein—which included Tom Brokaw's best seller *The Greatest Generation* and the construction of the WWII memorial on the National Mall, as well as *Ryan* and Terrence Malick's *The Thin Red Line* (1998). Goldstein himself places the phenomenon directly in the context of the Senate's "ritual caning" of President Clinton.[14] Indeed, *Saving Private Ryan*'s theatrical release coincided with the Monica Lewinsky scandal that led to President Clinton's impeachment, lending yet another valence to the film's anxious portrayal of American masculinity and its creation of a new, more traditionally masculine screen image for Hanks.

As Anthony Giardina opined in *GQ:* "Simultaneous to our fixation on the wanderings of the president's penis, we were given images of 19-year-old boys having their guts splashed before our eyes . . . Where they sacrificed, we indulged."[15]A conventional wisdom quickly developed that Americans' renewed interest in WWII was the result of baby boomer self-flagellation. But *Saving Private Ryan* earned a reputation as more than mere nostalgia, since the film's violence was assumed to give audiences unfamiliar with "real" warfare an understanding of war's human cost. *Ryan*'s official press junket celebrated this purported revision of the war film genre, which the film's producers argue deglamorizes death, if not war itself. Spielberg and screenwriter Robert Rodat structure the film's narrative around three deaths, and the increasing intimacy of those deaths reveals the film's interest in vulnerability without that vulnerability being gendered female.

Saving Private Ryan also undermines the audience's traditional understanding of male sacrifice by structuring its narrative around death on the one hand and the stories men tell themselves about women on the other. In this context, the absent Private Ryan becomes the focus of the narrative, and finding him closes off the questions the film raised about male vulnerability.[16] In order for the symbol of the tattered American flag (which both opens and closes the film) to resonate with the "sacrifice" the film catalogs, vulnerable bodies other than Ryan's need to be removed from the scene. And in order to close off these questions about vulnerability, the soldiers' bodies must be left behind. The film spends its final twenty minutes retraining its audience to *resist* the spectacle of vulnerability it had spent the previous two and a half hours establishing. The inevitability of this abandonment appears early in the film, in the present-day Normandy graveyard scenes that frame the central narrative, set during World War II. The graveyard frame opens with a close-up of the American flag faded out with the sun behind it. The sun washes out color and backlights the flag, making it both bright and faded. This will become a visual symbol for memory and sacrifice, the two concepts the film most wants to tie to patriotic symbols of the American nation. In one of the film's opening shots, an aging veteran breaks down crying in front of a grave. But, as the Omaha Beach invasion will soon establish, male tears are not the marker of vulnerability in this film; blood and injuries are.

Critics have called the Omaha Beach sequence "a blood- and gut-spilling range of cinema verité that would make Sam Peckinpah blanch."[17] Violent enough to spark an FCC debate about violence on television when *Ryan* was aired unedited on Veterans Day,[18] it is visually disorienting and aurally unrelenting; the only sounds are bullets, water, and screams of agony. This aural focus on suffering—labored breathing, crying, screaming—is central to what I identify as male vulnerability, and it lays the groundwork for a change in the way male spectacle has traditionally worked.[19] Ina Rae Hark argues that genres focused on physical conflict between men (Westerns, epics, war dramas) depend upon "episodes in which a male protagonist's enemies make a spectacle out of him."[20] But Spielberg's Omaha Beach sequence cuts the human enemy out of the equation and relentlessly focuses on physical injury itself making a spectacle out of men, placing the camera's focus on the details of death. The eerie underwater sequences focus the viewer's attention on this specifically visual spectacle. They provide a respite from the stomach-turning sounds of the above-water battle, but only to increase the suffocating horror of the experience as men drown, weighed down by their gear. Film critic Gary Kamiya has called this sequence "so corrosive, so subversive of all logic, all morality, all stories, that it devours the story that follows";[21] but this misses the ways the film channels the "corrosive" effects of this kind of spectacle. It does not subvert logic and morality so much as it hijacks them, creating its own logic and its own morality in ways that undermine our expectations about vulnerability. In *New York Magazine,* David Denby describes this effect as "cruel magnificence," calling it "one of the greatest, most appalling things ever done in movies. Not just the violence, but the strangeness of it, is overwhelming."[22] In my view, this filmic effect most clearly separates the Omaha Beach sequence from the narrative that follows. The structuring deaths later in the film retain the graphic violence but abandon the strangeness that the disorientation of the beach landing causes. Those later deaths, after Spielberg has established audience identification with the soldiers, involve male vulnerability without hallucination and cruelty without magnificence.

The beach landing's hallucinatory effect depends on a camera that rarely differentiates between the men, just as the German machine gun (behind which the camera is frequently positioned) does not. The camera relentlessly searches out spectacles of the body's vulnerability. Bodies leak and spill; a still-living man's guts lie piled next to his body as he screams, "Mama." An injured soldier that squad medic Wade tries feverishly to save is hit in the head by a bullet from a German machine gun. This war film cliché—a dark joke—sets up the actual activity the film's plot documents. Spielberg's camera does not linger on men fighting, or saving, but on soldiers watching each other die, rehearsing again and again the vulnerability of their own bodies. But the narrative's insistence that, as the film's advertising campaign announced, "the mission is a man" creates a backward sacrifice structure: the lives of many are sacrificed to save the life of one. The film's ending elides this structure, replacing it with thc traditional one-for-many sacrifice structure, with a final image of the elderly Ryan and his children and grandchildren standing before a single grave.

Lester Friedman points out that the film's Normandy frame establishes an unsettling confusion about point of view in the Omaha Beach sequence, since the elderly man in the graveyard is not revealed to be James Ryan until the film's end.[23] To understand how Spielberg's film works in terms of the iconography of vulnerability, we must try to uncover what kind of experience Spielberg's abrupt shifts in point of view, narrative style, and ideology create for the viewer. After the Omaha Beach sequence, a far more traditional narrative begins. The death scenes of Private Carpazo (Vin Diesel), Private Mellish (Adam Goldberg), and medic Wade (Giovanni Ribisi) structure this narrative, a familiar formulation from WWII combat films that works to raise the stakes of the squad's eventual rescue of the missing Ryan. More importantly for my purposes, the increasingly visceral horror of each death progressively undermines the stoic, duty-bound masculinity represented by Captain Miller. The first of these structuring deaths—Carpazo's—happens in a bombed-out French village where the squad finds a frightened, trapped family. This introduction of women and children, particularly the family's terrified little girl, appears to give audiences an image of vulnerability the way they expect to see it: young, helpless, and female. But the squad's interaction with the family makes it clear that protecting them is not the justification for the mission. Carpazo wants to help the refugees, who ask the Americans to take the children to safety with the Allied troops.

The scene's dialogue—Carpazo insists that taking the child he's holding down the road to safety is the "decent" thing to do, while Miller snaps, "We're not here to do the decent thing; we're here to follow fuckin' orders"—matters less than the visual image of tall, broad-shouldered Carpazo cradling a small girl. This image inverts when it turns out that the truly vulnerable body is not the child's, but the man's. Carpazo falls, leveled by a hidden German sniper; the moment is followed by a long, difficult-to-watch sequence where the squad, including medic Wade, cannot reach the dying Carpazo because the sniper remains hidden. Spielberg's camera hides the scene where Wade finally reaches Carpazo's body, focusing on the girl hysterically hitting her father. The French father's inability to protect his family from war mirrors the squad's inability to reach Carpazo's body in time to help him. The child is active (hitting, yelling) while Carpazo lies, unable to move, still vulnerable to the sniper's bullets. The camera forces spectators to confront the moment of his physical suffering, not to imagine Wade's ability to help him. Carpazo's emotional vulnerability to the plight of a family in a war zone where the domestic space has been destroyed leads to his body being made vulnerable. Only Miller's military restraint ("That's why we can't take kids") protects the body from its own vulnerability. Carpazo is the first character to be sacrificed in the search for Ryan, and after the spectacle of his death, the squad openly questions the efficacy of the mission. Walking away from Carpazo's corpse, the tough-talking Brooklyn-Irish Private Reiben—played by 1990s indie auteur Ed Burns—mutters, "Fuck Ryan." This dialogue, voiced by a visible representative of Generation X, the only one of the young actors with serious name recognition in 1998,[24] begins to establish the film's substitution of Ryan for the American civilian population in general and the film's audience in particular. The film asks whether the protection of people who don't understand the sacrifice is worth the cost of these agonizing deaths. By substituting a single soldier for this faceless collective, Spielberg has it both ways, voicing the cynical point toward which the film barrels for most of its running time (it's not worth it) while endorsing the film's eleventh-hour embrace of Ryan.

Saving Private Ryan's single ideological subversion of the traditional war film is the way it shows male vulnerability in the absence of women or feminized men that would keep that vulnerability coded female. But the conservative narrative needs a release valve for the consequences of this subversion, so the film becomes increasingly interested in stories the men tell about women. These stories attempt to rewrite men's vulnerability back into a narrative of male control, withholding, and exploitation. Spielberg thus primes his audience for Wade's death with a scene where the men swap stories as they camp in an abandoned church. Wade tells a story about his mother as a young medical intern, coming home late at night, and his own childish impulse to feign sleep rather than talk with her. In the story, he has control and the ability to wound other, more vulnerable people, despite the film's attempt to use his guilt over the memory to attract audience sympathy.[25] Captain Miller, a different type of man from the young soldiers, will not tell the story of his family or his home. He withholds it, just as Wade withheld his company from his overworked mother. The squad has a running bet as to Miller's home-front profession, and his reluctance to share this information indicates that he exists outside the storytelling structure that unites the younger men, an insistence that his type of manhood sees but does not tell. It is a sign of the film's ultimate rejection of the male body as a site of vulnerability that in the ending graveyard frame the now-elderly Ryan withholds Miller's story from Ryan's family. Ryan models Miller's style of manhood, not Wade's.

The sight of Wade's body being riddled with bullets the next day is similarly withheld from the spectator. Spielberg's camera shows only the aftermath, as the men rip open his shirt to expose his bleeding chest. Blood seeps out of multiple bullet wounds; they cannot wipe it off fast enough, and the camera focuses obsessively on Wade's face and bloody torso, intercut with close-ups of the panicked men surrounding him. In several tight medium shots, the men press their hands into his chest and stomach to try to stanch the bleeding. The composition of the film frame in this sequence is nearly identical to Stanley Kubrick's framing of Cowboy's death in *Full Metal Jacket*. Spielberg's visual reference to Kubrick and the antiwar tradition he represents gains extra ideological resonance when we consider that Spielberg infuses this sequence with far greater emotional weight than Kubrick gives it. Kubrick reserves the full horror of the body's vulnerability for the death of the female sniper who shot Cowboy, while Spielberg rests that weight directly on the bleeding male body.

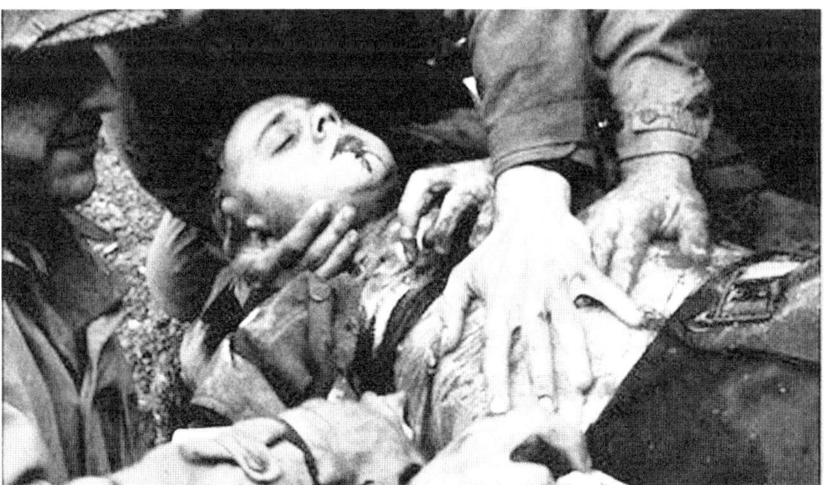

Figure 10 Wade dies

This is the second time in *Saving Private Ryan* that Spielberg makes visual reference to American film history. In the sequence showing Mrs. Ryan learning of the death of three of her four sons, Spielberg pays homage to *The Searchers* (1956) and John Ford's iconic shot of the landscape framed by a door, with a waiting woman standing just inside the threshold. As the film's narrative progresses, Spielberg's visual references grow increasingly darker—a communal shot of failed caretaking here replaces Ford's vision of the solitary antihero visually alienated from hearth and home. The other soldiers lack Wade's knowledge of how to deal with multiple gunshot wounds, and the sickening image created by shots of their hands ineffectively covering his body makes the site of the physically vulnerable male body also a site of male emotional and professional failure. After requesting an overdose of morphine, Wade cries, "I don't wanna die. Mama? Mama? I wanna go home. I wanna go home. Mama! Mama! Mama—Ma—Mama," an aural return to the dying soldiers on Omaha Beach. Critics often argue that the scene that follows this one, where squad members capture a German soldier, beat him, and want to execute him, is structurally important because of the moral questions it raises about killing unarmed prisoners. I view the scene where Wade dies as more crucial to the visual structure of a film more interested in establishing vulnerability than in establishing moral choice. When to kill matters less in this film than how to die, and how the spectacle of male vulnerability affects the ethics of war.

After the unsettling visceral experience created for the viewer by Wade's death scene, Spielberg desperately needs the reintroduction of a female presence to contain the film's anxieties about male vulnerability. The stories that follow, one about Miller's wife, the other about Ryan's mother, reassert the narrative that has been in tension with the camera's focus on vulnerable men. These narratives are the film's clumsy attempt to paper a traditional dichotomy of female vulnerability and male stoicism onto the scenes that precede and follow them.[26] The ability to tell a story, and to replace the sight of the dead body with a reminder of the absent domestic space (the dark space where Mrs. Ryan stands), thus begins to emerge as the film's answer to the problem of vulnerability.

Reiben, angry that Miller and the soft, bookish Corporal Upham (Jeremy Davies) stopped him from killing the German soldier who shot Wade, threatens mutiny. This confrontation, threatening violence within the squad, finally prompts the story of Miller's life at home. He is an English teacher—a teacher of stories—and *his* story, the film suggests, is the only antidote to the violence that threatens to erupt.

MILLER: So I guess I've changed some. Sometimes I wonder if I've changed so much, my wife is even going to recognize me whenever it is I get back to her. And how I'll ever be able to—to tell her about days like today. Ah, Ryan—I don't know anything about Ryan; I don't care. The man means nothing to me. He's just a name. But if . . . you know, if going to Ramelle and finding him so he can go home, if that earns me the right to get back to my wife, well then . . . then that's my mission. (*To Reiben*) You want to leave? You want to go off and fight the war? All right. All right, I won't stop you. I'll even put in the paperwork. I just know that every man I kill, the farther away from home I feel.

Hanks delivers this speech in his familiar everyman diction with a vocal register a bit deeper than the one he used for the romantic comedies that solidified his film stardom. But audience awareness of those roles, and the nice-guy persona Hanks perfects in them, becomes crucial to the sense created for the spectator that we're seeing something new. If Hanks's character is an English teacher forced by the war to carry a gun, Hanks as a performer is here asked to model a far different style of masculinity than the one that had made him famous. Spielberg negotiates this shift by contrasting Hanks's new persona as Miller with the collective presence of the young squad members. After Miller gives this speech, the camera shows him backlit, dragging a body to its shallow grave. This body is probably Wade's, though the light does not permit certainty. Now, Wade is just a body, waiting to be dragged offscreen. The supposedly redemptive effect of Miller's speech only works with the body absent. The spectacle of war must be framed in terms of a waiting woman, not the body of a man who just died calling for his mother. The speech itself not only writes choice back into the soldier's contract (a choice that didn't exist for soldiers in World War II any more than it did for soldiers in Vietnam), it obscures the film's actual moral calculus. Every man he buries, not every man he kills, makes Miller feel far away from home. Dying, not killing, prompts the horror of vulnerability that stories about women must try to obscure. Fittingly, then, soon after losing Wade the men find Ryan, another son waiting to talk to his mother.

Matt Damon's appearance as Private Ryan two-thirds of the way through the film has an accumulated meaning for the contemporary viewer of *Saving Private Ryan* different from that created for a 1998 audience. Damon was largely unknown when Spielberg cast him as Ryan, though by the time the film premiered the Academy had nominated him for Best Actor for *Good Will Hunting* (1997) and had awarded him an Oscar for Best Screenplay along with writing partner Ben Affleck. Once he appears onscreen, Ryan—grief-stricken over the news of his dead brothers—balks at abandoning his squad, which has been ordered to protect a bridge against heavy odds. Ryan's reaction to the news of the squad's sacrifice, and his refusal to "abandon [his] post," signal Spielberg's intention to switch the film's focus to Ryan, toward the narrative concerns of storytelling, and away from anxieties about male vulnerability. When Ryan resists Miller's offer of protection, Reiben angrily interrupts:

REIBEN: Hey, asshole! Two of our guys already died trying to find you, all right?
RYAN (*to Miller*): Sir?
MILLER: That's right.

RYAN (*walking over to Reiben and the squad*): What were their names?

MELLISH: Irwin Wade and Adrian Carpazo.

RYAN: Wade and . . .

MELLISH: Carpazo.

Ryan's desire to know the names of the men who died to find him shows that he understands and respects their sacrifice. Ryan names the spectacles of vulnerability the audience has witnessed ("Wade," "Carpazo") connecting the audience and Ryan in shared recognition of this *specific* sacrifice and the knowledge of vulnerability it entails. It serves as proof, both for the squad and for the audience, that Ryan is worth the sacrifice made for him, and it begins Spielberg's attempt to include his audience in the film's salvific project. *Saving Private Ryan* establishes the naming trope in an earlier scene where the exhausted squad jokes and banters while sifting through a pile of dog tags from dead soldiers, looking for Ryan's name. Wade had angrily reminded his comrades that those names represented people who were now dead. That Wade himself, along with Carpazo, is now just a name to be recounted highlights the film's obsession with the exchange of bodies, not the military strategy that makes holding the bridge important. This dynamic becomes more apparent when Ryan insists he doesn't deserve special treatment:

RYAN: It doesn't make any sense. It doesn't make any sense, sir. Why? Why do I deserve to go? Why not any of these guys? They all fought just as hard as me.

MILLER: Is that what they're supposed to tell your mother when they send her another folded American flag?

RYAN: Tell her that when you found me, I was here, and I was with the only brothers that I have left, and that there's no way I was gonna desert them. I think she'll understand that. There's no way I'm leaving this bridge.

Here, Ryan appears to voice the film's inversion of vulnerability: the other vulnerable men, not his waiting mother, deserve his protection. Ryan chooses "brothers" over mother, but the dialogue's focus on what story they should "tell" if he dies brings the narrative back to the question Miller posed over Wade's dead body: "how I'll ever be able to—to tell her about days like today." The "her" switches from Miller's wife to Ryan's mother, but both attempt to replace the dead body with a story about women.

Ryan's own story about home mirrors the third act's attempt to replace soldiers' physical vulnerability with stories about women and the stoic masculinity they require of men. Ryan confesses to Miller that he cannot remember his brothers' faces. Miller tells him to think of something specific, like Miller's own memory of "my wife pruning the rose bushes in a pair of my old work gloves." Ryan then tells a misogynist story about himself, his brothers, and their cruelty toward an "ugly" girl named Alice Jardine. Gary Kamiya, echoing many critics in otherwise glowing reviews of the film, calls Ryan's speech "one of the movie's few moments of artificiality."[27] But critics like Kamiya who dislike this story but admire the film miss something about the film's structure and the way these mininarratives work in Spielberg's larger ideological project. The stories serve the compensatory function of distracting attention from vulnerable male bodies with stories about women being made vulnerable by men.

What critics and audiences have seen as *Saving Private Ryan*'s unsettling effect is actually the consequence of its violent shift away from its revision of vulnerability. It encourages audiences to read the male body as a site of vulnerability, then reverses this logic through the increasingly visible importance of the stories men tell about war and about women. But in addition to replacing the visual emphasis on male vulnerability with a narrative focus on female vulnerability, Spielberg must also resolve the problem of sacrifice *Ryan*'s plot has established as a central concern. Having cataloged the relentlessly painful displays that are the cost of saving Private Ryan, the film must find a way to leave those bodies behind. It must shift the audience's focus from Carpazo's, Wade's, and Mellish's deaths toward Miller's death and the scores of people on the home front that his sacrifice purportedly "saved." In order to do this, the film makes its lone statement about World War II's political context, the piece of the moral puzzle that Spielberg had, up until this point, largely ignored.

The death scene for Private Mellish that Spielberg films differs drastically from the one that appears in Robert Rodat's shooting script. In the script, Mellish is shot by a German soldier who "darts into [his] path"; Upham promptly shoots the German soldier, and Reiben joins Upham in staring at the bodies.[28] The Private Mellish death scene in Ramelle that appears in the final version of *Saving Private Ryan* registers a far deeper and more political critique than the random senselessness with which Mellish dies in the original script. For the final battle, Mellish places himself on the second floor of a bombed-out house, relying on skittish Corporal Upham to bring him ammunition. At the climactic moment, Upham, unable to muster physical courage, cowers on the stairs with the now-useless ammo as Mellish struggles hand-to-hand with a German soldier. Earlier in the film, Carpazo had found a Hitler Youth knife on a dead German soldier and offered it to Mellish. Mellish renames the knife a "Shabbas challah cutter," and the object comes to represent Mellish's Jewishness in the ritualistic context of Shabbat. Mellish's struggle with the German soldier represents a turn away from the film's storytelling structure and a return to the violence and ritualism of the film's first half. And in this context, the knife again becomes an important symbol. After a series of disorienting, violent close-ups, Mellish pulls out the Hitler Youth/Shabbat challah knife, which the two struggle over at excruciating length. In a close two-shot, framed as an embrace, the German soldier slides the knife into Mellish slowly, whispering "shhh . . . ," his voice nearly a caress.

The spectacle of this scene, with its intimate, penetrative violence, becomes ideologically horrifying as well when we realize that Mellish is killed with the

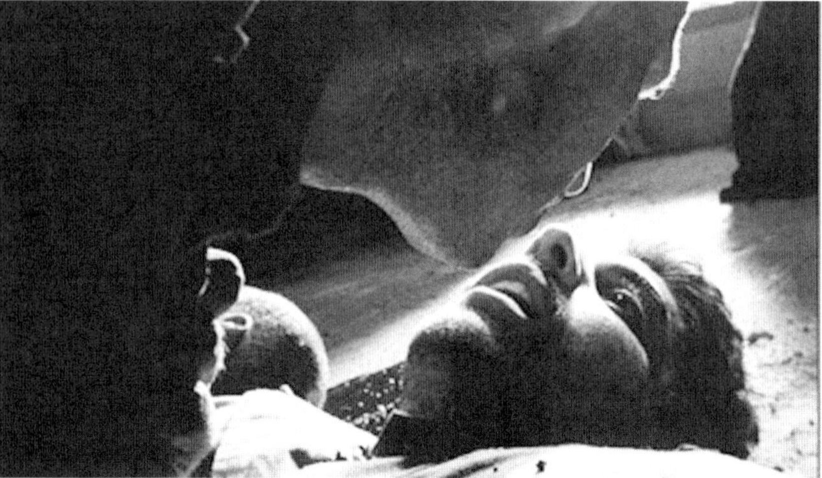

Figure 11 Mellish dies

Hitler Youth knife, now robbed of its potentially redemptive meaning, while Christian, liberally educated Upham cowers on the stairs outside, too afraid to intervene. Upham sinks on the stairs, crying, and the exiting German soldier brushes past him, deciding (together with the film) that he is not worth killing. Putting aside the irony of a Nazi soldier passing the film's own moral judgment on Upham, this scene provides a shocking moment in an otherwise ideologically predictable film. This movie emphasizes "saving": when you can't save, you witness; when you can't witness, you mourn. The fact that when the squad's sole Jewish soldier dies nobody tries to stop it, nobody witnesses it, and the soldiers who would have mourned it are already dead is a politically powerful indictment of America's inaction during the first five years of the Holocaust.[29] Yet Spielberg seems eager to disavow this critique. Given the celebration of American victory in World War II that is *Saving Private Ryan*'s crowd-pleasing goal, this political critique must be swept aside, much like the anxieties about male vulnerability the first two acts raised. Literally and figuratively, Mellish's body must be left out of sight.

The film's closing graveyard frame attempts to provide the audience with an emotional release from this tension. But the attempt lacks moral and emotional weight, since Reiben—as the only member of the original squad other than Upham to survive—is the witness whose mourning ought to matter, not Ryan's. To insist on ideological closure (and to shut off the potentially subversive critique it opened with Mellish's death), the film has to name Ryan the final witness. With his dying breath, Captain Miller tells Ryan to "Earn this . . . earn it." Miller's sacrifice buys James Ryan's manhood, purchased over the body of a dead father figure whose body never seems vulnerable the way the younger men's had. In these final scenes, *Ryan* trains its audience to resist the spectacle of vulnerability it had earlier established. The dying Miller speaks stoically to Ryan as the male body figuratively closes back up while he speaks.

The Normandy frame finishes the transition from the inverted sacrifice structure to the sacrifice structure the war film narrative traditionally demands—one for many. This compels the presence of Ryan's family at Miller's gravesite in Normandy. Miller is the sacrifice; Ryan and the generations of his family who otherwise would not have been born are the beneficiaries.

> RYAN: My family is with me today. They wanted to come with me. To be honest with you, I—I wasn't sure how I'd feel coming back here. Every day I think about what you said to me that day on the bridge. I've tried to live my life the best I could. I hope that was enough. I hope that, at least in your eyes, I've earned what all of you have done for me.
>
> MRS. RYAN: James. (*Reading the name on the cross*) "Captain John H. Miller."
>
> RYAN: Tell me I've led a good life.
>
> MRS. RYAN: What?
>
> RYAN: Tell me I'm a good man.
>
> MRS. RYAN: You are.

Despite the much-criticized sentimental tone of this closing frame, *Saving Private Ryan* is not about the certainty of having "earned it," for either the WWII generation it ventriloquizes or the baby boom generation whose members wrote, directed, and starred in it.[30] Instead it dramatizes the tenuous position of the "new" man—one who can tell stories about rose bushes as well as vulnerable male bodies—as a husband, father, and son, even as it catalogs the costs of physical sacrifice for a nuclear family that the movie implies can never really understand. Spielberg insists upon a traditional sacrifice structure at odds with his film's most viscerally powerful images. Thus he must back away from the dynamic that offers the Mellish/Upham interaction as a metaphor for America, instead offering the Miller/Ryan dynamic—the good father and the grateful son. *Saving Private Ryan* is at the same time ambivalent and certain: ambivalent about what the spectacle of vulnerability asks of men, but certain about women's inability to reassure them of its value. What the film itself wants to offer, though, is a respite from the question of male physical vulnerability through a collective absolution for the stories we tell ourselves about war. Viewers may balk at the aesthetics of Ryan's appearance in the graveyard rather than Reiben's, but ideologically the film requires Ryan's presence and Reiben's absence. In its final frames, the film celebrates Ryan, the character who, like the audience, was not part of the squad but understands and honors its sacrifice—Spielberg's final exercise in wish fulfillment. The film's salvific embrace thus includes the audience, and the narrative encourages us to believe that it is a tragic but unavoidable circumstance of war that Mellish's body is left behind. The image of Ryan's grateful family standing in near-mute awe of his status as veteran states the film's overt thesis: on the battlefields of Europe, a specifically American form of masculinity was born, and the appropriate response to it is gratitude. But there remains an uncomfortable sense, which the sea of white crosses cannot quite erase, that something else happened in Europe during those years, a spectacle of male vulnerability harder to repress than the tears that threaten to overcome Private Ryan.

Training the Body: *G.I. Jane* and the Sexual Politics of Resistant Vulnerability

Ridley Scott and Demi Moore create a spectacle in *G.I. Jane* perhaps even more disruptive to traditional notions of gendered vulnerability. The incendiary iconography of a buzz-cut, beaten Moore that graced the film's poster signaled a different use of her physicality than the one that sold issues of *Vanity Fair* in the early years of the decade. In September 1996, eleven months before *Jane*'s premiere, Moore appeared on the cover of *Cigar Aficionado,* and the title of the accompanying article proclaimed, "No Apologies, No Regrets: From the Roles She Plays to the Cigars She Smokes, Actress Demi Moore Makes Her Own Choices." Moore, holding the makeshift phallus on the cover and puffing away at it in the photographs inside, this time speaks for herself from the *Jane* set. Mervyn Rothstein's article collapses her star persona with the role she's shooting when the magazine goes to press: "'It's a Cuban Montecristo Joyita,' the soldier says, taking a long, pleasurable puff. The voice is assertively strong—and distinctly feminine. 'I prefer the panatelas, though I've tried the Montecristo No. 2, the torpedo. It's a little big for me but I like it.' The name on the back of the chair: DEMI MOORE."[31] Rothstein's tongue-in-cheek tone is typical of the cigar jokes that would proliferate the year after *Jane*'s release, when President Clinton came under congressional investigation for having used a cigar as a substitute phallus with Monica Lewinsky. But Moore is framed here as anything but an intern catering to powerful men.

The female body as a site of debate about military policy and women's place in the "warrior culture" gained traction in the 1990s. A month after Moore appeared naked and pregnant on the cover of *Vanity Fair,* the Tailhook Association, a private organization of retired U.S. Navy pilots, held its thirty-fifth annual symposium at a Las Vegas hotel. Thousands of active and reserve naval personnel attended the conference, and it caused a significant public relations disaster for the navy when dozens of female navy pilots accused male officers of sexual assault and harassment. The controversy over "the Tailhook incident" is emblematic of this moment in several ways. The naval aviators attending the conference (and manning the "gauntlet" through which female officers were allegedly forced to walk) had a hold on the American popular imagination about the military incommensurate with their number due to the popularity of Tony Scott's 1986 film *Top Gun*. But these pilots were also a symbol for a changing military at the end of the twentieth century. The September 1991 Tailhook symposium was the first meeting of the group since the end of the first Gulf War, which had relied on U.S. airpower, not ground troops, for a victory light on American casualties. The Tailhook incident also provided a flashpoint in the ongoing debate about the gender integration of the military, as the bodies of the assaulted female officers became an integral part of the controversy. The female officer most visible in the case was "Victim #50," whistle-blower Lieutenant Paula Coughlin, a navy helicopter pilot and the kind of officer Demi Moore played in *A Few Good Men* (Rob Reiner, 1992) as well as in *G.I. Jane*.

But if the Tailhook incident framed the female service member as a vulnerable body in danger of sexual assault by the aggressive sexuality of "elite" servicemen, *G.I. Jane* tries to move the debate from the hotel rooms on the home front to the training grounds of the SEAL/Combined Reconnaissance Team (CRT) program. Scott and Moore accomplish this by telling a new story about the United States military, revising both the Vietnam-era vision of boot camp as psychic violence and *Saving Private Ryan*'s vision of a male military where women are sisters, wives, or mothers. *G.I. Jane*'s negotiation of these tropes happens around the spectacle of the female body in pain. *Full Metal Jacket* focused these reactions most intensely on the vulnerable body of the Asian female; *Ryan* attempted to shift the spectacle, to open the vulnerability of the male body to audience scrutiny, only to disavow the project altogether in favor of a traditional, safe masculinity. If *Saving Private Ryan* used Tom Hanks's bland, reassuring solidity as a salve for the radical vulnerability of Diesel, Ribisi, and Goldberg, *G.I. Jane* makes its controversial star, Moore, herself the object of the film's radical revision of vulnerability, arguing that the bleeding body—male or female—should not automatically register as vulnerable.

One of the Tailhook scandal's unfortunate legacies is the public assumption, manufactured by opponents of women in combat, that expansion of women in combat roles during the 1990s came as the result of pressure on the military to become "politically correct" in the wake of sex scandals like Tailhook. This legacy provides the context for *G.I. Jane*'s political argument in favor of women's equality, which it establishes filmically in two ways: by refiguring combat service not as stain or trauma but as a neutral step on the ladder of military advancement,[32] and by retraining its audience's reaction to violence against women. The film accomplishes this second goal by setting up two reversals of the audience's expectations. First, it rewrites being beaten as a sign of strength, not vulnerability. Then it reappropriates the image of a woman being beaten by a man as signaling respect, not domination, figuring male desire to protect women from violence as insidious condescension. These reversals are central to the film's project. *G.I. Jane* seeks to erase the memory of Lieutenant Paula Coughlin and to replace it with Moore's Jordan O'Neil, hoping to rewrite Moore's own star image in the process. Though the film was not the huge commercial success that Moore hoped would end rumors of her waning box-office appeal, we need only consult the titles of the scores of articles written in 2009 about the blurring "front line" in Iraq to see the centrality of Scott's film and Moore's Lieutenant O'Neil to our collective cultural consciousness.[33] The film's plot figures women as physically equal to men, not desiring or needing the gender-norming special treatment the film posits as the real cause of women's continued inequality in the armed forces. Its iconography, and Scott's use of spectacle, however, demand a real shift in the ways the mainstream audience reads violence against women.

G.I. Jane's theatrical release in 1997 came amid press rumors of strain in the Moore-Willis marriage and widespread speculation about Moore's growing reputation as a bad box-office bet. Moore figures in much of this press as a star who needs to be "given her shot," which gives the film's plot an extra frisson of metafilmic resonance. O'Neil becomes the first woman to attend Navy SEAL training, the most elite and physically rigorous training program the U.S. military offers. Though O'Neil is the unwitting pawn of Senator DeHaven (Anne Bancroft), who uses her as a test case for the full gender integration of the military, the bulk of the film focuses on boot camp, where O'Neil earns the respect of her fellow recruits and Master Chief Urgayle (Viggo Mortensen). This structure—political machinations underlie the central narrative of growth and acceptance—allows the film to bring its realist narrative into tension with the audience's cultural responses to violence against women. In order to maintain the realist narrative's pleasures, it must therefore subvert audience expectations about violence and the female body, culminating in the film's famously gender-bending showdown between O'Neil and Urgayle. That this scene addresses O'Neil's near-rape at the hands of her drill instructor in the visual language of male-on-male rape gestures toward the film's unspoken historical context: the Don't Ask/Don't Tell policy debated in the years leading up to the film's production. In the mid- to late 1990s, laws about women in combat were not changing, but the DADT policy was changing the public face of the military. The film explicitly compares the racial integration of the military to gender integration—an African American recruit tells O'Neil that she's the "new nigger on the block"—but is unwilling to see homosexual soldiers as the next group fighting for inclusion. *G.I. Jane* offers, in the aftermath of Tailhook and an increasingly emotional debate about the new DADT policy, a reassurance to audiences that the military is not broken and that female advancement and the military "warrior culture" are not actually in conflict. But that reassurance comes at the price of renegotiating society's most cherished ideas about the female body in peril.

Film critic Kenneth Turan writes in a *Los Angeles Times* review that *G.I. Jane* "shows why Moore is indisputably a star and why the studios have difficulty knowing what to do with her," likening her performance as O'Neil to "the physicality of a Joan Crawford in combat boots."[34] The studios were not alone in their confusion over Moore's combination of conventional female beauty and lack of clearly defined vulnerability. Screenwriter Danielle Alexandra wrote the film specifically for Moore, enthusing in the film's press kit that "as I wrote the screenplay, I thought of the personal and physical strength that Demi has as an individual, a survivor, a woman, an achiever—an actress." Ridley Scott films a scene that mirrors this casting process, choosing the body of the woman that will stand in for the political battle over the gender integration of combat forces. Senator DeHaven and her staff pore over the photographs and service records of a number of female officers they might choose as "G.I. Jane." As Scott's camera shows a picture of an extraordinarily lean female runner, DeHaven purrs, "perfect—only do a chromosome check," and the photo of a female power lifter with large, muscular thighs meets with derision over the possibility of seeing *that* face "on the cover of *Newsweek*." DeHaven snaps, "She looks like the wife of a Russian beet farmer!" To audiences immersed in the contemporary debate about gays and lesbians serving openly in the military, the image of the female power lifter has a very different valence—DeHaven means not that she looks like a beet farmer's wife but that she looks like a lesbian. This anxiety about the gendered, sexualized image of women in the military drives the characters' choice of O'Neil, whose photo DeHaven approvingly notes is "top-drawer . . . with silk stockings inside." What kind of image "G.I. Jane" will present to the public about women in the military is Scott's metafilmic commentary on the images of military women circulating in the mid-1990s but also on the images circulating about Demi Moore herself.

The film's early scenes seem designed to separate the O'Neil character from Shannon Faulkner, who became the first female cadet at the Citadel after filing a gender-discrimination lawsuit. Faulkner resigned after less than a week due to emotional and physical exhaustion, making her the mid-1990s poster girl for "special treatment." But it's not merely the specter of Faulkner and Coughlin that the film seeks to banish—it is also the Vietnam-era image of combat experience as psychic scar. Action films in the 1980s often figured their protagonist's bitterness and cynicism as a result of war trauma sustained in Vietnam.[35] O'Neil's anger, in contrast, results from being denied combat experience; she was told that naval submarines did not have bathroom facilities for women. Once at SEAL training, she hews to this line. She's not there to "make some kind of statement" but to "get operational experience." O'Neil repeatedly insists that she craves "operational experience" of the kind that her male contemporaries gained in the First Gulf War because it is "the key to advancement." In refiguring combat as professionalization, Scott takes a crucial first step toward reorienting the way his audience reads violence, particularly violence against women. These early, verbal explanations of O'Neil's motives are crucial to tying the film's visual strategies to its political point about feminism. "Special treatment," not male violence, is the enemy of women's equality.[36]

When *Striptease* premiered in 1996, Moore was filming *G.I. Jane*. Her red-carpet appearance at the New York premiere featured her with a shaved head, mimicked by tomboy haircuts and matching dresses on the Moore-Willis daughters. *Striptease*'s display of Moore's body caused an uneasiness in the public press that I want to suggest stems partly from the gender dislocation of her shaved head and buffed-up body during the *Striptease* promotional junket. In a 1996 piece titled "Boom to Bust: Demi Moore, Nakedly Ambitious," William Leith discusses Moore's bared breasts in *Striptease* as a part of an arsenal: "Moore exposes her breasts. They jut out, firm and proud, like weapons, like John Wayne's gun, which was an extension of his body, too."[37] The comparison to John Wayne's body is instructive in light of the mid-1990s fascination with Moore's body. The film's delicate negotiation of Moore's gender—masculine but female—makes the movie's ideological embrace of military power and authority palatable. The film's appeal depends upon the transgressive celebration of masculine power centered in the female body. This desire structures the film's attitude toward its secondary female characters and demands that they be seen as foils to O'Neil, not comrades. O'Neil's gender marks her as a danger to the military's "official nonpolicy on women in combat" because she doesn't fit into the culturally accepted stereotypes of women in the armed forces. O'Neil insists she doesn't want to represent anything, but this is in itself a political position, and the film is too invested in creating a new visual iconography of female strength to be called apolitical. But because its politics work more transgressively in the realm of visuals than in the realm of narrative, *G.I. Jane* remains both fascinated by and uninterested in Moore's body as a spectacle. Ultimately, the film argues that equality can be purchased only through physical strength and transgressive speech. Political speech, and the avenues of power political feminism has insisted can open to women through that speech, must be disavowed.

For audiences fresh from the Tailhook and Citadel controversies to accept the pleasures of *G.I. Jane*'s traditional boot-camp structure, Scott must subvert his audience's response toward violence against women. Once O'Neil arrives at CRT, the film begins to establish its visual techniques, which will train the viewer to read physical abuse as respect. O'Neil's commanding officer, Captain Salem (Scott Wilson), clearly resents the integration mandate and does not respect her as the male trainees' equal. The film establishes this when he offers her tea and declares she needn't shave her head like the male recruits. By contrast, during a Hell Week training montage, Sergeant Johns (David Warshofsky) brusquely pushes O'Neil to the ground seconds before Sergeant Pyro (Kevin Gage) steps on a male recruit's back to force him underwater. This rough "equality" works so that, while the sergeant's snide remark about O'Neil "playing with [her] hair" and fellow recruit Cortez's (David Vadem) sexual taunting register as discrimination (being singled out), the sergeant's roughness with O'Neil's body registers as respect (equal treatment).

It is important to the film's political investments that military authority and hierarchy, which might at first seem hostile to O'Neil, are ultimately positive. Once O'Neil shaves her own head and tells Captain Salem that she will no longer tolerate the "double standard" that allows her more lenient goals but instead wants to go "head to head with the men," he gives her the respect he withheld during their previous meeting. This embrace of military hierarchy also means an embrace of the anti-individualist logic boot-camp films depend upon. These films' goal of achieving what Yvonne Tasker calls an "undifferentiated maleness" demands that characters give up traditional markers of both identity and privilege, class privilege being most important here, since officers in SEAL training are placed under the near-complete power of drill sergeants they technically outrank. Women's desire to take up previously male subject positions has usually been explained by mainstream films in terms of power. *G.I. Jane* complicates this question by placing O'Neil in a "male" position that involves a loss of power familiar to the boot-camp genre but unfamiliar to most female-empowerment films. *G.I. Jane* visually and narratively recodes the relationships between violence, control, and power, so that loss of control and subjection to violence becomes a form of power. This formulation is not entirely new to American film,[38] but when it is coupled with the way film has trained audiences to see violence against women, the combination is both volatile and political. In order for this reversal to work, the film must establish O'Neil's toughness and allow audiences a crowd-pleasing glimpse of the famous transformation of Moore's previously feminine body.

The mainstream press expressed confusion about the counterintuitive way Scott's camera treats Moore's body; the *Sunday Times*'s Caris Davis opined that "Demi Moore in army fatigues" meant "Hollywood has turned its back on overt sexiness" and that "Moore's GI Jane" epitomized "joyless sexual denial."[39] What might at first appear to be typical press misreading of female strength coded positively becomes more complicated when placed in the context of Tailhook's combustible mix of traditional female sexuality and military "warrior culture" run amok. *G.I. Jane* attempts to negotiate the line between Paula Coughlin and "joyless sexual denial" by displaying O'Neil's physical transformation from an officer who is a sexual partner to men to a warrior who is their equal. Directly following her decision to enter SEAL CRT, Scott inserts a scene of O'Neil bathing with her naval officer boyfriend, Royce (Jason Beghe). The sequence shows the couple in the tub, surrounded by candles and wineglasses. Moore's body is submerged, feminized but not visible. As Royce washes her feet, O'Neil declares that she's "not interested in being some poster girl for women's rights." At this moment, Moore/O'Neil disavows the connection to Coughlin and the other military "poster girls" she physically resembles. When Royce storms out of the bathtub, irritated by her constant refusal to "ask [his] permission," she orders, "Get your dick back in here!" Her substitution of "dick" for "ass" in this phrase highlights the power that having (or being able to claim) a "dick" possesses for Scott and Moore in shifting from the Coughlin iconography to the new iconography telegraphed by Moore's *Cigar Aficionado* cover. The one scene Scott shows of O'Neil and Royce together *after* CRT indicates the shift in power that comes with this changing iconography. In this scene, she sits on the porch, sporting a shaved head and bruises, smoking a cigar and drinking whiskey as the morning light flushes the porch.

G.I. Jane shows its audience the transformation from long hair to buzz cut, from white wine to whiskey, in a training montage in the middle of the film that intercuts scenes of O'Neil training alongside the men and scenes of her working out in private. Here the film's ambivalent attitude toward O'Neil/Moore's body emerges. In any scene where men are present (nearly every scene in the film), the camera refuses to fetishize the femaleness of Moore's body. But in private, in motion, the camera lingers over her taut abs, her smooth, strong legs, and the breasts that jut like weapons. In the private scenes, the audience is invited to admire both the strength and the sexiness of O'Neil's new body, filmed to highlight both her sweaty musculature and her heaving chest, masculinity and female sexuality joined in a single spectacle. But this spectacle is privileged—the audience sees it, Urgayle and the men do not. This serves two purposes: it acknowledges that the physical strength the film posits as earning O'Neil the right to attend CRT is created, not "natural," but it also insists that this effort be hidden. While proving herself, O'Neil must train on the sly, presenting the fruits of that training as "natural" to the men from whom she is still trying to win acceptance. This visual discourse of physical strength is contrasted in the montage with the supposedly equalizing power of firearms. Several montage scenes show the class learning to quickly assemble a "chopped-down version of the M-16 assault rifle," an activity that, by the end of the montage, O'Neil has mastered better than her male counterparts. The only effective way to waterproof the gun is to slip a condom over the barrel—as if we needed another reminder of what the gun stands for. But this is not the kind of phallus O'Neil needs, and, the film ultimately implies, the equality of a gun barrel is not the kind of equality she needs either.[40]

Amy Taubin, in an admiring *Village Voice* review of the film as an exhilarating "gender-fuck," is one of the few reviewers to note Ridley Scott's nationality, arguing that as "a British filmmaker working in Hollywood, Ridley Scott reenvisions classic American movie landscapes through alienated eyes." Following the training montage's ideology of equality through physical strength, Scott exposes Moore/O'Neil's body in a shower scene that shows "woman as spectacle, but the spectacle is a gender bender that scrambles the iconography of top and bottom, butch and femme, exploding male and female identities in the process."[41] In the scene, O'Neil showers; the camera lingers on her exposed body and on Urgayle in the shadows, watching. When he begins speaking, she's alerted to his presence, and her face registers irritation at his words, but not at his gaze.

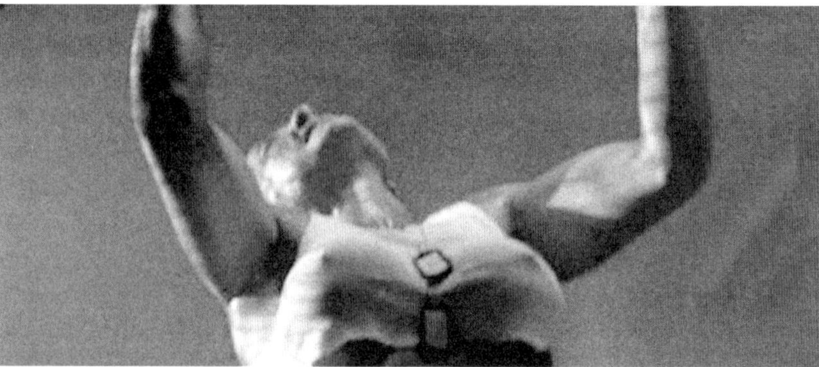

Figure 12 O'Neil trains in private

URGAYLE: The Israelis tried it. Women in combat. Seems the men couldn't get used to the sight of women blown open. They'd linger over the wounded females, often trying to save those who obviously couldn't be saved, often to the detriment of the mission.

O'NEIL: You were given the Navy Cross, right? Can I ask what you got it for? (*She turns off the water.*)

URGAYLE: Since it bears on this conversation, I got it for pulling a 240-pound man out of a burning tank.

O'NEIL: So, when a man tries to rescue another man, he's a hero, but when he tries to rescue a woman, he's just gone soft. (*She wraps a towel around her waist.*)

URGAYLE: Could you have pulled that man clear? (*She shrugs.*) Lieutenant, you couldn't even haul your own body weight out of the water today!

O'NEIL: Permission to get dressed, Master Chief?

Urgayle here voices both of the film's competing questions about women in the military. The question of physical strength and mental endurance ("Could you have pulled that man clear?") is purportedly Urgayle's objection to O'Neil, but this scene asks the more compelling question of what it means for men to watch women suffer, whether men can (or should) "get used to" it. This is the first in a series of scenes about men watching women, and though we're primed by convention to read Urgayle's voyeurism as a violation, O'Neil doesn't treat it as one. This is just a clearer example than most of a move the film makes frequently: O'Neil earns respect—from Urgayle, the men in her class, the film, and, presumably, the viewer—by the extent to which she reacts "like a man." In this sense, it is important that, standing naked in front of the clothed Urgayle, she grabs a towel and wraps it around her waist, like a man. Meanwhile, the scene's dialogue sets up the movie's intervention into mid-1990s debates about women in the military, conflated here with the recently instituted Don't Ask/Don't Tell policy. The film's ambivalence mirrors both the public outcry about Shannon Faulkner's "double standard" at the Citadel and the 1993 debates about DADT, with their focus on "unit cohesion." "Unit cohesion" and the yet more vague term "morale" are thinly veiled code for the social attitudes about gender and the military's masculinist structure implicit in the policies that keep women from serving in combat positions and keep gay men and lesbians from serving openly.

Although the Department of Defense had supported 1986's *Top Gun,* with its randy fighter pilots and traditional gender roles, early drafts of the *G.I. Jane* script sent to the navy met with resistance, particularly the viciousness of the training sequences and the dramatization of Survival, Evasion, Resistance, and Escape (SERE) training, where O'Neil and the other recruits are captured and taken to a simulated prisoner-of-war camp. SERE training had made a brief appearance in the early 1990s during the Tailhook scandal, with claims that the accused pilots were able to thwart investigators because they had learned how to withstand interrogation during the SERE course. As chapter 6 will discuss, this interrogation training has become central to the current debate over torture at Abu Ghraib and Guantánamo Bay, but for my purposes here, Ridley Scott's choice to stage O'Neil's showdown with Urgayle during the film's SERE sequence is important because the film's visuals set the scene in Vietnam. Location manager Mary Morgan chose Hunting Island State Park in South Carolina to stand in for the Florida swamps where the narrative tells us the training takes place precisely because of the visual connection to Vietnam: "Hunting Island is a great double for the Mekong Delta." The camp's bamboo cages and thatched-roof huts are meant to set this scene in Vietnam, with all of its politically fraught allusions for American film audiences, but also to self-consciously tap audience discomfort about the American soldier's capacity for sexual violence. Scott's establishing shot of the SERE interrogation hut is nearly identical to Michael Cimino's establishing shot in the Russian roulette POW sequence in *The Deer Hunter*. The charged discourses this setting raises—a female body in a space coded as Vietnam—primes the audience to read O'Neil's potential sexual vulnerability through the lens of the Asian woman who, raped or killed, was so central to the emotional impact of *Casualties of War* and *Full Metal Jacket*.[42] But the film rejects that connection. Here O'Neil's masculine performance becomes most volatile, and her lack of vulnerability most counterintuitive, in a near-rape scene during the SERE mock-interrogation. The film's two discourses of women's equality, its visual strategies in terms of the abused female body, and its sexual tensions collide with the political question of unit cohesion in a sequence Kenneth Turan calls an "unpleasantly graphic [display of] physical violence."[43] The SERE sequence occurs roughly two-thirds of the way through the film, after it has established the equality nexus through which O'Neil offers her body for punishment like a man's. But, although the scene hinges on a woman threatened with sexual violation turning it into power, O'Neil claims that power physically and verbally, not legally or politically. Audiences are primed to see the camp as a space oppressive of—and sexually frightening for—women. O'Neil reclaims that space, which serves as both a pleasurable moment of female power and an antidote to the legacy of trauma its Vietnam context raises for American audiences. *G.I. Jane* presents the space of Vietnam cleared out of *all* Asianness, reading the connection between Cold War and post–Cold War military bravado and Vietnam not as a space of American masculine victory over the Asian enemy, as *Rambo: First Blood Part II* (George P. Cosmatos, 1985) had, but as a space of the tough woman's victory over working-class men.

That Scott and Moore stage this sequence, with its incendiary iconography, in the context of Vietnam marks their desire to move the debate about the gender integration of the military out of the congressional hearing room and into the interrogation room. This move has stakes more controversial than anyone involved with *G.I. Jane*'s production could have anticipated now that SERE training—particularly the waterboarding that *G.I. Jane* dramatized without much controversy—has become fodder for those trying to justify torture. But *Jane* will make its commentary on the politics of the Middle East later in the film; the interrogation scene that takes place at SERE instead allows the film to renegotiate honorable masculinity and revise female vulnerability. Muscle-bound, laconic Instructor Pyro grows increasingly uneasy with Urgayle's physical assault on O'Neil. The camera vacillates between two scenes in conversation: the holding pen where the male recruits hear O'Neil being beaten outside of their field of vision, and inside the hut where Pyro attempts to stop Urgayle from beating the already bloodied O'Neil.

> PYRO: Jack . . .
> URGAYLE: What? You got a problem with this, Max? (*Pyro nods.*) Then get the fuck outta here! Get out!

Pyro and the imprisoned recruits are united visually as men who watch and ideologically as men who don't want to see a woman beaten. Crucially, this aligns Pyro and the recruits with the social structure that asks for "special treatment." Urgayle alone, it seems, respects O'Neil enough to treat her like a man.

> URGAYLE: You think we should go easy on women, Lieutenant? Do ya?
> O'NEIL: Fuck you.
> URGAYLE: I'm so glad we agree. (*He slams her head against the door and tosses her out of the hut into the view of the holding pen. He takes her to a trough of water and forces her head under.*) *To the men:* Two fire teams are still in the woods. Who's gonna give me a fix on 'em? Anyone can stop this. Just give me one good piece of intel, and it ends right here.

Scott's camera cuts jarringly from close-ups of Urgayle's face and O'Neil's submerged head and shoulders as she struggles to static long shots of the recruits behind the bars, watching. This scene's formal interest in the politics of spectatorship becomes more complicated as narrative tension mounts. The longer O'Neil refuses to "break," refuses to appear vulnerable, the more camera closes in on the caged men, eventually shooting them in close-ups that mirror the camera's treatment of Urgayle and O'Neil at the water trough. The moment that Urgayle shifts strategies, banking on male vulnerability in the face of female suffering as the threat to "unit cohesion" that will ensure the recruits' failure, he drags O'Neil across to the holding pen, crossing over the specular space until she is pressed directly up against the bars that separate her from the men, that cage them as spectators. If coming face-to-face with the image of female suffering does not have Urgayle's desired effect on his audience, he assumes his next tactic—sexual assault—will. And it is here that the identification Scott's camera has established between the caged men and the screen audience starts to unravel. Urgayle bends O'Neil over a table, her hands still bound behind her back, taunting, "Ever think about what happens when you're captured, Lieutenant?" He pulls out his knife and cuts the belt that holds up her pants. O'Neil maintains heroic ironic distance ("Oh yeah, just like the men do"), but "taking it like a man" does not involve taking it like a woman. Even when she's about to be raped, the scene is set up visually like male-on-male rape, registering the homosexual panic the film will not acknowledge.

During this sequence, which takes several uncomfortable minutes of screen time, Scott's camera turns less frequently to the caged men, drawing the film's spectator closer to the action without the mediating distance of the cage. In a series of close-ups, Urgayle kicks O'Neil's feet apart and yanks down her pants. As actual sexual violation seems to loom, and the men watching prepare to spill their secrets,[44] O'Neil fights back, knocking Urgayle to the ground. At the precise moment when the film's visual strategies are about to demand that its hero rape its heroine, O'Neil comes through with the backward head butt that breaks Urgayle's nose and saves the film from its unwillingness to follow through with its own logic. It is absolutely crucial to the film's political stance about special treatment that we're encouraged to believe Urgayle might have raped O'Neil, and that those who would have stopped it before she had a chance to stop it herself are consigning her to what George W. Bush would call the soft bigotry of low expectations. Of course, it is only through a nearly hysterical disavowal of the possibility of male-on-male rape that the film is able to see this kind of violence against O'Neil as a form of equality. After all, Urgayle did not try to rape any of the male recruits he interrogated. But the film's argument for gender equality at the expense of rejecting gays in the military requires this half-acknowledgment. Scott has successfully moved the debate out of a hearing room in Washington, DC, and into an interrogation hut in the imagined landscape of Vietnam, but he must still erase the specter of "unit cohesion" that marks the real-world similarity between the debates around women serving in combat units and LGBT soldiers serving openly. The threat to O'Neil's body that Scott's camera registers remains technically heterosexual but visually homosexual, registering both the film's uneasiness with its protagonist being treated as a woman and its nervousness with sex as a traditional site of female vulnerability.

O'Neil, hands still tied behind her back, fights Urgayle in the kind of bloody, macho set piece familiar to both prison and action films, necessary to establish the ethical demands of the masculinity Scott wants to extend to O'Neil. After Urgayle levels O'Neil with a particularly vicious punch, he staggers over to the men in the holding pen, who turn their backs on him in disgust: "You're a real fuckin' hero, man."

> URGAYLE: Guys—I'm saving her life. And yours. Her presence makes us all vulnerable. I don't want you learning that inconvenient fact under fire.
>
> O'NEIL: (*struggling to her feet*) Master Chief . . .
>
> URGAYLE: Lieutenant! Seek life elsewhere.
>
> O'NEIL: Suck my dick.

Screen audiences familiar with Ridley Scott's 1991 hit *Thelma & Louise* will recognize O'Neil's final line here as the taunt uttered by *Thelma & Louise*'s would-be rapist Harlan, causing Louise (Susan Sarandon) to shoot him, setting the film's feminists-on-the-lam plot into motion. In *G.I. Jane,* as in *Thelma & Louise,* Scott is interested in the power of speech acts to function as violence, which is crucial to *Thelma & Louise*'s justification of Louise's action.[45] Here, Scott gives the female hero the rapist's line, having exorcised the specter of Tailhook and the American public's ongoing discomfort with rape as a site of women's vulnerability. In this famous moment, O'Neil claims the "dick" that will make her an accepted part of the group, gaining a rhetorical victory over Urgayle, but not over the perspective he has raised about male vulnerability. He is the only male character who has consistently treated O'Neil with what the film figures as equality, and the visceral exhilaration of O'Neil's defiance hides the fact that this scene actually validates his perspective. Urgayle makes specific reference to vulnerability, but not the vulnerability of the female body. The real danger is men's vulnerability to the way they are socialized to protect women.

Viggo Mortensen's performance as Urgayle is central to the way Ridley Scott intends to figure military masculinity. Mortensen is physically slight when standing next to the other instructors and the male recruits, but his feral energy and commitment to the film's counterintuitive ethic of violence mark him as the film's most potent symbol of the masculinity it wants to extend to O'Neil. After the interrogation, Scott inserts a scene where Pyro lectures Urgayle: "It was out of line in there. It ain't gonna happen again." The scene's dialogue implies that spectators are meant to side with Pyro, but Scott's visuals side with Urgayle, who nonchalantly snaps his broken nose back into alignment. Here, as in so many other places, the film's narrative logic and its visual logic are in conflict. *G.I. Jane* takes a debate about men's emotions and frames it as a debate about women's physical equality, while male emotions about that equality remain contested. Once again, *G.I. Jane* mirrors the actual debate about gender integration: it pretends to be about whether women can do it physically, while *actually* being about whether men can handle it emotionally (Urgayle tells Pyro: "She's not the problem. We are."). *G.I. Jane* answers the first question but not the second. Even in places where the script criticizes Urgayle, the film as spectacle celebrates him and the kind of unqualified masculinity he represents.

Critics who confuse the film's radical gender politics with a disdain for the military frequently misread the Urgayle character. Anthony Lane writes in the *New Yorker,* "It goes without saying that Urgayle is a monster; Hollywood, with its liberal innocence and, at the same time, its craving for regular savagery, has never bothered to rid itself of the convenient delusion that people in positions of military authority are by definition implacable brutes."[46] Lane misreads the film's posture toward the U.S. military and toward this character, but Lane's assumption that any male character who treats a female character's body this way is "by definition" an "implacable brute" is merely evidence of how counterintuitive a response Scott, Moore, and Mortensen are asking from their audience and how deeply ingrained our assumptions about female vulnerability onscreen remain. The film does not portray Urgayle as a monster. On the contrary, it values Urgayle's perspective over any other, even over O'Neil's own perspective. But the film's narrative drive and its creation of a strong female icon come at the expense of the working-class male power he represents. O'Neil's victory over sexual violation comes not only over the body of the absent Asian female but also at the cost of masculinity, as figured by the noncommissioned officer Urgayle. The film posits women's advancement in the military occurring at the expense of working-class white men. As much as the film wants to establish physical strength and masculine stoicism as the markers of a real military officer, it is the officers' education that will actually afford them power in the armed services, while Urgayle and his macho cohorts will remain NCOs. It is therefore central to the Urgayle/O'Neil dynamic that she outranks him. She is an officer and he is enlisted, so while during training she calls him "Master Chief," after training is over, he will call her "Ma'am." Yvonne Tasker's otherwise insightful reading of *G.I. Jane* twice refers to Urgayle as O'Neil's "commanding officer." This misunderstands military hierarchy—Urgayle is not an officer at all. This matters, since *G.I. Jane* is unusually sensitive to and precise about class divisions in the military and the importance of rank and hierarchy to those distinctions, primarily because they are important to the film's point about women's advancement in the military. During CRT, the privileges of the recruits' ranks are suspended; when conniving politicians force O'Neil out of training,[47] she regains her status as a lieutenant, but this is not the kind of power the film is interested in. In order to really treat her like a man, to give her access to what the film identifies as the privileged space of real integration, it has to strip her (and the other recruits) of the class privilege afforded by their status as officers. The movie's careful attention to this process reveals that it is ultimately less interested in feminist debates about female equality and the dangers of patriarchal power structures than it is in claiming the military's rigid hierarchy as a space of egalitarian meritocracy.

But not all segments of the culture industry invested in the military see it as a proving ground for women's equality. Director-producer and army veteran Jerry O'Brien complained at the time of the film's release, "You insult all of the men who achieved their SEAL badges when you imply a woman can do it . . . I think women's liberation is fine, but there are parameters . . . Women need to know their place. I don't know where that place is for sure (they choose so many), but I'm sure I know where it is not—and that is at the training facilities at Coronado, Calif. (SEALs); Fort Benning, Ga. (Airborne Rangers); and Fort Bragg, N.C. (Special Forces)."[48] If *G.I. Jane* imagines a military where a woman's place is in SEAL training, it must still find a place for her outside of training, where violence is not a game or a test. *G.I. Jane* was filmed between the first and second Gulf Wars, and the long, contrived denouement where Urgayle leads the trainees on a real-life mission in Libya combines Cold War and post–Cold War fears about the United States' position in the global power structure and marketplace. But it also means to evoke for American film audiences a war with few American casualties, to replace the Vietnam context of the POW training sequence with a Desert Storm context, where American women didn't die in the desert. In the Libya sequence, O'Neil lies in wait, holding a knife, as an enemy soldier looms, unaware of her presence. Urgayle, covering her with a sniper's rifle, refuses to trust that O'Neil can handle hand-to-hand combat and shoots the man who menaces her, alerting the Libyans to the Americans' presence and getting himself shot in the process. At this crucial moment, Urgayle denies O'Neil the opportunity to slit a man's throat, to prove that she can kill like a man in addition to carrying comrades like a man and taking it like a man. Soon after this denial, she manages to drag the wounded Urgayle to safety, answering the question (raised by the image of Shannon Faulkner at the Citadel and posed by Urgayle in the shower) about physical equality but leaving open the real question about male emotions on which the political issue of military integration rests.

It is worth asking what ideological work a film that tries this hard to reprogram our response to seeing the female body abused is doing in terms of the question DeHaven asks O'Neil: how do we teach the public to find female casualties in war acceptable? *G.I. Jane*'s answer is to train its audience to see female suffering as equivalent to male suffering, no more horrifying and no less. In this respect, the otherwise conservative *G.I. Jane* is considerably more subversive than the critically praised *Full Metal Jacket*; the latter's viscerally horrifying final scene absolutely depends upon our seeing a woman dying in agony as more horrific than a man dying the same way. Because of, not despite, its impatience with "political" feminism, *G.I. Jane* is charmingly contemptuous of the idea that women need to be protected. The new iconography of female suffering and strength that Scott and Moore create in this film posits a very specific theory of female strength: a strong woman (a real feminist) doesn't complain when the drill sergeant barges in on her showering or beats her up in a training exercise. Central to this ethic is that, even when she is naked or abused, we never really see O'Neil powerless—thwarted, but never really vulnerable. Even in the attempted-rape scene, she's figured as powerful. Yvonne Tasker points out that "male violence against women has typically functioned within the Hollywood cinema as a signifier of evil. Feminism has proposed a rather different understanding of violence against women in relation to institutionalized male power, often expressed through metaphors of physical strength versus weakness."[49] *G.I. Jane* attempts to rewrite these associations, reading a specific kind of violence against the female body as progress, and the man who enacts that violence not as "evil" but as a closet egalitarian, whose presentation of his own Navy Cross to O'Neil tucked in a copy of D. H. Lawrence poems functions as the closest thing this film has to a romantic finale. But after Urgayle has given O'Neil's military career his blessing, the film doesn't know what to do with him. He limps out the door on crutches, and the camera focuses on O'Neil's face, its expression of dewy victory an oddly dissonant moment in a film more interested in its heroine's muscles than in her heterosexual attachments.

G.I. Jane's vision of a female officer who proves herself in ground combat in the Middle East seems eerily prescient in light of the number of women who served on the front lines in Iraq and Afghanistan during the first decade of the twenty-first century. Though women are still barred from the infantry, artillery, and Special Forces branches, the counterinsurgency tactics demanded by U.S. occupation of both countries means that "combat" is being redefined unit by unit and often street by street.[50] The shifting attitudes toward women in combat that have been gaining anecdotal strength in recent years make Moore's Lieutenant O'Neil seem less an exercise in wish fulfillment than she might have seemed in 1997. During the years directly following the end of the Cold War, economic globalization and technological advances in the machineries of commerce and war were fast making traditional masculine strength less necessary for male success. The anxieties this continues to raise about stoic, muscular masculinity leads, in my view, to both the patriotic retreat from vulnerability we see in a popular film like *Saving Private Ryan* and the class ossification we see in an ambivalently feminist film like *G.I. Jane*. Though Jeanine Basinger says that *Saving Private Ryan* is, "to paraphrase Kirk Douglas speaking to John Wayne in *In Harm's Way*, 'a gut-bustin,' mother-lovin' honest-to-God World War II combat movie,'"[51] the production of vulnerability in both *Saving Private Ryan* and *G.I. Jane* raises the question of what all of this gut-busting and mother-loving accomplishes, and where both discourses lead us in thinking about gender, violence, and vulnerability. The shift *G.I. Jane* would have us make in the way we conceive vulnerability brings us back, in this century, to the question of combat-force integration that is the film's ostensible subject. As I write, the American public *is* accepting female casualties in war, far more docilely than commentators of any political persuasion had anticipated. And antiwar voices have not mobilized the imagery of the suffering female body with quite the intensity that the war film as a genre has suggested they might. The resistant vulnerability Spielberg and Scott helped to create in the 1990s may have trained audiences to speak and think about the costs of violence in new terms. As the following chapters will explore, the resistant vulnerability that popular culture is beginning to recognize might at least teach us to ask the question.

4

Matthew Shepard's Body and the Politics of Queer Vulnerability in Boys Don't Cry *and* The Laramie Project

A year after Matthew Shepard's murder in Laramie, Wyoming, in the fall of 1998, Andrew Sullivan unleashed a firestorm of controversy about what he termed the "marketing" of Matthew Shepard. Sullivan alleged that "the marketing of Shepard is . . . a damaging symbolic statement about who gay men still are in this culture." Sullivan *says* that marketing Shepard as representative of gay men in America allows the larger culture to view gay men as "weak, effeminate stereotypes," but he appears to *mean* that it posits gay men as vulnerable—and to be labeled vulnerable is to be seen by the culture as a woman or a child. Sullivan asks why it is Shepard and not Billy Jack Gaither or Private Barry Winchell, also victims of antigay murders, upon whom American culture so fixated its memorializing attention. While suggesting that the media discusses Shepard as "a child rather than an adult," Sullivan argues that frequently circulated photos "depict him crouched sparrow-like on a waterfall, gazing cherubically into the distance . . . The point of this iconography is to divest Shepard of any maturity, any manhood, any adult sexuality." Gaither and Winchell, Sullivan posits, "suggest a gay world that is strong and grown-up and mainstream—exactly the kind of world that has no need for pity."[1] When we think about why Sullivan—a tireless advocate for LGBT equality, despite the controversy he often courts—balks at the iconography of vulnerability, we see that it is because Sullivan imagines the vulnerable body as in need of "pity." Culture codes this body female in opposition to the signifiers of strength and adulthood that Sullivan problematically labels "mainstream."

But this debate about what Matthew Shepard's body signifies is not limited to the blogosphere—it exists equally on small and silver screens, in the culture and in the courts. In 1999, JoAnn Wypijewski reported in *Harper's:*

> Among the weighty files on the proceedings against [Shepard's killers Aaron] McKinney and [Russell] Henderson in the Albany County Courthouse is a curious reference. The state had charged, as an "aggravating factor" in the murder, that "the defendant[s] knew or should have known that the victim was suffering from a physical or mental disability." The court threw this out; Judge Jeffrey

> Donnell, who presided over Henderson's case, told me he assumed it referred to Shepard's size (five foot two, 105 pounds) but was legally irrelevant whatever its intent. In a sense, it is sociologically irrelevant as well whether the prosecution regarded Shepard as crippled more by sexuality or size, since by either measure he was, in the vernacular of Laramie's straight youth, a wuss.[2]

Judge Donnell "assumes" that the state case labeled the physical traits that cause Sullivan to refer to Shepard as a "sparrow-like" waif a "physical disability."[3] Sullivan disagrees with other LGBT-rights activists over which perceived gender norms most effectively aid the struggle for equal rights. But this disagreement depends upon American culture's social and legal association of the vulnerable body with a frightening—here actionable—lack of agency. Sullivan objects to the image of the gay male as victim because Sullivan, along with the modes of cultural production I investigate throughout this book, thinks that victimization is something that happens to women. *Boys Don't Cry* (1999) and *The Laramie Project* (2002), both based on horrific murders of queer people in the rural West, attempt to uncover what the vulnerable body signifies. The queer body poses a stark challenge to the politics of vulnerability that I have traced throughout this project, since it disrupts the heterosexist assumptions about special vulnerability of the female body. In order to uncover the politics and possibilities of queer vulnerability, this chapter will investigate the strategies of exposure and erasure that reveal how central the problem of embodiment remains to the project of transgressing social norms. *Boys Don't Cry* negotiates its protagonist's radical vulnerability by exposing star Hilary Swank's gendered body, while *The Laramie Project* removes Shepard's victimized body from the screen altogether.

Shepard's murder was part of the cultural landscape into which Kimberly Peirce's *Boys Don't Cry* was released in 1999. The film, which takes as its subject the rape and murder of transgendered teen Brandon Teena, was known throughout most of its production by the working title *Take It like a Man*. This abandoned title exposes the volatile intersection of violence, sex, and gendered vulnerability that makes this film the subject of such fierce debate among feminist scholars and queer theorists. This debate has most often centered on the film's portrayal of its transgendered protagonist and whether or not the film's romance plot ultimately works to label Brandon Teena a lesbian driven to cross-dress by "internalized homophobia."[4] I am less interested here in the (mistaken) labeling of Brandon's sexuality as "lesbian" than in the increasingly horrific vulnerability of his body as it is increasingly gendered female. But this is far from a simple trajectory in the film, or in the politics of transgendered identity into which the film wades. I argue that *Boys Don't Cry* uses Brandon's exposure and rape at the hands of men to gender vulnerability female, but that this process depends upon the tense mixture of fear and sympathy Peirce carefully constructs around her film's working-class characters. Cynthia Fuchs labels "respect for all its characters and situations" *Boys Don't Cry*'s most significant achievement: "Small town Nebraska has never looked so seductive as it does through Brandon Teena's eyes."[5] And, indeed, Brandon's gaze infuses Falls City with both a glamour and a poignancy that marks queer vulnerability as a function of both homosocial and heterosexual desire. Examining Hilary Swank's performance as Brandon reveals the ways that the protracted, unsettling focus on Swank's naked body during scenes of his exposure and rape uses the viewer's sudden, explicit awareness of that body's *femaleness* to heighten audience investment in the character, whom Peirce had previously resisted gendering. Furthermore, the odd sympathy of Peter Sarsgaard's performance as the ringleader of the men who rape and murder Brandon amplifies and complicates this effect. Taken together, Swank's and Sarsgaard's performances reveal the film's uneasy, deeply transgressive investment in the operations and costs of rural, working-class masculinity—a masculinity that brings us always back to the question of the gendered body.

We have seen the way that Method acting and its claims to psychological realism have become associated with male actors, often at the expense of performance styles and character arcs associated with the feminine. In *Boys Don't Cry,* Swank's deeply immersive Method performance enacts the same effect on the audience that Brandon's "performance" of masculinity enacts on the other characters in the film. Peirce's camera, while showing us the act of binding breasts and stuffing underwear that constitutes the production of Brandon's masculinity, never shows us "Teena Brandon," only Brandon Teena. Rachel Swan, in a strategy adopted by many who try to make sense of the film's confused and confusing retreat from Brandon's masculinity after his rape, argues that the film ultimately repositions Brandon as female:

> On the one hand, *Boys Don't Cry* pays homage to the performative nature of gender, to the idea that a sexed body can vacillate between gender identities. In the film's multi-layered theater, Brandon's masquerade was played out by Swank, who also had to reinvent herself in a generative process of gender construction. Nonetheless, our culture's neurosis with regard to sex-gender symmetry demands ultimately that Brandon be castrated and re-positioned in a female body. This occurs not only in the film, but also in the real-life reincarnation of Brandon Teena as the "sexy babe" Hilary Swank.[6]

But in the same way that Brandon's performance of masculinity is prone to slippages *throughout* the film, not only in its devastating third act, Swank has only been marginally successful at "reincarnating" as a "sexy babe." She has been unable to attract box-office or critical success playing "straight"—*The Affair of the Necklace* (2001), *The Black Dahlia* (2006), and *P.S. I Love You* (2007) each struggled at the box office, and her second Oscar for Best Actress came when she once again played it tough as a female boxer in Clint Eastwood's *Million Dollar Baby* (2004). Both the film's use of violence to gender the body female and the apparent cultural preference for Swank in roles that use her androgynous beauty to embody violent martyrdom make legible our cultural investments in the boundaries of that body, and particularly in its vulnerability to harm.

The film's plot begins after Brandon begins living as a man, following him from Lincoln to Falls City, Nebraska, where he befriends John Lotter (Peter Sarsgaard), Tom Nissen (Brendan Sexton III), and Lana Tisdel (Chloë Sevigny). The film dramatizes Lana and Brandon's love affair and the violence that erupts when this makeshift family discovers Brandon's biological gender. An influential strain of the scholarly criticism on the film argues, as Melissa Rigney does, that "*Boys Don't Cry* rationalizes both Brandon and the murders, explaining Brandon as a confused, closeted lesbian and the murderers as violent and intolerant 'white trash.'" But this is mistaken on both counts; Rigney's formulations ("closeted lesbian," "white trash") elide the tense, compelling tangle of desire and identification that marks Brandon's relationships with Tom and John and their collective construction of masculinity. Nearly all of these critics, disappointed with Peirce's seeming abandonment of Brandon's masculinity in the postrape love scene with Lana, read Brandon's "passing" (as a boy) as a convincing spectacle, both for spectators of the film and for characters within its diegesis. But how convincing is Brandon's portrayal of masculinity? Brandon holds eye contact for a little too long, eyes a little too wide, smiles a bit too quickly and too widely. Even in their first meeting—a fistfight in a bar—John is very physical with Brandon, caressing his face and manhandling his shoulders and chest in a way that makes not feeling Brandon's bound breasts seem like an act of conscious unknowing. Upon Brandon's arrival in Falls City, he quickly finds himself in a confrontation with a bar patron who menaces Candace (Alicia Goranson). The man shoves Brandon, calling him a "little fag," and Brandon enters the physical fight with abandon, throwing himself at his much larger assailant until John approaches to hold him up and hold him back.

This early scene establishes a dangerous intimacy between John and Brandon but also the pugilistic style of masculinity Brandon courts in his relationships with other men. "C'mon, stud—you got us into this," John says, grinning as he shoves Brandon back into the fray. John spends much of this scene with the front of Brandon's plaid shirt bunched in his hand. Given the force this shirt will accumulate as a signifier of Brandon's masculinity, John's seemingly constant desire to touch it, straighten it, and yank Brandon around by it posits Brandon's maleness as created not just by Lana but by John as well. Once they flee the bar into an alley, John inspects Brandon's face, holding it in his hands to inspect a bruise left by the fight, smiling softly as he predicts, "You're going to have a shiner in the morning." The close camerawork in this scene, and Brandon's legible delight at seeing the developing bruise when he turns to inspect his own reflection in a window behind him, signal his new status as a fighter. It's these shifting signifiers of masculinity that so complicate the issues of desire and identification that operate both within the film's diegesis and in the way Peirce positions the viewer in relation to this spectacle. "You don't have to be a lesbian to identify with Brandon Teena," Rachel

Swan argues. "In fact, his unflinching, two-fisted maleness seems to throw a punch at the category of 'butch lesbian' while consolidating a 'straight male' cowboy hero ideal."[7] But, of course, this film never really engages the category "lesbian"—Peirce, for most of the film's running time, treats the "fact" of Brandon's biological gender the way Brandon himself seems to view it: as a miscue with his "authentic" self, not as a signifier of "truth." Rigney wants to place *Boys Don't Cry* into a trajectory of Hollywood representations of female masculinity that includes *Bound* (1996) and *Set It Off* (1996).[8] But this formulation ignores Brandon's own sense of his sexuality and his gender, and the careful way that Peirce's film positions the viewer in relation to Brandon's masculinity. For Peirce, the project of construction creates John and Tom's masculinity as well as Brandon's.

"If you're going to get into fights over girls like Candace, you gotta learn a few moves," John advises Brandon, grinning and shadow-boxing as Candace stands by watching them both. Though it appears to be just a particularly explicit version of Sedgwick's triangulation—the chemistry in the scene is between John and Brandon—John's comment here is a foreshadowing of the woman who *will* form the focus of both attachment and tension between them, Chloë Sevigny's Lana Tisdel.[9] Lana is often read as the one character who knows the "truth" about Brandon, but I would suggest that part of the repressive panic that John and Tom spiral into is the horror of delayed recognition. It's part of the cultural unknowing by which inarticulate, violent men can accept a biological girl as one of the boys and be half-in on the ruse, or where Lana's mother (Jeannetta Arnette) can admire the physical beauty of her daughter's boyfriend and declare him "handsome," as John looks on in a mute tangle of identification and desire. As seen through Peirce's camera, Swank's ethereal androgyny makes Sarsgaard's adult masculinity seem threatening, both to Brandon and to the female characters in the film. Two things important to the film's construction of vulnerability are often missed in critics' focus on Brandon's gender performance and the romantic relationship with Lana. First, Brandon's seemingly uncontrollable desire to hang out in rough bars with a rough crowd, to court a dangerous intimacy with men like John and Tom, is absolutely central to Brandon's masculinity. Second, Brandon's lanky, loose-limbed tomboy charm is a mixture of the categories "masculine" and "feminine" of which John and Tom are inferior copies, and Lana and Candace aren't the only ones who desire the different style of masculinity Brandon represents. John remains fascinated by Brandon, even as he fears Brandon's usurping his place in Lana's family. The tangled, dysfunctional sexual tensions and familial dynamics of Lana's household nearly veer into redneck parody, but Sarsgaard's performance salvages the film's portrayal of these characters and codes the domestic space of the Tisdel home as a haven as well as a locus of danger. Speaking of Lana and her mother, John tells Brandon, "This here's my real family, even if it isn't my real home." In the face of the complicated dynamic involving these wounded, unstable men, the scholarly description of Brandon as a lesbian suffering from internal homophobia falls apart.

It's not just in relation to Lana and the other women he dates that Brandon wants to be male, and part of the film's tense power comes from John's willingness to include Brandon in this surrogate family. John refers to Brandon by a series of endearments, "little buddy," "little man," "little dude," and these endearments are more than a halting form of intimacy; they're markers of the different kinds of pleasures and desires that the camera's gaze in this film constructs. Peirce's camera obsessively frames characters looking out of windows, imprisoned behind doors, caught in the lens of the camera Brandon uses to photograph his new "family." But the camera's gaze is not the only one operative here, and Lana's desiring gaze isn't the only one the film privileges. There's a measure of narcissistic identification in the constant, eroticized eye contact between John and Brandon, but the frequent tenderness of John's gaze is a visual sign of the dangerous vulnerability that John's rage will attempt to contain, once Brandon's gender is *legible* in the scene of his exposure in the Tisdel family's bathroom.

Academic critics nearly always write from the end of this film, from the image of Tom and John once they've committed horrific acts of violence that make them irredeemable as characters. But the frequent scholarly descriptions of John and Tom as "villains" who "delight" in exposing Brandon erases the complex and shifting character of gendered vulnerability operative for most of the film's running time.[10] These misreadings ignore the film's actually very transgressive investment in working-class masculinity. In its pathologies and violence, yes, but also its woundedness and appeal—an appeal made very real for the audience by Brandon's own approximation of it. These competing tensions explode in the first moment in the film that explicitly genders Hilary Swank's body female. John and Tom, prompted by Candace to search for Brandon's literature on sex-reassignment surgery, confront Brandon in Lana's home. "Are you a girl, or are you not?" John asks over and over, eventually leaning over Brandon, cupping his face as he growls, "I should fucking kill you for lying to Lana." Lana pushes John off of Brandon and replaces Brandon in the frame, looming over John. "Do you trust me enough to let Brandon show me? Then I'll tell you," she promises, which sets up a complicated relationship between seeing, saying, and knowing that threatens to unravel the film's carefully constructed emotional structure. Brandon and Lana then retreat to the seemingly safer space of Lana's bedroom, where she refuses to let Brandon "show" her his body. Peirce gives the viewer a surreal eyeline match of the night sky as Lana says, "Don't be scared. Look how beautiful it is out there . . . That's us. We can just beam ourselves out there." This dialogue sets up Lana as the author of the "beaming" that allows Brandon to appear in two places at once, visually, in the exposure scene that follows.

Tom and John drag Brandon into the bathroom and strip him. Here, Brandon/Swank's body is exposed to both the viewer's and the rapist's gaze, as Lana, author of the film's sympathetic female gaze, refuses to look. This creates a transgressive identification between the viewer and Tom and John, particularly John, who

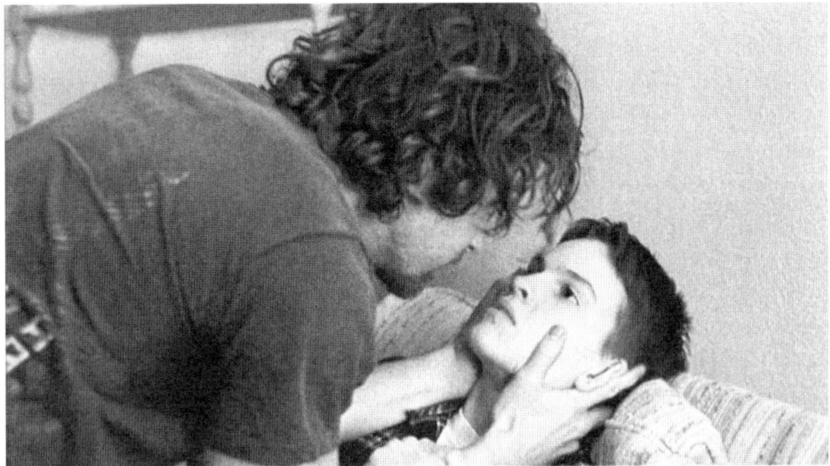

Figure 13 John confronts Brandon

Figure 14 Lana intervenes

can't pull down Brandon's underwear and then holds Brandon in a strange near-embrace as Tom does it for him. But I want to suggest that Peirce undercuts this scene's subversive potential by resorting to a strategy long familiar to war films and action cinema—using an image of the vulnerable *female* body to elicit audience sympathy and protectiveness. The visceral shock for the audience in seeking visible "proof" of Swank's female body is also the shock of *feeling* this character's physical vulnerability in ways that Peirce's camera had previously resisted. The classing and queering of vulnerability that the film had accomplished for much of its running time here begins to shift, turning a film about transgendered identity into a female tragedy for both Brandon, whose naked body is now the object of audience pity and protectiveness, and for Lana, whose only way of protecting Brandon is not to look.

At this moment, Peirce inserts a shot of Brandon making eye contact with a spectral version of himself that stands, clothed, behind Lana's mother, looking at the exposed Brandon.[11] Judith Halberstam argues that this moment solidifies what she calls the film's transgendered gaze. "The transgendered gaze is constituted as a look divided within itself, a point of view that comes from two places (at least) at the same time, one clothed and one naked. The clothed Brandon is the Brandon who was rescued by Lana's refusal to look: he is the Brandon who survives his own rape and murder; he is the Brandon to whom the audience is now sutured, a figure who combines momentarily the activity of looking with the passivity of the spectacle."[12] But this scene's focus on the nude lower body—all of a sudden explicitly gendered female—allows the audience to read a very different Brandon: the one standing naked in the bathroom, the one now forcefully positioned by Peirce's own gaze as "she." Halberstam argues that the reveal scene "serves both to destabilize the spectator's sense of gender stability and to confirm Brandon's manhood at the very moment that he has been exposed as female / castrated,"[13] but I want to suggest that this moment actually splits off the "female" Brandon so that the audience's pity and protectiveness can by projected onto *her*. The exhilarating, risky bravado of Brandon's characterization throughout the film remains with this "safe" Brandon, allowing the coming sexual violation to be posited as something that happens to women.

Boys Don't Cry asks viewers to invest in the specific horror of sexual threat against the body—in the moment of the reveal scene, for the first time explicitly gendered female. Gendering Brandon during the rape is a kind of cultural shorthand for the vulnerability Peirce needs to establish for Brandon in order for the narrative to work as melodrama. Peirce intercuts the rape scene with a wrenching interrogation scene where Brandon reports the rape at the police station. The sheriff bullies Brandon into saying the word "vagina"; Swank's halting over the word draws a searing line between the physical act of violation and this second, violent stripping of the ability to self-label. The sheriff forces Brandon to say the word, but Peirce herself seems to think that audiences need to see a vagina in order to feel about the rape scene the way we're "supposed" to feel. But if we read the rape as John and Tom's brutal attempt to shove Brandon into the category "female," what are we to make of John and Tom's desire to read Brandon as once again male in the rape's horrifying aftermath? I argue that we can read this scene, and John and Tom's counterintuitive behavior afterward, in the context of the masculine rituals that structure the film's first half. In that earlier section of the film, John and Tom involve Brandon in the male bonding ritual of bumper skiing that involves enduring physical pain, "taking it like a man." As John introduces Brandon to the bumper-skiing crew, his sardonic public declarations—"This here's Brandon. He's a mean prizefighter from Lincoln, so be careful what you say to him"—alternate with his more intimate instructions to Brandon: "Don't let 'em scare you. You can do it." John has removed his shirt, so as he leans in toward Brandon to whisper this encouragement, his naked upper body is the object of the camera's uneasy and fascinated gaze. The stripping on and off of clothing in this early sequence sets up a trope that the film will continue—nudity is coded as dangerous. Because of the "secret" we know Brandon hides, clothes are a form of safety. In the dysfunctional construction of masculinity these characters prize, the rape and its aftermath occupy a particularly Gothic place on this continuum, which allows John and Tom to call Brandon "little buddy" and "little dude" after raping him.

After raping Brandon face-to-face in the back of the car (intercut with the sheriff forcing Brandon to say the word "vagina," removing any ambiguity about the rape's logistics), John yells, "Take her. Take her!" at Tom. The two subsequent attacks are more logistically ambiguous; Tom rapes Brandon from behind outside the car, and Peirce's camera withholds the third rape from our view. Critics often read this entire sequence as the moment in which John and Tom castrate Brandon.[14] But the language of castration shockingly oversimplifies the scene and the ways it implicates John and Tom in a queer vulnerability that Peirce has temporarily stripped from Brandon himself. This different queer vulnerability solidifies afterward, when John and Tom reclaim her as "he." In the aftermath of the rape, the camera reveals Brandon lying in the fetal position on the ground, Hilary Swank's slender shoulders and bound breasts looking as "female" as Swank's body ever looks in this film, posited visually as female at the moment that it's most vulnerable. By the time we see a pair of boots walking toward Brandon's still form, Peirce has taught us to fear more violence, but instead Tom covers Brandon with the flannel shirt that has symbolized Brandon's masculinity throughout the film, saying, "Come on, buddy. Up. Let's go." He keeps an arm around Brandon as Brandon pulls up his jeans and eases back into the shirt. "You okay?" Tom asks softly. "C'mon, let's go." This is one of the film's most unsettling moments, because it lays bare the self-deception at the heart of masculinity for biological men as well as for more liminal figures. David M. Jones, calling for an interrogation of whiteness in the film's construction of a Hollywood drama out of the raw material of Brandon Teena's murder, suggests that *Boys Don't Cry* "[represents] rural, Midwestern, working-class whiteness as an exotic, demonic force."[15] Jones is right that both popular media accounts of the crime and scholarly work on *Boys Don't Cry* figure John and Tom's masculinity as "demonic," but this scene's ambivalent mixture of masculine endearments with threats of violence if Brandon doesn't "keep our little secret" reveals the conflicting impulses at the center of John and Tom's self-fashioning. They must refer to Brandon as "her" in order to rape and later kill him, but in order to help him back into the car, they must reclaim Brandon as "him."

It seems to me indicative of the film's vulnerability politics that the rape scene is more viscerally upsetting than the scene where John and Tom murder Brandon and the bystander Candace. Peirce focalizes the murder scene through Lana, who watches in powerless horror. But the film doesn't end with Brandon's murder. We hear Swank's voice—since Brandon's death relegated to the semidiegetic space of the letter Lana takes off of his body—over shots of the passing Nebraska countryside that seem to be from the window of a car. Brandon's voice promises, "I'll be making a trip out on the highway before too long," but when the car finally appears in the frame of Peirce's camera, it's Lana's face we see behind the wheel. She fulfills for the viewer Brandon's dream of a "trip out on the highway," a ghost of a smile on her face as we hear Brandon's final farewell to her. The screen goes to black with white lettering, and we learn that John Lotter waits on death row while Tom Nissen serves consecutive life sentences. But a stark white-on-black message after the final image but before the final credits chillingly undercuts Lana's victory: "A few years later, Lana Tisdel had a baby girl and returned to Falls City to raise her." This is the moment where the film finally becomes a specifically *female* tragedy—a formulation that both includes and excludes Brandon himself. Lana hits the open road at the film's conclusion, but only to bring a girl-child back to Falls City, tainting any sense of satisfaction the audience feels at the news of John's and Tom's incarceration. But this turn toward female tragedy obscures the specifically queer vulnerability that's always under the surface of Brandon's self-fashioning. I agree with Halberstam that there's a way the boy Brandon remains untouched. But that's not wholly positive; it keeps the transgendered figure somehow apart from the hard, messy embodiment that the film ascribes to women. And the political implications of this retreat from the more complicated model of vulnerability suggested by both Swank's and Sarsgaard's performances becomes more important in a cinematic landscape that continues to replace the vulnerable bodies of (non-American, nonwhite) men with images of women. If *Boys Don't Cry* uses a transgendered gaze to keep Brandon safe from the violence that embodiment opens up to women, *The Laramie Project* keeps the violated body offscreen altogether. I have argued throughout this book that the logic of replacement is one of the central ways vulnerability is constructed onscreen and in the public imagination. *The Laramie Project*, HBO's 2002 film version of Moisés Kaufman's 2000 play, does not replace the violated body but instead removes it from view.

In an analysis of the mainstream media's narrative about Shepard's death in the wake the event, Brian L. Ott and Eric Aoki argue that "the news media's tragic framing of the event works rhetorically and ideologically to relieve the public of its social complicity and culpability; to reaffirm a dominant set of discourses that socially stigmatizes gay, lesbian, bisexual and transgendered (GLBT) persons; and to hamper efforts to create and enact a progressive GLBT social policy."[16] While *The Laramie Project* as both a play text and a film works hard against ignoring "social complicity and culpability" in the way Ott and Aoki suggest, its impulse to remove the vulnerable body from view minimizes the complicity viewers might feel in the crime, particularly once Kaufman gives us a fictionalized version of himself and the other members of the Tectonic Theater Project (TTP) as point-of-view characters. Scholars like Jennifer Petersen suggest that Matthew Shepard serves as a locus of public identification in the weeks and months after his murder,[17] but the structure of *The Laramie Project* shifts that identification from Matthew to the remaining residents of the town, particularly Joshua Jackson's bartender, Christina Ricci's budding activist, and Jeremy Davies's aspiring actor. This means that the vulnerable queer body functions solely as a conduit for the sentimental project of "feeling right" that the film will dramatize.[18]

Jay Baglia and Elissa Foster worry that "*The Laramie Project* confirms for liberal audiences what they already believe—that violence and hatred are wrong," suggesting that the HBO film, in particular, offers its audience absolution. They imply that *The Laramie Project*'s play script uses the "aesthetics of documentary" while "employing techniques associated with experimental or political theater. Brechtian alienation emerged in resistance to the illusions of realism, and, as a technique, it is intended to constantly remind the audience of the constructed nature of what they are seeing."[19] But the antirealist impulse of the play's strategy of using the same actor to play multiple parts is softened in the HBO film, making discrete the boundaries, for instance, between the TTP interviewers and the Laramie residents they interview, boundaries that the play's casting strategies collapsed. The "distinct frames of cultural memory" through which Thomas R. Dunn argues the LGBT community "strategically remembers" Shepard are presented in the film as a series of genre-specific frames:[20] the television frame through which we see actual footage of Tom Brokaw reporting on the attack, the fourth wall of the theater stage where we watch Davies's character perform in *Angels in America,* and finally the frame of Kaufman's own camera, which puts us in the last shot of the film in Matthew Shepard's own perspective on the fenceline in the dark.

In order to see how a historic event is framed by the media and then more specifically by Kaufman's film as a redemptive spectacle, we can look at the film's representation of the University of Wyoming's Homecoming parade, held on October 10, 1998. The film, like Kaufman's play, focalizes the parade through Laramie resident Harry Woods (Bill Irwin), who announces that he's "52 years old. And I'm gay." Kaufman's camera begins inside Woods's apartment, which he tells us has windows on opposite sides, facing both the northbound and southbound streets on the parade route, from which he will watch, unable to join in because of a cast on his leg. The camera fades out on a close-up of Harry's face to fade in on a long shot that shows the hall of the apartment and Harry in his cast, looking out a window, framed himself by the doorframe to the room. In this scene's camerawork, Harry Woods's body—absent from the parade—seems to stand in for Matthew's own, the cast on his leg serving as a visual marker of his body's vulnerability. Woods narrates seeing the tag at the end of the parade, "a group of people walking behind a banner for Matthew Shepard." For a few moments, the camera moves to the marchers' eye level, bringing the viewers' attention to several of the film's most important characters. Then Woods narrates walking to the opposite window of the apartment to see the parade come by again ten minutes later: "And I saw the most incredible thing. As the parade came down the street, the number of people marching for Matthew Shepard had grown, like five times. Can you imagine? The tag at the end was bigger than the entire parade." We see the crowd through the slightly disorienting view from Harry's window, then in among the crowd again, this time in closer shots; this movement from behind the window to in front of the action is an example of a visual strategy the film uses often, a framing and reframing that makes it unclear whose spectral position the viewer inhabits. Although *The Laramie Project* frequently moves its setting back and forth between Laramie and Fort Collins, Colorado, where Matthew lay comatose in the hospital, the parade the film dramatizes is the University of Wyoming parade, not the Colorado State University homecoming parade, held the same day in Fort Collins. At that parade, a float sponsored by Pi Kappa Alpha and Alpha Chi Omega featured a scarecrow hung with signs reading "I'm Gay" and "Up My Ass."[21] The combination of antigay slurs on the float and the disturbing imagery—made more potent by the frequent news media descriptions, in the days between the attack and the parade, of Matthew's body appearing "like a scarecrow" on the deer fence—is another representation of Matthew's absent body in the public record, but this is not the story *The Laramie Project* wants to tell about what Matthew's missing body means. As the University of Wyoming parade rounds the corner to become visible again out Harry Woods's window, Woods says, "I thought to myself, 'Thank God I got to see this in my lifetime.' And my second thought was, 'Thank you, Matthew.'" Thus *The Laramie Project* figures Matthew's absent presence as a kind of social balm, having moved beyond vulnerability to serve as an icon or a secular saint.[22] If Brandon Teena's vulnerable body onscreen produces the pity and protectiveness that cause viewers to label him "her," *The Laramie Project* needs the vulnerable body to accomplish a different kind of work, realized at the film's end with the appropriation of the final scene of Tony Kushner's 1993 play *Angels in America*.

Although McKinney's and Henderson's trials form much of the drama of *The Laramie Project*'s second act, and Dennis Shepard's speech in court granting McKinney life in prison instead of the death penalty is arguably the film's emotional climax, McKinney and Henderson are never characters the way John and Tom are in *Boys Don't Cry*—never the subjects of transgressive identification. This function is served instead by Jedadiah Schultz (Jeremy Davies), the University of Wyoming acting student who transforms over the course of the film into an advocate for LGBT rights. For most of the film's running time, the visual representation of human rights activism is Romaine Patterson (Christina Ricci), the Laramie teenager whose "Angel Action" at Shepard's funeral shielded his family and friends from the protest led by professional homophobe Fred Phelps.

But by the film's end, the visual representation of Romaine's Angel Action is replaced by the imagery of Kushner's *Angels*, as Jedadiah performs Prior Walter's

Figure 15 Angel Action

Figure 16 *Angels in America*

final speech in a University of Wyoming production of the play.[23] Jeremy Davies's voice begins over the shot of the Wyoming landscape: "The dead will be commemorated and will struggle on with the living," he declares as the image of the landscape fades into an image of his face in profile before showing us the whole stage, with Kaufman's camera positioned as if the film's audience has a seat among the crowd at the theater. A stylized set shows a replica of the Angel of the Waters statue atop the Bethesda Fountain in New York's Central Park, the angel's wings mirrored by a larger set of wings extending across the backdrop. "We won't die secret deaths anymore," Prior Walter promises, "we will be citizens." The final part of this speech is audible as the camera cuts between a series of shots of the TTP interviewers bidding farewell to Laramie residents, preparing to leave. As the TTP crew climbs into their car, ready to hit the highway that provides *Boys Don't Cry* with its closing image, they ask each other if they've ever been "out to the fence." As their car pulls away, Kaufman's camera returns to Doc O'Connor (Steve Buscemi) telling the story of how Matthew spoke of Laramie's sparkling lights. The final image of the film is a long shot of the Laramie skyline, with Doc's voice narrating: "Matt was right there in that spot, and I can just picture—in his eyes—I can picture what he was seeing. The last thing that he saw on this earth was the sparkling lights of Laramie, Wyoming." Laramie's lights very, very slowly fade out, in a closing that is a significant departure from the play script, which the film has otherwise scrupulously followed. In the play text, Doc's speech about Matthew looking at Laramie's lights is followed by a short scene titled "DEPARTURE" that ends with TTP member Andy Paris saying that on their way to Denver, he looked in the car's rearview mirror, "and in the distance I could see the sparkling lights of Laramie, Wyoming." In the film, the artistic, ethnographic eye of the actor/journalist is replaced with what we can only see as Matthew Shepard's own gaze. And it is in this final shot that we can see a shadow of *Boys Don't Cry*'s more transgressive politics. *The Laramie Project,* having refused to present viewers with a visual representation of Matthew Shepard, closes by putting us in Matthew's spectral position, a disembodied version of Brandon's double-embodiment in the exposure scene. Instead of seeing Matthew ourselves, we see with his eyes, as Jeremy Davies, who played Corporal Upham in *Saving Private Ryan,* redeems himself for viewers by promising that "we will be citizens." It is precisely this question of citizenship and spectatorship that the television of the twenty-first century will take up in the wake of *Boys Don't Cry* and *The Laramie Project*'s gathering dark.

PART III

VULNERABILITY BEYOND THE BODY

5

The Violated Body after 9/11

TORTURE AND THE LEGACY OF VULNERABILITY IN *24* AND *BATTLESTAR GALACTICA*

When American Airlines Flight 11 and United Airlines Flight 175 crashed into New York City's World Trade Center on September 11, 2001, the production team behind Fox's new program *24* had already filmed the show's pilot, which includes a terrorist parachuting from an airplane full of passengers, which then explodes midair. The show debuted two months later, on November 6, 2001, and more than a decade later the show's focus on terrorism seems as prescient as the pilot episode's exploding plane seems eerie. *24* became a major hit for Fox, complete with a lively online following—including a site (*The Jack Bauer Torture Report*) devoted to tracking how many people the show's protagonist, Jack Bauer (Kiefer Sutherland), tortured or killed in a given twenty-four-hour period. Sutherland, often cast as a white supremacist during his career's fallow period between *Flatliners* (Joel Schumacher, 1990) and *24* (Fox, 2001–2010), suddenly found himself the icon of a cultural response to 9/11 over which he and *24*'s producers had very little control. This chapter opens with a brief discussion of *24* and its impact on the national conversation about torture and terrorism, then turns to the ways torture, rape, and humanness are theorized by the Sci-Fi Channel's reimagined *Battlestar Galactica* (2004–2009).[1] Both *24* and *Battlestar Galactica* position themselves as commentaries on twenty-first-century American politics: *24* centers on the fictional Counter Terrorist Unit (CTU), while *Battlestar Galactica*'s third season found the show's protagonists mounting an insurgency (complete with suicide bombings) against an enemy that seemed modeled on U.S. forces that were occupying Iraq as the third season aired. While I see *Battlestar Galactica* as a more controversial commentary on contemporary foreign policy than contemporaneous shows like *24*, *The Unit* (CBS, 2006–2009), and *Sleeper Cell* (Showtime, 2005–2006), the show matters to this project in the ways that it animates twenty-first-century debates about torture through the vexed issues of homecoming and rape with which the U.S. military has struggled since Vietnam.

24's and *Battlestar Galactica*'s divergent opinions about the ethics of torture make them important case studies of the early-twenty-first-century debate about vulnerability and the "war" on terror. But despite the ways that both shows reflect the historical specificity of the post-9/11 moment in American culture, their historical and ideological malleability along with their formal ambition position them as important texts in our narrative about the vulnerable body on television. *24* allows post-9/11 anxieties about borders and boundaries to take over its narrative, but uses its ticking-clock conceit to alter how its audience understands televisual time. Meanwhile, *Battlestar Galactica* uses television's long-form narrative format to expand its historical reach and to collapse our ability as viewers to easily delineate the boundary between the cultural trauma of Vietnam and the historical specificity of 9/11.

The Ticking Bomb: *24* and the Ethics of Torture on Television

Americans' post-9/11 willingness to think about torture as a tool in the "war on terror" was not greeted with complete enthusiasm by the professional military brass. In November 2006, West Point dean Patrick Finnegan met with producers of *24* to express his displeasure with the show's celebration of torture and the "toxic" effect it had had on students at the United States Military Academy. "I'd like them to stop," he told an interviewer. "They should do a show where torture backfires."[2] As any one of *24*'s legion of devoted fans can tell you, torture rarely backfires on the Counter Terrorist Unit's Jack Bauer. Although Bauer and his colleagues at the fictional CTU sometimes torture the wrong people, the dozens of people Bauer tortures in a twenty-four-hour period more often than not give up vital information, allowing Bauer to thwart assassination attempts (seasons one and eight), biological warfare against American cities (seasons two and seven), nuclear attacks (seasons three and six), nerve-gas threats (season five), and dirty-bomb plots (season eight).[3] For our investigation of both vulnerable bodies and the show's cumulative effect on its audience—which will suggest that the wrong question has been asked all along—we must attend to both the show's narrative strategies and the way it fictionalizes torture. The gimmicky-but-brilliant real-time conceit distorts the audience's imaginative understanding of how torture works, and the show defines torture as the infliction of physical pain, sidestepping the potentially thornier issues of cultural or sexual humiliation that remain central to contemporary public debates about torture.

Each season of *24* takes place in a single day. The episodes unfold in "real" time, with a digital countdown leading into and out of each commercial break and frequent use of a split screen so viewers can catch important action going on simultaneously in different plot threads. These strategies help create the adrenaline-fueled pace the show's narrative depends on, but they also create a *compression* of time that confuses the emotional and psychological pacing television audiences are trained to expect. A season of *24* offers viewers the pleasures they expect from high-concept television—season-long romantic arcs, emotional character development—but these strain credibility given the show's insistence that the season's action has taken only one day.[4] While this disjunction is merely implausible in terms of the characters' romantic intrigues and familial dramas, it creates a more troubling dynamic as regards the show's frequent use of torture. Since each season's major story arc must resolve within twenty-four hours, the information Bauer wants from the people he tortures nearly always involves the ticking-bomb scenario. *24* head writer Howard Gordon has admitted, "The premise of *24* is the ticking time bomb. It takes an unusual situation and turns it into the meat and potatoes of the show."[5] The ticking-bomb scenario isn't merely the way *24* imagines torture—it was also the most frequent justification used by Bush administration lawyers during the show's first six seasons to find loopholes in the United Nations Convention Against Torture, which states unequivocally: "No exceptional circumstances, whatsoever, whether a state of war or a threat of war, internal political instability or any other public emergency, may be invoked as a justification for torture."[6] Despite the picture painted by *24*, torture takes time. As ethicists and military analysts alike have argued for decades, the feelings of despair and disorientation that most experts argue are necessary for "effective torture" take, on average, a year, not twenty-four hours. Furthermore, revelation of the abuse at Guantánamo Bay of prisoners who had been held in American custody for more than five years exposes the extent to which the ticking bomb is a political sleight of hand with serious ethical consequences.

But it is not difficult to see why *24* frames torture this way. The reluctant decision to torture in order to save innocents frames violence in its most emotionally palatable light. *24* creator and executive producer Joel Surnow argues: "We've had all of these torture experts come by recently, and they say 'You don't realize how many people are affected by this. Be careful.' They say torture doesn't work. But I don't believe that. I don't think it's honest to say that if someone you love was being held, and you had five minutes to save them, you wouldn't do it. Tell me, what would you do? If someone had one of my children, or my wife, I would hope I'd do it. There is nothing—nothing—I wouldn't do."[7] By equating official torture with masculine protection of women and children, Surnow neatly conflates the decision *not* to torture with the denial of familial bonds and responsibilities. His formulation also abandons the very basis of the rule of law—that it is *not* the family members of potential victims who are asked to make legal decisions about torture's ethics and efficacy. But this conflation of torturer and decision maker often characterizes the way *24* uses torture. Jack Bauer, with his steely determination to protect American interests and his ability to torture without appearing cruel, provides a soothing cultural palliative to actual U.S. Army MP Charles Graner, the Abu Ghraib ringleader who has been quoted declaring: "The Christian in me says it's wrong, but the corrections officer in me says, 'I love to make a grown man piss himself.'"[8] Bauer, by contrast, embodies the "liberal fiction of the conscientious interrogator" that law professor David Luban argues "overlooks a division of moral labor in which the person with the fastidious conscience and the person doing the interrogation are not the same."[9]

24 remains deeply invested in the fiction that decision maker and torturer are the same person, as evidenced by the producers' insistence that the show takes torture seriously and that Bauer's actions have taken a clear emotional and moral toll on the character. Jane Mayer quotes Gordon arguing that "Jack is basically damned."[10] This defense of the show's moral seriousness shifts the question from "Does torture work?" or "Is torture justified to advance national interests?" to the sexier but less honest question "How much are *you* willing to sacrifice for democracy?" Jack Bauer, the show implies, is willing to sacrifice his *very soul*. Of course, this is not a new trope in American popular culture. The 1992 box-office hit *A Few Good Men* (Rob Reiner) features a crowd-pleasing performance by Jack Nicholson as a Marine Corps colonel willing to do "what people don't like to talk about at parties" to protect Americans. While *A Few Good Men* sacrificed Nicholson, sending his character to jail and giving a purported victory to Tom Cruise's navy lawyer and the rule of law, *24* makes the "Nicholson" character the hero. *24* constructs its torture scenes carefully in order to maintain audience sympathy for and identification with Bauer. The show's villains are portrayed as sadists, while Bauer is a willing but fiercely utilitarian torturer. In the season-four episode "12:00 a.m.–1:00 a.m.," Bauer and his CTU colleagues capture Joe Prado (John Thaddeus), a middleman who has information on the whereabouts of a terrorist with a stolen nuclear warhead. The terrorist mastermind has anonymously tipped off "Amnesty Global" about the man's capture, knowing that the human-rights organization will thwart Bauer's attempts to interrogate Prado. At CTU, Bauer chides the Amnesty Global lawyer, David Weiss (Evan Handler), for not being willing to sacrifice his moral comfort for national security:

BAUER: You and I both know that your client isn't clean. And that he conspired to steal a U.S. nuclear warhead—

WEISS: All my client wants is due process.

BAUER: Mr. Weiss, these people are not going to stop attacking us today until millions and millions of Americans are *dead*. Now, I don't want to bypass the Constitution, but these are extraordinary circumstances.

WEISS: The Constitution was born out of extraordinary circumstances, Mr. Bauer. This plays out by the book, not in a back room with a rubber hose.

BAUER: I hope you can live with that.

That "these people" will not stop attacking Americans *today* is crucial to Bauer's decision to torture. When the weak-willed and ineffective new president asks Bauer to wait twenty minutes so the he and the Justice Department can "discuss" the issue, Bauer snaps, "This thing could be over in twenty minutes!" To get around the legal niceties of a human-rights organization that wants the suspect treated humanely and a chief executive who wants twenty minutes to decide whether authorizing the torture of an American citizen will be his first official act as president, Bauer resigns from CTU so that he can torture Prado "as a private citizen." Once Bauer finally has Prado where he wants him—off the CTU site, away from the pesky Amnesty Global lawyer—the ubiquitous *24* time clock at the bottom of the screen flashes "12:58:13." The clock indicates that there are two minutes left in this episode, so audiences are primed that Bauer's methods will have to be quick and brutal. As the distinctive *24* music pounds, the camera cuts quickly between CTU, the terrorists consolidating their plan, and Bauer breaking Prado's fingers. Even with the frequent use of split screen, the camera never stays on one scene for longer than a couple of seconds, ratcheting up the sense of time slipping away. At the beginning of the episode, a CTU agent had insisted: "I want this man broken in minutes, not hours." As the actual torture sequence shows, it takes Bauer fewer than fifty seconds of screen time to "break" Prado, who gives up what he knows about the terrorists' location. In addition to finessing the decision to torture at all, the speed of this action makes the violence itself easier to watch. The quick cuts and split screens are disorienting, but they make the torture more viewable by either withholding the crying, gasping, and ragged breathing we read as markers of the body's vulnerability, or by cutting away from these sights and sounds before the viewer can absorb their ethical import.

For all of his ethical fluidity, the show cannot allow Bauer to cross certain lines, so *24* depicts torture as the infliction of physical pain (gunshot wounds, electric shock, broken fingers), not humiliation or sexual violence. This reveals both the show's macho ethic and the bright line the show's producers want to draw between torture and depravity. In terms of the show's attitudes toward vulnerability and gender, sexual violence is the point at which torture becomes depravity. Jack will break Prado's fingers to preserve national security, but he won't rape anyone. This is a crucial difference between Bauer, a "good" torturer, and the "bad" torturers Bauer fights. In the show's first season, Bauer's wife was raped by terrorists holding her and Bauer's daughter prisoner. When Bauer has custody of a terrorist's daughter in season two, he threatens to infect her with a virus that will cause her to die in excruciating pain, but he doesn't threaten to rape her. Presumably, even for Bauer, national security is not worth rape. While the show clearly thinks of itself as an equal-opportunity user of violence (women are sometimes the perpetrators and sometimes the victims of torture), the show's avoidance of the gendered, sexualized violence audiences associate with the actual "war on terror" shows its investment in traditionally gendered notions of vulnerability. *24* wants to retrain our responses to torture, not to gendered vulnerability.

To place the Jack Bauer character in cultural context, we must briefly return to *A Few Good Men,* a film (based on the 1989 stage play by Aaron Sorkin) that now seems oddly prescient for introducing Guantánamo Bay (Gitmo) into the cultural lexicon more than a decade before it gained international infamy as a post-9/11 prison colony for detainees from Afghanistan. In *A Few Good Men,* Nicholson's character, Colonel Nathan Jessup, commands Guantánamo Bay. In the film's famous courtroom showdown between Jessup and Cruise's Lieutenant Daniel Kaffee, Jessup turns Gitmo into a symbol of the harsh tactics he claims Americans want to happen behind the scenes. Ostensibly, *A Few Good Men*'s narrative brings Gitmo back under the United States flag, banishing Jessup and the rogue tactics he represents, which are embodied most clearly by Jessup's lieutenant, Jonathan James

Kendrick, played by a pre-24 Kiefer Sutherland. But *A Few Good Men* frames Guantánamo Bay in the American popular imagination as a place apart from the United States and the rule of law, a sort of legal limbo that has become all the more serious since 2002, when a military prison was opened at Gitmo, housing prisoners in a territory whose physical remove from the mainland United States allows the U.S. government to claim that its prisoners are not protected by either the Geneva Conventions or the United States Constitution.[11]

Battlestar Galactica and Question of the Human

This question of United States territory—where it begins, how far it extends, and what can be done by its agents—becomes both more complicated and more explicit in *Battlestar Galactica*. The original series *Battlestar Galactica* premiered on ABC in May of 1978, attempting to capitalize on the popularity of 1977's *Star Wars* with its scrappy, ragtag band of "rebels," in contrast to *Star Trek,* with its sleek jumpsuits and clean command structure. But if both *Star Wars* and the original *Battlestar Galactica* imagined an enemy of gleaming white storm troopers or robot Cylons, the reimagined *Galactica* (2003) raises the stakes. Now the Cylons (still machines, still "the enemy") "look like us." The show's Cylons are machines that were created by humans, rebelled, "evolved," and now look human. In the miniseries that served as the show's pilot, the Cylons attack and destroy all "human" life except for the small remaining Colonial fleet. We follow this band of "survivors," led by the Battlestar Galactica, the last remnant of the Colonial Fleet, on the run from the Cylons. Two aspects of this setup are central to my argument: the Cylon "terrorist" enemy that looks human but isn't, and the "constant state of war" that both allegorizes the contemporary "war on terror" and sets up the Galactica as a space like Guantánamo Bay. Galactica is connected to the old Colonial government that existed before the Cylon attack, but apart from it, too, requiring the characters constantly to negotiate their social and governmental structure in the face of legal uncertainty and physical threat.

Science fiction's often-discussed use of both aliens and robots as allegories of racial otherness makes *Battlestar Galactica*'s use of machines and *not* aliens to make its point about racial prejudice telling. This choice reveals not just an anxiety about race (though the pilots' casual use of the slur "toaster" recalls similar slurs against Asian and Middle Eastern populations in both Vietnam and Iraq), but also an anxiety about the mechanization of war, particularly so in the wake of the U.S. Air Force–driven First Gulf War and the anxiety it produced about human sacrifice and suffering.[12] The show is fascinated with the Cylons as "machines" that don't have wires and computer chips under their skin but flesh and blood and bone. These are organic robots, to such an extent that calling them "machines," as the more Cylon-phobic members of Galactica's crew often do, merely alerts the viewer to the instability of these labels. The confusion and angst this creates around what it means to be human, what it means to have a body, and ultimately what it means to be gendered makes *Battlestar Galactica* a rich site for a discussion of our cultural attitudes toward the military body post-Vietnam and post–Gulf War I.

While *Battlestar Galactica*'s premise and major story arcs reference both the war in Iraq and the issue of global terrorism, the show's treatment of the military and of gender relations has its most explicit context in representations of Vietnam. *Galactica*'s fantasy of an enemy that looks human but isn't enables a different imaginative engagement with Vietnam than films like *Deliverance* (1972), *Apocalypse Now* (1979), or *First Blood* (1982). The show shares these films' anxieties about the body and about the soldier's psychological and spiritual isolation as well as their empathy for the position of a military that seems more separated than ever from the civilian population it protects. Films like *Full Metal Jacket* (1987) and *Casualties of War* (1989) frame the trauma of Vietnam as a story about American male violence against Vietnamese women, so it should be no surprise that much of the specter of the diseased military in American popular culture revolves around representations of sexual trauma. And although rape has been used as an instrument of war throughout the history of armed conflict, international laws and social customs that prohibit rape in war have been based on the idea that women are noncombatants. Vietnam was the first large-scale American conflict in which this assumption was explicitly undermined in the view of America's television screens. Countless memoirs and reports from returning veterans, as well as films like *Casualties of War* and *Platoon,* dramatized the American soldier's confusion and trauma when women hiding among the civilian population turned out to be Viet Cong. The paranoia about who is and is not the enemy thus became written into the cultural text of Vietnam in American culture, particularly around the site of the Asian female body.[13]

Galactica's vision of a Cylon enemy that looks human and blends into the fleet's population harnesses anxieties about "the enemy" and collapsing distinctions between military and civilian populations that have their clearest cultural expression in 1970s and 1980s films about Vietnam. But, unlike the narratives of female absence and victimization we saw in chapter 2, *Galactica* imagines a postgender military where women are as likely as men to be combatants and female vulnerability registers the same way male vulnerability does. To take just one example, *Galactica* strips the word "sir" of its gendered connotations; the term is used by Galactica's enlisted crew to refer to officers of both genders. And this military appears to have abandoned an investment in women's special vulnerability. In one of *Battlestar Galactica*'s first episodes, female pilot Starbuck punches fellow pilot Apollo during an argument, and he punches her back, without any of the anxieties about gendered vulnerability audiences would usually expect. Lieutenant Kara "Starbuck" Thrace (Katee Sackhoff) is the show's clearest example of the post–*G.I. Jane* fighting woman and the purest illustration of the show's postgender ethic when it comes to women in the military. Sackhoff's casting in the *Battlestar Galactica* miniseries caused controversy among fans of the cult 1978 series. In the 1970s *Galactica,* Starbuck was played by Dirk Benedict as a womanizing, cigar-chomping hotshot pilot. The producers of the reimagined *Galactica* cast Sackhoff, switching the character's gender, while making few other changes to the character. Sackhoff's Starbuck is a cigar-smoking, tomboyish hotshot pilot, though the character's sexual promiscuity and alcoholism (played for comedy by Benedict in the 1970s) take on a considerably darker tone here. But while *G.I. Jane* portrayed Jordan O'Neil's emotional blankness as an important feature of her status as a postgender woman, *Galactica* treats Starbuck the way it treats its male characters.[14]

The show's frequent Starbuck-in-peril storylines ("You Can't Go Home Again" in season one, "The Farm" in season two, and Starbuck's imprisonment by the Cylon Leoben at the start of season three) are less a function of the show's investment in female vulnerability than a carryover from the 1970s series, where Dirk Benedict's Starbuck frequently got himself captured or lost and had to be retrieved by Apollo (Richard Hatch) and Commander Adama (Lorne Greene). The current *Galactica* maintains the emotional bonds between the three, with Sackhoff's Starbuck, Jamie Bamber's Apollo, and Edward James Olmos's Commander Adama forming the show's central ad-hoc "family." But when this Starbuck is injured ("You Can't Go Home Again"), captured ("The Farm"), or imprisoned ("Occupation" through "Exodus, Part II") she manages to save herself, usually by stabbing someone, and the show treats her physical injuries as difficulties to be soldiered through, not as debilitating traumas. This is true even when the violence is gendered (as it is in "The Farm," where Starbuck is held by the Cylons, who want to forcibly impregnate her) or psychological (as it is during her third-season imprisonment by Leoben in a nightmare vision of heterosexual domesticity). But most importantly for my purposes, *Galactica* portrays the aftermath of these violations the way audiences are used to seeing male trauma portrayed in war films, action films, and sports dramas. As the mental and emotional toll on her rises, Starbuck drinks, fights, behaves insubordinately, and eventually pulls herself together after a show of tough love and physical aggression from her commanding officer and father figure, Admiral Adama.

Here, vulnerability is rewritten not as male/female, but as human/Cylon. Women are not especially vulnerable, but humans are. This becomes vexed when we examine the show's divergent treatment of the human women and the Cylon female models. The humans ("real" women) are members of a nearly postgender society, but gender, and the possibility of gendered violence, become increasingly central to the show's commentary on the Cylons' "humanness" and its counterintuitive investment in their vulnerability. But before we get to rape and its place in both *Galactica*'s engagement with the legacy of Vietnam and its construction of gendered vulnerability, it is worth considering the season-one episode "Flesh and Bone," which engages the ticking-bomb scenario so central to *24*'s depiction of torture. *Galactica* reimagines that scene, using it to set the stakes of Cylon vulnerability. As David Luban points out: "In the real world of interrogations, decisions are not made one-off. The real world is a world of policies, guidelines, and directives. It is a world of *practices*, not of ad hoc emergency measures."[15] While *24* blurs this distinction (Jack does not follow policy guidelines when he tortures—he makes time-sensitive decisions that rules must be broken to save lives), *Galactica* opens "Flesh and Bone" by outlining the chain of command that leads to Starbuck torturing one of the male Cylon models, Leoben. Once the Galactica learns that Leoben has been captured, the decision to torture comes at two removes—President Roslin (Mary McDonnell) orders Adama to see that the Cylon is "interrogated." Adama argues against it, believing that interrogation will not yield any useful intelligence. Roslin orders him to do it anyway, and he assigns Starbuck, believing her more capable than his other officers of withstanding Cylon attempts at psychological warfare.

Figure 17 Apollo, Starbuck, and Baltar

The scene's camerawork and dialogue announce its difference from the adrenaline-fueled torture scenes characteristic of *24*. Instead of cutting away from the filmic markers of human vulnerability, *Galactica*'s camera focuses on the sweating, shaking, and bleeding that mark cinematic representations of suffering and that *Galactica* establishes as markers of the human. The human-looking models (called "skin jobs" by the humans) are not the only class of Cylon. Cylon society is a hierarchy with the humanesque models at the top, metal robot models at the bottom, and the Cylon Raiders, fighter jets that are hybrids of "machine and animal," occupying an oddly liminal space.[16] But the show asks for our ethical engagement only with those Cylons that look human—possessing bodies with skin and flesh. In Judith Butler's evocative terms, "The body implies mortality, vulnerability, agency: the skin and the flesh expose us to the gaze of others, but also to touch, and to violence."[17] Crucially, the one way that the Cylons are *not* human is in the body's promise of mortality. Cylons cannot die; when one body expires, they wake up (in a womblike cocoon of fluid) in a new, identical body, a process the show calls both "downloading" and "resurrection." The tension between these two terms, and the theological connotations of "resurrection," illustrate the ambivalence with which the show approaches the Cylons and the possibility of their humanity. While their vulnerability to pain confuses the human/machine dichotomy, their invulnerability to death marks the Cylons as not-human, both for the Galactica crew and for the show's audience. Although we have seen the term "vulnerability" signifying differently throughout this project, Butler's important formulation in her book *Precarious Life* ties vulnerability to loss. Though unstated, her use of the term almost always describes a vulnerability to death, to the ultimate fact of our mortality. *Battlestar Galactica* raises different questions: What is the place of physical pain in our responsibility to others? Where does vulnerability to death figure into this equation? And, ultimately, what are the boundaries of the human?

Starbuck's decision to torture Leoben in "Flesh and Bone" changes the stakes of the ticking-bomb scenario, since Leoben's status as a "machine" blurs the ethics of both torturing and "killing" him. Leoben himself establishes the ticking-bomb scenario, claiming that he has planted a nuclear warhead in the fleet, set to go off in nine hours. The show frames Starbuck's willingness to torture him as a gamble about the Cylons' desire to think of themselves as human. As the camera focuses on the sweat beading Leoben's brow, Starbuck muses:

> Machines shouldn't feel pain. Shouldn't bleed. Shouldn't sweat . . . See, now a smart Cylon would turn off the ol' pain software right about now. But I don't think you're so smart. (*Starbuck signals a guard standing behind Leoben; the guard brutally strikes him.*) Here's your dilemma. Turn off the pain, and you feel better—but that makes you a machine, not a person. See, human beings can't turn off their pain. Human beings have to suffer. And cry. And scream. And endure.

> Because they have no choice. So the only way you can avoid the pain you are about to receive is telling me exactly what I want to know. Just like a human would.

Starbuck's dialogue and this scene's visual focus on Leoben's blood and ragged breathing frame physical vulnerability to torture as part of what it means to be human. Unlike *24*'s torture scenes, with their jumpy camerawork and pounding soundtrack, *Battlestar Galactica*'s camera lingers on bodily fluids—the blood that cakes Leoben's face, the sweat that covers both him and Starbuck. This difference can be explained in terms of the shows' ideological investments. *24* sees torture as something practiced under pressure because its point is political: Americans should be grateful to have a man of action like Jack Bauer willing to protect them at any cost. But *Battlestar Galactica*'s point is existential and theological: the point at which a "machine" can question the facts of its own existence is the point at which it deserves our sympathy. As is evident at the episode's conclusion, this Cylon's ability to feel pain is not enough to make him human, in the eyes of the Galactica crew or the viewer. That step comes when Starbuck discovers that Leoben can die. When Leoben's resolve proves resistant to beatings and simulated drowning, Starbuck posits that fear of death makes Leoben willing to talk:

> I think that you're afraid. You're afraid that we're a long way from home. What if you don't transfer all the way back? What if when you die here, you really die? It's your chance to find out if you're really God or just a bunch of circuits with a bad haircut . . . Someone's programmed you with a fairy tale of God and streams and life ever after, but somewhere in that hard drive you call a brain is a beeping message. Error. Does not compute. I don't have a soul. I have software. If I die, I'm gone.

Starbuck's sarcasm about Cylon belief in a single God is typical of the Galactica crew. One of the show's most interesting topical valences is that the humans are either atheists (like Adama) or polytheists (like Starbuck), while the Cylons are devout monotheists. The show keeps this distinction constantly in the viewer's consciousness by having the humans utter awkward curses ("gods damn it!") in contrast to the Cylons' talk of "trusting God's plan" and "believing in God's love." But though Starbuck's clumsy attempt to goad Leoben into confessing the warhead's location fails, this speech outlines the debate that that haunts "Flesh and Bone." Once Starbuck asks if Leoben is too far from home, Cylons and their vulnerability will never be treated in quite the same way by the show.

If Leoben really is vulnerable to death—as the episode's climax shows us—that makes him grievable. President Roslin switches tactics after Starbuck is unable to torture information out of Leoben:

> ROSLIN: I apologize for what you've been through. Take his restraints off. Do it!
> LEOBEN: Thank you.

ROSLIN: I can do more. I can guarantee your safety; I can order your release. We are running out of time, we have only four minutes until your bomb goes off. I've come here to tell you that this conflict between our peoples does not have to continue. It can stop right here with us. We have to trust each other. Trust me. I think you know you can. Tell me what I need to know, and you will live.

LEOBEN: The warhead doesn't exist. I made it up. The lieutenant was right—I was too far out. I didn't want to die, so when I got caught I made up a story to buy some time.

ROSLIN: I see. Thank you for the truth.

LEOBEN: Thank you, Madame President. (*Starbuck starts to walk away.*) Don't be too hard on Kara, she was just doing her job. The military—they teach you to . . . dehumanize people.

ROSLIN: I'll take that into consideration.

Starbuck had insisted, "It's a machine, sir. There's no limit to the tactics I can use," when Roslin objected to the sight of the bloodied and waterboarded prisoner. When Roslin orders the guards to "put him out the airlock," however, Starbuck claims that she "can't do that—not after he told the truth." Roslin's answer shows the fluidity of the Cylons' moral position for Starbuck, the loyal soldier, and Roslin, the utilitarian president. Roslin's displeasure with Starbuck's interrogation techniques does not undermine her certainty about Leoben's status: "Yes I can. And I will. Lieutenant, look at me. You've lost perspective . . . But you're right—he's a machine. And you don't keep a deadly machine around when it kills your people and threatens your future. You get rid of it." Starbuck, on the other hand, begins to question this strict machine/human dichotomy: "He's not afraid to die. He's just afraid that his soul won't make it to God." The discovery that Cylons can bleed and sweat and suffer fails to shift Starbuck's perspective. But the discovery that Cylons can doubt grants Leoben an ethical standing in her view that he lacks in Roslin's. Roslin puts Leoben out the airlock, and in the pilot's locker room Starbuck prays for him: "Lords of Kobol, hear my prayer. I don't know if he had a soul or not. But if he did, take care of it." Starbuck's "long way from home" doesn't just refer to Leoben. Galactica's crew is a long way from home, too, and that emotional dynamic sets the stage for *Battlestar Galactica*'s engagement with the vulnerable body and the specter of Vietnam in the three-episode arc "Pegasus," "Resurrection Ship I," and "Resurrection Ship II."

Rape in the Uncanny Valley

These mid-season-two episodes mark the show's movement toward the questions of gender and rape that *Battlestar Galactica* uses both to raise the stakes of audience confusion about the Cylons' ontological status and to address an important subtext of any contemporary representation of the military: the specter of Vietnam.

Of Vietnam's many cultural legacies, the image of the American soldier as rapist has particular currency for twenty-first-century audiences familiar with viewing Vietnam through the lens of 1970s and 1980s films about the conflict. One of its other clearest legacies is the sense of a deep political and affective split between the military and the domestic civilian population it protects. This mutual distrust and anger gives dramatic heft to the trope of homecoming central to so many Vietnam War films and novels. This theme of homecoming and what I see as its dependence on narratives of rape bring gender and the limits of resistant vulnerability into the show's ongoing conversation about what it means to be human. *Battlestar Galactica*'s fantasy of military technology that looks human forces us to think about recent theorizations of what the category of the "human" means in our current historical moment. Butler argues that the aftermath of September 11 can be thought of as the problem of vulnerability, what she calls "the problem of a primary vulnerability to others, one that one cannot will away without ceasing to be human."[18] Our vulnerability *to* others and the vulnerability *of* our bodies—this is the central question about the legacy of Vietnam that shows like *Battlestar Galactica* force us to confront.

The humanoid Cylons come in twelve models, with hundreds of copies of each model. As we have seen, Leoben, one of the male models, plays a key role in "Flesh and Bone," but for the majority of the show's first two seasons, the most visible Cylons are two female models, a model #6, a statuesque blonde played by former Victoria's Secret model Tricia Helfer, and a model #8, played by Grace Park, who during the first season is a sleeper agent in the Colonial Fleet, Lieutenant Sharon "Boomer" Valeri. It's important to the episodes I'll discuss in this chapter that some of the copies—particularly the Sharon Valeri copies—at first don't even know they're Cylons. They look, seem, and *feel* human, to the extent that they think they *are* human. Both #6 and #8 are central to the narratives of homecoming and rape that I discuss in this chapter, and their physicality—Helfer's nearly comic-book femininity and Park's athletic build and Asian heritage—become central to the show's meditation on gender in the post-Vietnam military. In the casting of both Helfer and Park, we can see American anxieties about Vietnam reflected back as anxieties about rape and the vulnerability of female bodies that American culture always ends up imagining as white. Popular representations of Vietnam in the 1970s and 1980s often used the American soldier's sexual violence against Vietnamese women as a symbol of the moral chaos produced by the war. We have seen the ways that *Full Metal Jacket* uses the dying Vietnamese sniper to make this point, and many of the returning-veteran films of the 1980s registered anxiety about the possible savagery toward women the Vietnam vet brought home with him. *Casualties of War* exemplifies one familiar trope, telling the story of the American soldiers who rape and murder a Vietnamese woman and the one soldier who tries to protect her. *Battlestar Galactica* takes this familiar Vietnam narrative and splits it, introducing

Figure 18 #6 and #8

another battlestar full of humans (rapists) that allows the show's protagonists to protect Park's body instead of exploiting it.

"Pegasus," which originally aired on September 23, 2005, before a four-month midseason break, opens with the discovery of another battlestar (the Pegasus) that the fleet didn't know had survived the Cylon attack in the miniseries. The isolation and bunker mentality of humanity's surviving remnant is a recurring trope on *Battlestar Galactica,* so finding the Pegasus and realizing there are other human survivors registers as a moment of wonder and catharsis. At the sight of the Pegasus, Apollo declares it's "like a dream." But what kind of dream is this? And what does it tell us about the American cultural imagination of both the military and the legacy of Vietnam in the midst of the "war on terror"? Admiral Helena Cain (Michelle Forbes), the Pegasus commander, announces, "Welcome back to the Colonial Fleet." This serves as both a greeting and an ominous reminder to the Galactica's crew and the show's viewers that the Galactica and the Pegasus are floating outposts, part of the structure of laws and regulations that governed the Colonies when they existed but that are endangered in this postapocalyptic scenario. A reunion with the Pegasus brings the Galactica "home" to the Colonial Fleet, a move reminiscent of the scores of Vietnam representations that put these moments of homecoming at their center. This arc in the middle of the show's second season is important because I read the Pegasus as a sort of nightmare-mirror vision of a post-Vietnam military that didn't "learn" what the show will suggest are the "lessons" of Vietnam, particularly as regards gender and rape. Many viewers see the Pegasus arc as a critique of prisoner abuse at Gitmo and Abu Ghraib, and indeed the show offers a trenchant analysis of intramilitary debates about the humanity of the "enemy." But the specific forms of emotional manipulation around the sight of the female body in danger or in pain, and the replacement in this drama of the Asian female body with both the white female body and the body of the white soldier (coded as American), have their most specific cinematic parallel in fictions about Vietnam. Indeed, *Galactica*'s ideological fluidity and its collapsing of distinct moments in U.S. military history are part of its success as an allegory.

The Pegasus presents viewers with a military full of conscripts, a violent, megalomaniacal commander, and a crew with a penchant for violence against women. If this reminds us of 1980s films about Vietnam, from *Apocalypse Now* to *Casualties of War* and *Full Metal Jacket,* it ought to. In addition to its commentary on the politics of rape in war, these episodes are important to our current political moment for what they say about unchecked executive power. But perhaps despite the series of prisoner-abuse scenes I will discuss (and despite her name), Admiral Cain isn't a two-dimensional villain. Nor is she the most visible female commander on the show. The "Pegasus" arc lasts only three episodes—Cain is murdered at the end of "Resurrection Ship II"—and President Roslin and Starbuck are both far more indicative of the show's complex representation of women and power. Cain's cold insistence on military regulations and her insensitivity to Cylon suffering merely align her with the rest of the Pegasus crew and serve as further examples of the show's gender-blindness when it comes to its human characters. But reading the Pegasus and its officers and crew as a fantasy of America without the Geneva Convention, and absent the "lessons" purportedly learned in Vietnam, allows us to see *Battlestar Galactica*'s commitment to gender-neutral vulnerability breaking down at the site where the definitions of male and female, and human and machine, break down—the site of sexual violence. Acknowledging Cylon humanness allows audiences to (however obliquely) acknowledge the humanness of the "enemy" in war and therefore the immorality of torture. But the show's most visceral statement against torture, and acknowledgment of Cylon vulnerability, occurs around the spectacle of rape. At the moment the show highlights the Cylons' gendered vulnerability to rape, it asks for the viewer's full engagement with them as persons. This creates an ethical paradox: in acknowledging the humanness of the animae, and therefore the injustice of torture, the show falls back on gendering vulnerability female.

In order to deal with the legacy of Vietnam and the thorny questions it raises about civil-military relations, *Battlestar Galactica* makes *sexual* violence (or its threat) the thing that can humanize a machine. But this also brings us back to the question of gender that the show's "they look like us" conceit puts at the center of debates about who, exactly, is the enemy. Sharon and Six are both military prisoners when the episode "Pegasus" opens—Sharon in the Galactica brig, Six in the Pegasus brig. They are also different "models" of femininity in the egalitarian future *Battlestar Galactica* imagines. Cylon "women" tell a different story than human females like Starbuck and President Roslin, or, more accurately, *two* different stories, one civilian (Six) and one military (Sharon). Here, the Asian female body, so often in the Vietnam context a specter for both the American male soldier's aggression and his trauma, is visually positioned as one of them—as a soldier. But she's a soldier who is also the enemy. Importantly, this Asian female body is the object of male desire but not a fetish; that position is occupied by Six in her iteration as a figment of a human's imagination. That human is Gaius Baltar (James Callis), the fleet's brilliant but squirrelly vice president, whose romantic involvment with this Cylon leaves the question of his loyalties constantly open.[19] The screwball-comedy banter between Baltar and Six (whom no one else can see) provides one of the few sources of comedy in the show's consistently dark second season. This raises the emotional stakes of the scene where Baltar examines the Pegasus's "Cylon prisoner."

The camera follows Baltar, imaginary Six, and Admiral Cain through the corridors of the Pegasus to the brig where they're holding an as-yet-unidentified Cylon prisoner. This registers as a moment of anticipation for the show's regular viewers. We have been told that there are twelve models, but at this point in the show's run, we only know what six of them look like. The viewer expects another model to be revealed; as Baltar approaches the brig, imaginary Six coos, "I wonder who the Cylon will turn out to be. Stranger? Familiar face? Trusted friend who suddenly turns out to be the enemy?" Admiral Cain tells Baltar that she wants him to "examine it as soon as possible; see if you can glean anything from it." The Pegasus crew's insistence on seeing Cylons as things ("it" instead of "she") withholds this Cylon's gender until the dramatic "reveal" moment, where the camera cuts from imaginary Six's suddenly horrified face to the bruised, bloodied prisoner inside the brig: another model #6, looking considerably more vulnerable without the slinky dresses and the platinum-dyed hair audiences are used to seeing on imaginary Six. This #6, the Pegasus prisoner, is eventually called "Gina"; the sight of Gina, the same model that has seemed so plastic and otherworldly in Baltar's imagination,

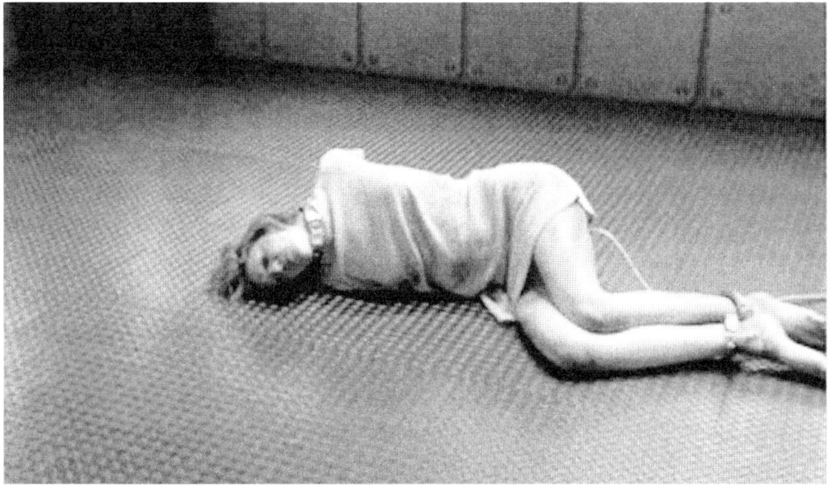

Figure 19 Gina in the Pegasus brig

provides the audience's first glimpse of Tricia Helfer registering as more than a figure of fantasy.

Baltar and Six enter the brig, circling the unresponsive prisoner. Six says that Gina's been "abused" and "tortured," but the aspect of this that the show focuses on is that she's been raped. Baltar's "examination" of Gina's inert body yields "no obvious sign of head trauma," as Gaius explains to the indifferent Admiral Cain:

> It suffered no serious head injuries, therefore no physical damage to its neural pathways or cognitive reasoning centers. But it is quite clearly traumatized. Which would suggest that its current condition is psychological in nature. Had you thought of that? No. It shows that Cylon consciousness is just as susceptible to the same pressures and cleavages as the human psyche. It can be manipulated in the same fashion. Simply put, Admiral: You have already used the stick. It's time to use a carrot.

This speech frames Gina's emotional trauma in terms of a torture debate that would replace Cain's brutal tactics with the more Geneva Convention–approved psychological manipulation (the "carrot") that the fleet's laws presumably demand. But on an affective level, the show's use of Gina's broken body and Baltar's uncharacteristically humane response to it connects sexual violence to gender and ultimately to humanness. If torture scenes in *24* work to disassociate torture from cruelty, framing it as a utilitarian tactic a society under threat would do well to utilize, the aftermath of Gina's torture at the hands of the Pegasus crew does important work to reestablish the link between torture and sadism. The Gina storyline sets up an obvious comparison between the good military (the Galactica crew) that treats its female Cylon prisoner humanely and the bad military (the Pegasus crew) that abuses her. But beyond that, this episode tells a different *kind* of story about the military—not how the enemy becomes dehumanized, but how it's rehumanized, as we'll see in the next scene, through the specter of rape.

Sharon (#8) has been a prisoner in the Galactica brig for the better part of season two, and the reunion with the Pegasus (the return of the "bad" military) cements her status as both a romantic interest for Lieutenant Karl "Helo" Agathon (Tahmoh Penikett) and a "person." Midway through "Pegasus," a convivial scene of the Galactica and Pegasus pilots sharing clandestinely produced moonshine on the hangar deck quickly sours when the Pegasus crew banter about their sexual abuse of Gina. The scene in the hangar deck, where the Pegasus pilots become increasingly boorish and the Galactica crew increasingly uneasy, is intercut with quick, brutal shots of Sharon in the Galactica brig being attacked by an interrogator from the Pegasus.

> PEGASUS PILOT 1: Hey Chief (*offering him a glass*), you deserve a fracking medal—we haven't seen booze for months. This place is a frackin' party!
>
> PEGASUS PILOT 2: I heard you guys even got yourselves a Cylon. Heard she's a hot one, too. (*Pegasus pilots start laughing and catcalling—"gonna get me a little of the oh-yeah oh-yeeaahhh!"*)
>
> CHIEF: Hey, y'know what? That's enough, guys. Just shut up.
>
> PEGASUS PILOT 2: Oh, sensitive. So you got a soft spot for the little robot girl, huh?

The camera cuts to Sharon doing sit-ups in the brig. Lieutenant Alastair Thorne (Fulvio Cecere), the "Cylon interrogator" from the Pegasus, enters as ominous music begins to play, and Sharon backs away, demanding to know who he is. The dialogue from the next scene on the hangar deck starts over these images before the camera cuts back to Chief Galen Tyrol (Aaron Douglas) and Helo, who are growing more agitated.

> PEGASUS PILOT 2: Remember when Thorne put that "Please Disturb" sign up on the brig there? (*laughing, other pilots chiming in "I got in line twice!"*) Remember how she was just lying there, like, that blank look on her face, like (*does an ugly imitation of traumatized blankness*).
>
> SPECIALIST CALLY (female Galactica mechanic): Hey! Do you mind?! (*Storms out, glaring at the Pegasus pilots as they leer: "Oooh! Frisky!"*)

The caricature of military masculinity presented by the Pegasus crew demands a very different response to gendered vulnerability from the audience than this show usually does. After Cally storms out, the camera cuts back to the Galactica brig, where Thorne "interrogates" Sharon, choking and punching her while demanding information about the Cylon resurrection ship. She keeps insisting she doesn't know anything, and it's important to the scene's visceral impact that viewers assume she genuinely doesn't have the information Thorne seeks. Sharon has been involved romantically with Helo throughout the second season, and her free choice to align herself with humans instead of Cylons is one of the season's most emotionally significant arcs. Unlike Starbuck's harsh tactics against Leoben, Thorne's abuse of Sharon registers as utterly gratuitous, a reflection of a military that has completely dehumanized its "enemy."

In a series of increasingly quick cuts, the Pegasus pilots muse that "maybe Thorne will give us a chance with this one, too . . . I heard him say he's going to have to break her in a little first," while Thorne attempts to rape Sharon, and Chief and Helo race to the brig to stop the attack. This rush to the brig to "save" Sharon reverses the show's usual stance toward gender. The threat of rape against a character who isn't—technically—a woman but looks like one leads to this frenzy of conventional male protection.[20] As this sequence demonstrates, the show wants to see rape as categorically different from other forms of abuse. Specialist Cally, the female mechanic who protests and leaves during the description of Gina's rape, had herself shot and killed a female Cylon prisoner earlier in the season. Having her voice the Galactica crew's disgust evidences the "special" place the show wants to assign sexual violence in regard to conventions of war. Chief and Helo make it to the brig just in time, throwing Thorne off of Sharon, accidentally killing him when his head strikes the wall. This provides the episode's heart-thumping climax, and the alarmist music and shots of Sharon curling up in pain give the show's unambiguous ethical approval to killing a human man to save this "woman" from rape.

After this interrupted attack on Sharon, Galactica's Commander Adama apologizes to her, for the first time calling Sharon "her" instead of "it."

> COTTLE (Galactica ship's doctor): You do have a cracked rib, which means it's going to hurt like hell for a while. But I'm not seeing any signs of permanent damage from the attack.
>
> SHARON: The "attack." Is that what we're calling it now?
>
> ADAMA: They were not from the Galactica.
>
> SHARON: They were from the Pegasus. So what? What about Helo and Chief? I heard a rumor they were going to be executed.
>
> ADAMA: I'm not going to let that happen.
>
> SHARON: Well, how are you going to do that? Isn't Admiral Cain in command?
>
> ADAMA: What happened to you—
>
> COTTLE: Was unforgivable.
>
> ADAMA: Happened aboard my ship on my watch. And it's my responsibility. So I just want you to know that I personally apologize. (*To Cottle.*) See that she's okay, then back into her cell.

In addition to the questions this raises about how the show portrays gender difference, it's worth asking what kind of fantasy *Battlestar Galactica* peddles about executive authority in times of war. This is a military and a government where people in positions of power actually take responsibility for detainee abuse, for starters. So this makes "Pegasus," at base, a drama of failed military leadership. The newly vulnerable, and newly female, body is a direct result of Admiral Cain's megalomaniacal and overly ideological command. Pegasus, the military that didn't adjust after Vietnam, is a military adrift from civilian control.

This question of civilian control animates the aftermath of Chief Tyrol's and Helo's violence in defense of Sharon. Chief and Helo are being held in the Pegasus brig for killing Thorne when two Pegasus crew members enter and attack, hitting them with bars of soap wrapped in towels, in what seems a clear reference to the famous boot-camp "training" scene in *Full Metal Jacket*. The Pegasus XO, Colonel Jack Fisk (Graham Beckdel), arrives and stops the attack. He shouts at his men, forcing them to acknowledge the uniforms that identify Helo and Chief as "Colonial officers," then claims to not understand what he saw: "Because I think I saw you two knuckledraggers treating those two men like they were Cylons." Chief and Helo are prisoners in the same brig that houses the Cylon prisoners, but, as Fisk's dialogue in this scene makes clear, they're not similar targets of official violence. And this is where our discussion of the chain of command in the post-Vietnam military becomes blurrier, directly at the boundary of what it means to be female, or human, and what it means to be a subject who can be raped. The almost-cartoonish violence in this scene is important for what it *isn't*—it isn't rape, but it also isn't sanctioned. It's not official state violence in the way both earlier sexual assaults were. If Helo and Chief's rescue of Sharon in the earlier clip privileges "human" feeling above military hierarchy, the colonel's rescue in this scene is the triumph of military protocol and hierarchy over emotion. After Fisk has dismissed the two men, he turns to Chief and Helo, who thank him for stopping the attack.

> FISK: I don't want your thanks. I owe Lieutenant Thorne my life, as do many people on this ship.
>
> HELO: He was trying to *rape* a *prisoner.*
>
> FISK: You can't rape a machine, Lieutenant.

It's not until this moment, halfway through the second season of a show devoted to hot-button treatments of gender, violence, and torture, that we as viewers really become aware of the bizarre affective response this show demands from its audience. Technically, you *can't* rape a machine—that is central to the ways we define rape and the special place it has in our culture's discourses about violence and about gender. But the cross-cutting between Sharon and Six in the earlier sequence builds a frenzied emotional response to the threat of Sharon's rape. In the apology scene, both Adama and Galactica's doctor seem to believe that you *can* rape a machine, and indeed that the act itself gives #8 a status as woman (as "Sharon") that she lacked before. Rape is the specter around which the "good" military and the "bad" military get defined. This should hardly be news to anyone familiar with literary and filmic representations of Vietnam or second-wave feminist theory. The

Vietnam-era allegations of widespread rape of Vietnamese women by American soldiers, which have been a crucial and emotional part of the decades-long fight over Vietnam and its legacy, are perhaps the most visible remnant of this debate in American popular culture. But the status of rape in war (and as a war crime) has been the subject of ongoing feminist activism that has attempted to quantify what it means to be a woman, what a combatant is, and whether rape is, indeed, a gender-related crime.[21]

The spectacle of Gina's broken body and her traumatized psyche, particularly when the show places it in the context of the "Please Disturb" sign, forces Baltar to recognize her as female, as human, in a way that he hadn't before. And the regular viewer's emotional investment in Baltar's character arc implicates the audience in the show's uneasy formulation of "woman" as defined, in some real but unspoken way, as one who can be raped. Anthropologist Christine Helliwell's work on rape and sexual difference can provide a useful frame for how this show and popular discourses like it theorize rape and personhood. Helliwell questions Western culture's "ingrained presumptions concerning difference between men and women and, particularly, concerning men's genitalia and sexuality as inherently brutalizing and penetrative and women's genitalia and sexuality as inherently vulnerable and subject to brutalization."[22] I see this as a particularly interesting formulation when thinking about science fiction as a cultural form, since a show like *Battlestar Galactica* presents viewers with the fiction of nonhuman cyborgs that appear gendered. This makes the show's attempt to engage audience emotion with the Cylons' femaleness around the specter of rape especially troubling. Making rape a step on the path toward "becoming" female reinscribes the cultural commonplace that Helliwell attempts to challenge—that rape is something that happens to women.[23] In "Pegasus," gender emerges as the ultimate social construct, which allows rape (and emotions about rape) to become the thing that structures what it is to be a woman. Sharon's and Gina's vulnerability to rape makes them women, which therefore makes them human. The show's condemnation of the Pegasus crew and celebration of Chief's and Helo's masculine protectiveness attempts to assuage post-Vietnam fears about the military and its capacity for sexual violence (banishing Cain's "bad" crew and replacing them with Adama's "good" crew). And our feelings of revulsion at the sight of violence toward military prisoners is, indeed, positive. Our collective acknowledgment of both the fact that rape often remains a gendered crime and the sympathy due to those held in prisons means an acknowledgment of their vulnerability and therefore their humanness. But after presenting a moment of the new, postgender vulnerability, where humans are vulnerable and machines are not, *Battlestar Galactica* gives way to the old: as Cylon collapses into human, vulnerability collapses into femininity, as it always seems to do in a culture obsessed with and frightened by gender difference. And the implications of this are mixed. Sympathy with the suffering of prisoners is ethically useful, but this intense and emotional focus on these two female bodies also blinds us to military rape in our current moment, which *is* occurring—just not against a female enemy with the body of a Victoria's Secret model.

To understand the way this substitution works, we must turn to the ways that scholars have theorized the figure of the human machine, particularly the female cyborg, because it can help us see how this particular fantasy about Vietnam and the American military works in popular science fiction. Judith Halberstam analyzes the female cyborg, celebrating the "inherent artificiality" of a machine's performance of womanhood (what Donna Haraway calls the "machinery of gender"). Halberstam argues that "by merging so completely the familiar with the strange, the artificial with the natural, the female cyborg appears to evoke something unsettling, something that profoundly disturbs and frightens certain authors. We might call the effect produced by the cyborg 'uncanny.'"[24] Halberstam refers to Freud's notion of the uncanny as the terrifying spectacle that leads back to the familiar, the familiar become strange. But we can also usefully think about what roboticist Masahiro Mori has called the "uncanny valley," a hypothesis about human emotional response to artificial intelligence that looks human. Mori posits that response to humanoid robots gets more positive, more empathetic, as the machine appears more and more human, until a certain tipping point at which the response quickly becomes very negative as the machine appears almost exactly human but not quite. This "valley," then, is about our recognition of similarity and what Mori thinks is our emotional recoil from the close but imperfect reflection of ourselves. In a scene cut from the aired version of "Pegasus" but included in the extended DVD episode, Admiral Cain tells Baltar: "I can never get over how human they [Cylons] look." He replies, "Yes, it's uncanny, isn't it?" The uncanny valley here isn't just the distance between Sharon or Six and the Galactica crew, it's between the two crews: our actual military and the uncanny mirror vision of a military that didn't learn from Vietnam.

But the question of the Cylon and our collective responsibility toward her returns us to what Butler would remind us is the problem of the human. War has ethical costs *because* of the vulnerability of other bodies, the "enemy's" as well as ours. It's the confrontation with the humanity of the other that makes *Battlestar Galactica*'s meditation on the body and its vulnerability particularly trenchant for twenty-first-century popular culture's confrontation with Vietnam's legacy. The question *Battlestar Galactica* asks is what happens when lives that are not precarious are housed in bodies that are—bodies that look like human women. The show combines a science-fiction scenario where robots look like people and gender relations appear egalitarian with a Vietnam aesthetic that sees women, not men, as the victims of military sexual violence. This use of Vietnam matters because it allows the show to ignore the actual sites of military rape in the post-Vietnam era (military academies at home and prisons overseas). At the same time, it imagines a return to male violence (against other men) in protection of the suffering female body, complicated by the uncanny valley of the "women's" status as flesh-and-blood machines.

Battlestar Galactica places its most visceral commentary on terrorism, suffering, and the ethics of torture in the visual context of Vietnam—bringing the specter of Vietnam home to the war on terror. The fact that Vietnam's specter emerges in images of raped women and gendered vulnerability vexes the ethical thrust of this project. Though I have tried to complicate our easy protectiveness when it comes to women—our collective investment in women's special vulnerability—fictions of torture and of military prisons trouble this picture. Sympathy with the suffering body is an ethical good, especially in the context of torture, national security, and humanness that shows like *Battlestar Galactica* raise. But by imaginatively replacing Iraq's imagery (the male Middle Eastern body) with Vietnam's imagery (the Asian female body, and its imaginative corollary, the white woman), *Battlestar Galactica*—usually braver than any show on television about current events—again relies on a sentimental vulnerability that lets us off the hook.

Having insisted on the individuality of the female Cylons, and thereby their humanness, *Galactica*'s final seasons begin to question the primacy of individual subjectivity. Vulnerability, as we have seen, is always constructed relationally but has usually been about the discrete human body and the horror of its boundaries' violation. Slowly, however, *Battlestar Galactica* abandons its impulse to delineate the boundaries between Cylon and human. The human body's vulnerability is a function of its building blocks: blood and bone. By the fourth season, *Galactica* has virtually given up on the idea that the Cylons are machines. In the opening miniseries, the Galactica is figured as a relic of an earlier era in military technology. Set to be decommissioned, it survives the first Cylon attack because its computer systems are too old and outdated to be vulnerable to the Cylon plan to crash the integrated computer systems of the rest of the fleet. It turns out that the way the Cylons have moved forward technologically (they "evolved") is also a movement back, from technology to biology. Even their ships are alive, breathing and bleeding. And once this final barrier has been crossed, the anxiety about who is and is not a Cylon is revealed as the wrong question to have asked.

6

Vulnerability by Proxy

DEADWOOD AND THE FUTURE OF TELEVISION FORM

In the second episode of David Milch's HBO series *Deadwood,* Seth Bullock (Timothy Olyphant), former sheriff, future hardware tycoon, and erstwhile protagonist, tries along with his partner Sol Star (John Hawkes) to purchase a lot of land from saloon owner, murderer, and pimp Al Swearengen (Ian McShane). As Al approaches the table where Seth and Sol sit at Al's Gem Saloon, Seth stands abruptly and announces, "Sol's got my proxy." When Al asks, "Meaning him and me should talk without you?" Seth snaps, "That's what it means." As Sol and Al debate the efficacy of Al selling the lot outright, Sol insists that he and Seth are alone in their partnership in Star and Bullock Hardware, while Al fears that Wild Bill Hickok (Keith Carradine), newly arrived in town, is an unnamed partner. When Al suggests that Seth and Sol partner with him for the first few months of their operation, Sol hedges:

SOL: Seth won't accept it.
AL: I thought you had his proxy!
SOL: Just up to a point.
AL: See, that ain't my sense of proxy. That's what I'd want these few months for, till we agreed what things meant.

The substance of Al's anxiety in this scene is whether Wild Bill, "the A-number-one mankiller in the West," holds an "unnamed piece of the action," but, as will be typical of *Deadwood,* while the content of this conversation is about commerce, its substance is about the ability of one person to speak for another, to represent another's interests. And, as will also be typical of the show's attitude toward the efficacy of commerce, the scene ends with a display of Al's negotiating skills: "Here's my counteroffer to your counteroffer: Go fuck yourself."

Throughout this book, I have argued that a sort of cultural proxy is at work in the construction of vulnerability. One body's removal from the screen or the stage allows another body, often young, usually female, to take its place in the American cultural imaginary. *Deadwood* makes the logic of this substitution explicit, and the show's structuring premise—that Deadwood is a town with no law or enforceable contract and therefore a proving ground for the unbridled free market—seems to indicate that the show will concern itself with the gold mining, whoring, and boozing that structure its opening credits. But the show's first season slowly and subtly reveals this setup to have been what I call an affective miscue—a strategy that the serialized television of the twenty-first century uses frequently to encourage its audience to ask one question, only to reveal this to have been the wrong question to ask all along. Since 9/11, television has started to work through in narrative what we won't allow ourselves to think about in politics—the disruption of individual subjectivity. Al keeps claiming that he wants to be able to "operate in peace," but the arc of the series forces the viewer to realize that Al's business interests are not the interests that should engage us. And if there's any question left about where the viewer's affective response belongs in terms of capital, the question is removed when George Hearst (Gerald McRaney) arrives in Deadwood at the end of the second season. If Al's murderous impulses are mitigated for the audience by the contrast between Ian McShane's glorious, moving performance as Al and the cold menace Powers Boothe brings to his portrayal of Cy Tolliver, even Tolliver seems brushed with the stroke of humanity in comparison to Hearst, who declares: "My only passion is the color." The "color" refers to the gold that the miners who stake small claims in the South Dakota town pan out of the creek and that Hearst wants to harvest more efficiently by sinking shafts. "The earth speaks to me," he says, "tells me where to dig into her." The clear metaphor here, of the earth as a woman Hearst will penetrate, connects mining to the trade practiced by the town's prostitutes, but it also reveals Hearst's proclivity for seeing things only according to their monetary value.

This dynamic, and the way Hearst seems positioned as the corporate interest that will dispossess the small miners and the owners of local businesses like Al, Seth, and Sol, lead many scholars to read the show as a confrontation between different kinds of capitalism. Daniel Worden, for example, argues that Hearst represents corporate interests and the other characters represent individual entrepreneurship. But throughout the show's third season it is Hearst who is framed as both individualist and entrepreneurial, in stark opposition to the show's protagonists. Worden suggests that "Deadwood's residents relate to one another strategically and are quick to sever ties and create new ones as social and economic situations shift."[1] Yet tracing the long narrative of these characters' engagement with one another reveals something very different—that while several makeshift families like Al and his employees, Seth and Sol, Charlie (Dayton Callie), Jane (Robyn Weigert), and Joanie (Kim Dickens), *claim* that their actions and alliances are motivated by market forces, their actual behaviors, and the way the show asks its audience to engage with them, are motivated by something very different. Hearst alone is motivated solely by capitalism and "stark individualism."[2]

It is telling that in a show that makes "cocksucker" and "motherfucker" a seamless part of its unique and poetic language, the ugliest line in all three seasons is Hearst's manifesto of individualism: "My proper traffic is with the earth. And [in] my dealings with [people], I ought solely have to do with niggers, and whites who obey me like dogs." That the show so completely rejects Hearst's preferred form of interaction with others—a mirror of his vision of his "traffic with the earth"—forces our recognition that the show has abandoned the ethic suggested by its opening episodes. *Deadwood* frames its argument about the possibilities of a town without law as a capitalist's dream only to reveal that entrepreneurial individualism is a greater fiction even than law. In fact, *Deadwood* is very clear about the fact that everyone is *not* equal under the rule of the marketplace, particularly the Cornish miners, Chinese launderers, and prostitutes of all ethnicities that populate Deadwood's brothels and thoroughfare. Worden gestures toward this when he reads Al as a "hybrid force . . . bound by neo-liberal logic, yet gesturing to new values and commitments that stand in stark contrast to the short-sighted commitments of entrepreneurial individualism."[3] I suggest that instead of merely gesturing toward these new values and commitments, *Deadwood* radically rejects not only "entrepreneurial individualism" but the very concept of the individualized self. Robert Westerfelhaus and Celeste Lacroix label *Deadwood* a "ritual of disquiet," arguing that it "simultaneously expresses and provokes the psychological discomfort that comes from posing unsettling questions about important matters."[4] The cultural texts I have investigated throughout this book imagine new affective pathways beyond female vulnerability, but *Deadwood* imagines something even more—a pathway beyond the idea of the individual.

Deadwood can be read in this context as a crisis of failing bodies; plague-ridden, epileptic, and murdered bodies here provide us a way to think about vulnerability relationally. Just as Butler's *Precarious Life* offers us new ways to think about vulnerability and the social contract, *Deadwood* suggests new ways of thinking about long-form television narrative in relation to our ideas about the self. Much of the existing scholarly work on *Deadwood* deals with the show's relationship to history and with series creator David Milch as an auteur, and most of this work takes Milch at his word that the show's rich and elaborate profanity is "realistic."[5] But I argue that those elements that make the show difficult for some viewers—baroque language, the absence of episodic structure, seemingly incomprehensible plots about treaties and land annexation—allow *Deadwood* to say something about the violence that haunts the founding of America as a nation and that drives its westward expansion. The collective sins of slavery and the genocide of the Native American population are never far from the edges of the frame. The vulnerable communities, both in and out of the frame, become a point of reference for the kind of community that Deadwood could become as opposed to the duplicitous model of market capitalism represented by Hearst. Part of the way the show accomplishes this racial haunting is by figuring the camp itself as illegal, as an outlaw or fugitive space. Due to the 1868 Fort Laramie Treaty with the Sioux, the mining camp exists on what is, in 1876, when the show opens, technically "Indian land." Of course, the focus on these characters as treaty violators means that U.S. imperialism is figured, visually at least, as a government crackdown on the largely white miners and saloonkeepers, but the show's visual strategies and central metaphors never let the audience forget the exploitation of women and people of color. It does this by decentering the white male protagonist—first in the frame (visually), then by completely rejecting the idea of the individual that structures film and television as narrative forms.

The show's first episodes establish audience identification with Seth; the camera arrives in Deadwood with him, figuring Seth as the show's protagonist. His immediate tension with Al establishes the saloonkeeper as the show's villain (however magnetic and eloquent), especially given that Al commits one murder, orders two more, beats one of his prostitutes, and attempts to orchestrate the murder of an orphaned child within the show's first three episodes. But with Cy's arrival, the show has a foil onto which it can project negative feelings about Al's status as a murderer and a pimp. Al's trip to the Bella Union to assess the competition is important because it establishes Al as a vulnerable figure, a characterization that becomes increasingly evident through the season, despite the early miscues that seemed poised to establish Seth as a civilizing force and Al as a symbol of chaos. By the last episode of the season, Al is the central force in the formation of the camp's community. The story of "order rising out of the muck" hinges on a series of threats to the camp, most notably Wild Bill's murder, which leads to the show's most explicit statement about community, vulnerability, and the "body" of the camp.[6] At Wild Bill's funeral, Reverend Smith (Ray McKinnon)—a frontal-lobe epileptic who becomes the first season's version of a Shakespearean holy fool—makes a speech that ties the blood of vulnerable bodies to the vision of community as parts of a body:

> Mr. Hickok will lie beside two brothers. One he likely killed, the other he killed for certain and he's been killed now in turn. So much blood. And on the battlefields of the brothers' war, I saw more blood than this. And asked then after the purpose, and did not know. But know now to testify that, not knowing, I believe. Saint Paul tells us: by one spirit are we all baptized in the one body, whether we be Jew or gentile, bond or free. And they've all been made to drink into one spirit. For the body is not one man, but many. He tells us: the eye can not say unto the hand, I have no need of thee. Nor again, the head to the feet, I have no need of thee. Nay, much more those members of the body which seem to be more feeble, and those members of the body which we think of as less honorable, are all necessary. He—he says that there should be no schism in the body, but that the members should have the same care, one to another. And whether one member suffer, all the members suffer with it.

The show figures this intensely corporeal vision of the community—disembodied parts only making a whole body when they conceive of themselves as "members"—as the result of the "blood" that binds ex-lawman Wild Bill with the "brothers" he killed in previous episodes. Director Ed Bianchi's camerawork in this scene, with frequent close-ups of an increasingly agitated Seth, frames the concept of the community as body as a commentary on Seth's need to embrace his "part" in relation to that body: the position of sheriff, which he left Montana to escape and has consistently resisted since his arrival in Deadwood. The show understands this conflict as a matter of language, a language Seth does not yet speak. Following Seth and Sol back to the camp after the funeral, the Reverend asks Seth what he thinks his "part" might be. Seth insists that he doesn't know what the Reverend means, a repeated topic of conversation between them during their frequent postfuneral talks. The first time Smith presses Seth about his belief in his autonomy and individuality, Seth snaps, "If you're preachin' at me, Reverend, you need to put some more light on the text."

Season one is the story of Seth learning to speak the language, to recognize the "parts" of the body of the camp, and to throw "light on the text" of his dangerous delusion of himself as an independent agent. In *Deadwood,* at least for Seth, the operative fiction is not his difference from the hustlers and thieves that populate Deadwood's filthy thoroughfare and frequent its brothels. The more salient fiction is that a town with no official law frees him to be an individual, to work only for his own interest. What Milch would call the "illusion" of the self's isolation is the central motif that the show's "no law at all in Deadwood" gambit brings to the audience's attention. Seth's ethical education on this point, and his growing realization that we're always vulnerable in *relation,* posit that *Deadwood*'s central vulnerability is not that of individual bodies, but our vulnerability to others. Erin Hill's reading of corporeality and community in *Deadwood* uses Elaine Scarry's argument that pain is isolating and "unshareable" to argue that "body crises" in *Deadwood* involve characters "taking leave of their reality to inhabit a separate realm of bodily pain for a period of time, and returning from it changed in ways that go beyond the physical."[7] Hill sees these body crises as periods of powerlessness to be waited out, seeming to agree with Scarry that physical pain is isolating. In my view, *Deadwood* shows us that pain can serve a different purpose—to connect the vulnerability of an individual body to the larger body of the camp, to expose in a literally spectacular fashion the connectedness of all these bodies.

Deadwood was not the first series Milch pitched to HBO. He proposed a police drama set in Rome during Nero's reign; this show's pilot episode was set to end with the protagonist being ordered to arrest St. Paul.[8] Milch claims that his interest in the Rome project was to imagine "what it was like for the cop, and then for the cops to encounter a new organizing principle, which was faith."[9] HBO already had an agreement with Todd London to produce *Rome* (HBO, 2005–2007), so Milch went back to the drawing board and pitched *Deadwood.* Milch describes this as a change in setting, not ideology: "When I wound up in Deadwood, I just changed the organizing principle from the cross to gold."[10] But Milch's paratextual argument is itself part of the affective miscue the show uses to mount its argument in favor of radical communalism.[11] Is gold the show's operating principle? I would argue that it is not—particularly not after Wild Bill's body hits the floor in the show's fourth episode. Westerfelhaus and Lacroix argue that "though the town of Deadwood is no natural or social Eden, it is however an economic paradise of sorts for aggressive and unscrupulous capitalistic entrepreneurs, such as [Al] Swearengen and [Cy] Tolliver, who are willing to work hard, take risks, and to ruthlessly manipulate and exploit others."[12] The mistake Westerfelhaus and Lacroix make here is to take Milch at his word and to follow the horizon of expectation set by the show's first few episodes. In fact, the show almost immediately abandons any pretense of interest in capitalism or those who would make it their primary goal. For all of Al's talk about what's good for business, we scarcely see him make a move good for business during the run of the show, and particularly not after the first season. The show's visual syntax and ideological investments distance it from westerns, both traditional and revisionary,[13] but they also remove it from the debates about contemporary neoliberalism to which Worden, Westerfelhaus, and Lacroix would relegate it.

The show's credits sequence takes the setting of the western and removes it from the fixation on individuality and the physical space of the American West that usually animates the genre.[14] The credits intercut a horse galloping through the Black Hills with quick shots of the mining, bathing, and gambling that make up life in the camp. As the sequence nears its end, shots of a man's hand reaching up to touch a naked woman are intercut with the horse arriving in town, suddenly at rest instead of in motion. The final image of the credits sequence is, like the first one, a picture reflected in water: the Gem Saloon, and the horse looking at the camera, reflected in a puddle. But then the horse disappears from the reflection. The horse, along with the wilderness-as-redemption western it represents, has been removed from the iconography of this western. As the horse is leached out of the frame, *Deadwood* brings the western into the town, into the ideological structures of community and commerce that the hero of the western typically resists.[15] The show's central characters ride into town in pairs or groups, never alone, and the action almost never leaves the camp for the hills the horse gallops through in the credits. Instead of the plains, vistas, and rivers on which the male hero of the traditional western tests his mettle, *Deadwood* fixates on interior spaces, obsessively framing its characters looking out windows, or down from balconies, or striding outdoors onto the muddy thoroughfare. Removing the western from a focus on wilderness shifts the viewer's ideological expectations: it rewrites a genre about open space as an indoor drama of manners, centered on the saloon, the whorehouse, and the hardware business. *Deadwood*'s visual style differs from that of other westerns in its camera's preference for painterly shots of people clustered in groups, not the expanses of landscape and single horsemen characteristic of the genre.

Although the show's action does not leave the squalid mining camp for the better part of the first season, *Deadwood*'s pilot episode opens in the Montana Territory in 1876, where the camera takes us inside Seth's sheriff's office with its single cell. The establishing shot of the office and the cross-cutting between the horse thief inside the bars and the lawman outside of them places the viewer in the visual space of the western. The shot/reverse shot of their conversation, the show's first dialogue, shows us the prisoner from Seth's perspective, then Seth from his. The bars obstruct our view either way; visually, both are caged. When Seth looks out the window and sees the ex-horse-owner Byron Sampson (and the "dozen, shit-faced, backing his play"), he looks out, through bars, at the mob. He is the prisoner of another kind of justice, the lawless vigilantism that his status as sheriff demands that he thwart. This scene sets up Seth as the sole enforcer of the law against the mob. But this is a feint, a misdirection that is important to the show's views of the law, just as the vulnerability feint it later sets up with its central female characters is important to the show's construction of gender. In this scene, Seth attempts to regain control of what violence means, to take it back from the mob: "I'm executing sentence right now, and he's hanging under color of law." Since he cannot safely escort the prisoner past the mob to the scaffold across the street, Bullock strings the noose over the porch cross-beam, promising the condemned man: "I'll help you with your drop." The specter of mob judgment, which blocks their access to the scaffold and necessitates the makeshift hanging with an insufficient drop, forces Seth to wrap his arm around the man's waist in a half-embrace and jerk violently forward, breaking his neck so the man doesn't strangle. The mob wants to lynch the thief—to mark his body—so Seth's insistence that "he's hanging under color of law" requires physical contact with the writhing, twisting body in pain. As this opening scene illustrates, the "color of law" Bullock intends to represent doesn't protect the vulnerable body, it just makes the lawman a proxy for the mob. This sequence rewrites a classic western script: after Seth stands up to the community, only to become its agent, he rides off into the night, not alone, but on the back of his partner's wagon, which carries the shovels, pickaxes, and bedpans necessary for carving capitalist profit out of the "wild" Black Hills.

But rather than tracing the accumulation of this capitalist profit, *Deadwood* focuses on the inevitability of community, particularly outside the formal (and distorting) structures of state, church, and nuclear family. Milch is a famously hands-on presence on the *Deadwood* set (though he has never been credited as an episode's director), instructing the actors that "the modern situation is predicated upon the illusion of the self's isolation—that business of 'I'm alone, you're alone, we can bullshit each other when we're fucking or whatever else, but the truth is we're alone. Right?' Well, I believe that is fundamentally an illusion."[16] When framed this way, *Deadwood*'s odd juxtaposition of affect and violence, of nineteenth-century cadences and twentieth-century invective, of the sacred and the profane, begins to make sense. Ultimately, *Deadwood* does not focus on the vulnerability of individual bodies but on the community imagined as "parts of the body," and its vulnerability to the cleavages threatened by capitalism. *Deadwood* is about the place of the state (or in its absence the community) in our ethical responsibilities to others—particularly to the demands their vulnerability puts on us. Throughout the first season, *Deadwood* repeats the metaphor of the community as body, privileging the community over the single body and creating an identity that is communal instead of individual.

In a *New Yorker* piece that traces Milch's movement "from *NYPD Blue* to *Deadwood* by way of an Epistle of St. Paul," Mark Singer describes the show's taping of the second-season episode "Requiem for a Gleet," which climaxes with a narrowly avoided surgery for Al. "Milch had instructed the actors Ian McShane (Swearengen), Brad Dourif (Doc Cochran), Paula Malcomson (Trixie, a prostitute and Swearengen's occasional mistress), and W. Earl Brown and Sean Bridgers (Swearengen's henchmen Dan Dority and Johnny Burns) to approach the scene—five people struggling fiercely so that one of them might properly pee—as if the patient were a woman in labor."[17] While the childbirth metaphor might seem at first like a white male appropriation of female subjectivity, it is apt to *Deadwood*'s project because childbirth is the one form of physical pain that the culture seems to acknowledge is not unmaking for the female subject. Here, the communal effort means that pain is not isolating but instead generative. Milch offers what Singer identifies as his signature "garrulous but lucid stream of subtextual information—intellectually daunting, digressive, arcane, wittily profane":

> It isn't just about witnessing a woman suffering. It's about the cohabitation of the spirit—where you've gone out as fully in compassion as one human being can go to another. And all you're trying to do is help her through. In any operation, what you have to do is to persuade the patient to grant access to the patient's energy. The purest form of that is when you're trying to help a woman through labor.[18]

In keeping with the trajectory from *Macbeth* to *Kill Bill,* Milch figures vulnerability through an anxiety about wombs and wounds, here imagined as communal instead of individual. After spectacles of physical pain, *Deadwood*'s camera often ends on a beautifully composed shot of the community, the "parts of the body" that are galvanized, not isolated, by the specter of the body in pain.

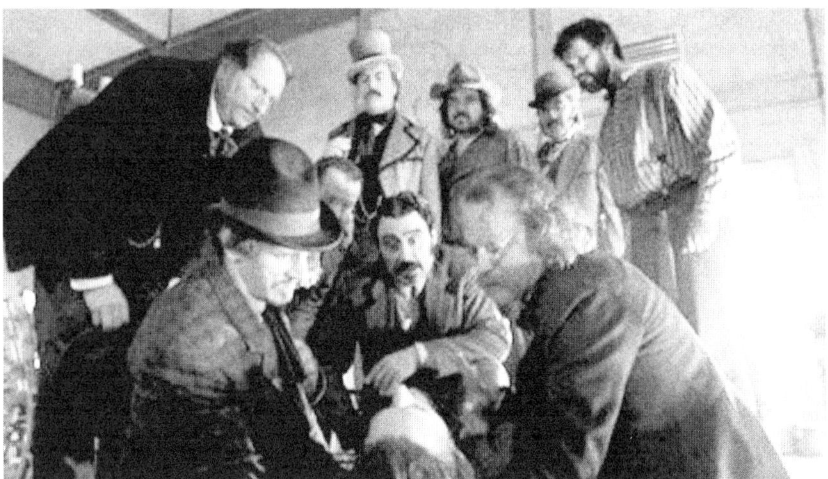

Figure 20 Camp elders gather to help Reverend Smith

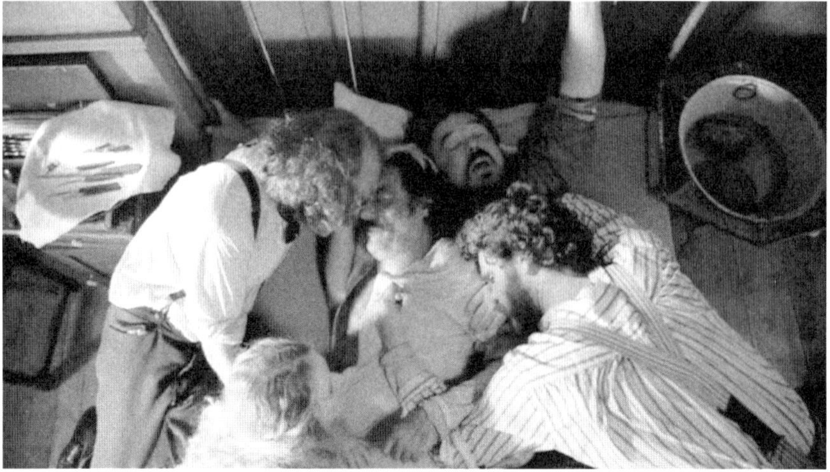

Figure 21 After "childbirth"

This revision of pain, injury, and what they signify becomes increasingly complicated when we consider how much of *Deadwood*'s action takes place in brothels. Trixie, a Gem prostitute and one of the show's central female protagonists, spends fully half of the first season with her face visibly bruised from two altercations in the show's pilot episode: one with a violent customer, whom she shoots and kills, and one with Al, who argues that prostitutes murdering customers is "bad for business." The complex and ultimately moving relationship between Al and Trixie mirrors the trajectory of the show as a whole. Instead of merely dramatizing the ways women are vulnerable to men, the show asks us to replace our assumptions about gender with new networks of sympathy based on class. The collective identity the show valorizes is classed, not gendered. We can see this most clearly in the audience's growing investment in Trixie and Al's mutually dysfunctional affection as Al is increasingly contrasted with Cy Tolliver. Audiences are encouraged to project their discomfort with Al's exploitation of his female employees onto Cy, the pimp without Al's gruff affection and paternal concern for the camp. This revision begins in earnest in the show's third episode, "Reconnoitering the Rim," when audiences first see Al placing his body under the control of someone else.[19] Alone in Al's office/bedroom above the Gem, Trixie scrapes calluses off of Al's feet with a straight razor.

AL: Not too fucking deep, huh?

TRIXIE: I won't.

AL: Trust. Hell of a way to operate, huh? Look at all the ins and outs of gettin' killed. Not too fucking deep! (*Trixie brushes the side of his foot and scrapes.*) Every fuckin' beatin' I'm grateful for. Every fuckin' one of them. Get all the trust beat outta you. Then you know what the fuckin' world is.

The scene's blocking (apparently Paula Malcomson's idea) undercuts his dialogue's bizarre attempt to rewrite his violence toward her, and to imply similarity between them as grateful recipients of educative violence. His dialogue conflicts with the visual image of his physical "trust" in Trixie with the razor. Trixie asks if he wants "the other foot" done, and he answers, "Yeah. Please." Milch has described this as "the first civilized exchange you see between them," and Malcomson specifically ties the razor to Trixie's singular knowledge of Al's vulnerability: "Ian [McShane] looked at me and said, 'Please.' The minute he said 'please,' I knew it was a new place for us."[20] This scene is shot in a very intimate series of close two-shots and alternating close-ups that visually mark it as a perverse love scene. Their eye contact at the end of this scene ends the episode and, in a serial text like *Deadwood,* creates an important context for the sequence at the end of the next episode, "Here Was a Man." Trixie wielding the razor establishes the link between physical vulnerability, intimacy, and danger that makes Wild Bill's murder in "Here Was a Man" the galvanizing event for the show's communal ethic.

This fourth episode serves as a turning point for the series in several important ways. It kills off Wild Bill, one of the central protagonists, and it places audience assumptions about both sex and violence into conflict with the show's argument about bodies in community forming the "body" of the camp.[21] *Deadwood* presents a model of community at odds with viewer desire—or at least at odds with how that desire is conventionally constructed by film and television. We can see this in how it negotiates Bill's death. *Deadwood* announces its difference in the framing of this moment, withholding shots of Bill himself, instead showing the community in pairs in a series of two-shots that obsessively frame people looking out windows or through doorways, drawing visual attention to the difference between interior and exterior space.

In the sequence that leads up to Bill's murder, the camera cuts between brief shots, none lasting longer than sixty seconds, of the episode's several threads: Seth and Sol building their hardware store, Alma (Molly Parker) and Jane attempting to cross the cavernous linguistic and social barrier between them, and Trixie and Al in Al's bedroom above the bar. A shot of Wild Bill with his back to the door of the #10 Saloon playing what will be his last poker game cuts to a shot of Alma at the window of her room narrating her marriage to Brom Garret (Timothy Omundson) in language that establishes marriage as merely legal prostitution. But Alma's voice precedes the visual cut so that the beginning of her speech—"My father was the best company"—is audible over the image of Bill's weary eyes and upright posture. Bill is, of course, nobody's father, and these characters' presence in an outlaw mining camp established only weeks earlier means that they are all adrift from the ties of blood and kinship that Alma's speech suggests are no refuge from the exploitation that happens in Deadwood's streets, brothels, and barrooms.

> My father was the best company. From the time I was ever so little—problems, or difficulties, or even sadness, no such thing. Not permitted. The evening I was presented to society, I found out later he'd been able to attend only by physically fleeing some dismal legal difficulty. In that sense, my marriage to Mr. Garret was a tremendous solution. Tremendous. At the ceremony, I remember Father whispered to me, "Darling, I can never repay you for what you are about to do, but I can repay everyone else." And he said, "To think of you, with him, in that godforsaken place, is almost unbearable."

Jane clarifies, "Meaning your husband?" and the camera cuts to a close-up of Alma's brittle, fragile face as she says, "And I said, 'Maybe he'll die.'" Directly after Alma says "die," the camera cuts to Al's climax; the juxtaposition of the modern and early-modern meanings of "die" ties Brom and Al as "husbands" of a sort to women whose positions, the show implies, are not very different. While this critique of nineteenth-century marriage does little to mitigate our awareness of the grim circumstances in which Al's prostitutes live at the Gem, it does complicate the viewer's attitudes toward the Al/Trixie relationship that becomes increasingly central to the show's vision of the community as parts of a body.

Alma's face and voice work in the scene as bridges; the first sounds of Al's and Trixie's sex scene are audible while the camera still holds Alma's face in a close-up so that when the camera enters Al's bedroom at the Gem, as if through the door, it is Alma's story of being sold in marriage to Brom Garret that forms the subtext of the sex between prostitute and pimp. The camera closes in on Al on top of Trixie, one of her legs wrapped around him, then cuts to a close-up of their hands, Al's hands holding Trixie's wrists at the headboard. These shots, interspersed as they are with similarly imagistic shots of the hardware store being built and Hickok walking down the thoroughfare to his death, create a confusing set of signifiers. The one disparate series of scenes intercut with the community formation between inhabitants of the Gem, the hardware store, and Alma's hotel room is a scene at the Bella Union, where Cy and Joanie argue over their sick friend Andy Cramed (Zach Grenier), who has just come to camp suffering from smallpox. The shot of Al's hands holding Trixie's to the headboard cuts almost immediately to an intimate shot of the town's doctor listening to Andy's strained breathing. Joanie sympathizes with Andy's plight, but Cy, who has spent the episode overpaying the doctor and the camp's newspaperman for their services, represents a style of masculinity that the show doesn't redeem by tying it to the working-class rogue masculinity Milch's shows consistently celebrate. The arrival of smallpox in the camp, creating scores of vulnerable bodies, cements Cy as an outsider, specifically by the way he treats the body in pain. Cy banishes Andy to the woods to die alone; when faced with a similar circumstance, Al calls a camp meeting to organize medicines and a pest tent. To Cy, pain is isolating, and the way he deals with vulnerable bodies is to banish them. The contrast this forms with Al creates an ethically dubious

Figure 22 Al and Trixie

but artistically effective sense of viewer affiliation with Al and the tactile, corporeal attitude toward bodies and pain that he represents.

This scene seems to double Trixie and Alma, prostitute and wife. But ultimately what the show's visual strategies suggest is not the doubling of discrete figures—the traditional way that television has shored up the idea of the individual and the structures of audience identification—but the situating of two characters as radically contingent. We can see in these fragments an obsession with the body's boundaries; each fragment dramatizes some breakdown of the body's control in orgasm, death, or plague. The camera bookends the moment of Bill's murder with shots of the important members of the community in order to signify that what's important in that scene is *not* the vulnerability of Bill Hickok's body but the relationship of the community to that body, about to fall from a shot in the back fired by Jack McCall (Garret Dillahunt). Once Jack flees the scene of his crime into the thoroughfare, episode director Alan Taylor crosscuts shots of his attempted escape with beautifully composed two-shots of the other characters coming to realize that something fundamental has changed. The in-between space between injury and death that we have seen throughout this book as so crucial to the construction of vulnerability is here hidden from the camera's view. This is a strategy we've seen before—but with the "famous" Wild Bill's removal from the show's visual field, we also see a retreat the myth of individualism that he represents and ultimately an unmooring of individual subjectivity itself.

Jane, Bill's best friend and the show's clearest representation of female masculinity, arrives at the #10, now deserted except for Bill's body, still slumped in the chair. Seth arrives at the door a moment before Jane and watches Bill's body fall. She remains in the back of the frame, drinking and tossing aside a whiskey bottle as

Figure 23 Seth and Sol

Figure 24 Alma and Jane

Seth kneels in front of Bill's fallen body, becoming himself the center of the camera's gaze. Once Bill's body falls, the camera replaces Jane with Seth as mourner, which is a representation of both the show's use of the vulnerable body and the way it unmoors emotions like grief from their traditional associations with the individual psyche. In *Deadwood,* vulnerability isn't just a quality of our bodies, it's a quality we respond to, and that response happens, in its most palpable form, collectively. The moment where Seth replaces Jane as mourner helps us see how *Deadwood* constructs the self relationally. In the next episode, when Bill's body is buried in the graveyard that overlooks the town, Jane will be restored to the position of mourner in relation to another discarded body. Vulnerable body parts become a site around which the vulnerable community is constituted. Thus *Deadwood* seems to posit—as most of art does, as our experience of life does—that vulnerability is a function of the corporeal body and its limits and failures. But with Bill's burial, the dead body, not actually vulnerable itself anymore, not sentient, becomes, as it's lowered into the grave, the harbinger of a new and more radical form of vulnerability.

Reverend Smith's metaphor—the mining camp as human body—is the central metaphor of this radical vulnerability, so it is fitting that his sermon on St. Paul's letter to the Corinthians comes at Bill's graveside. Hearst will attempt to replace this organic metaphor for the camp (as "body") with the metaphor of the camp as factory, which is why Hearst's expulsion from Deadwood provides the third season's narrative arc. At the end of that sermon, the Reverend says, "Let us sing 'How Firm a Foundation' as Mr. Hickok is laid to rest." A guitar and violin start to play the hymn, and the voices of the mourners, a least half a beat behind the graveside musicians, sing the words as the camera cuts between close-ups of Seth and Sol lowering the casket into the ground and a perspective from the distance that we eventually see is Jane's watching the funeral from the hill. It would seem, visually, that Jane is excluded from the "body" of the camp by her physical distance from the action and by the alcoholic spiral that has kept her away from the camp since Bill's death. But, once again, the show's narrative juxtapositions work to break down barriers between self and other.

Near the end of the episode, Jane returns to the smallpox-ridden Andy, who has been thrown away to die in the woods. She brings water to him from the creek but finds him lying motionless, glassy eyes fixed. "Are you dead?" she shouts, then pours water from her canteen into his gaping mouth. As he gasps and spits, she grins triumphantly. "Yeah, there you are! Choking and coughing just like the rest of us." She sits on the ground next to him in the clearing, and as the camera keeps its distance, circling them as if it were an animal wary of approaching, she tells him she's seen Alma's husband's body being kept cool in the creek, "tethered, wrapped up, and floating like a lure for some huge fucking fish." Jane continues, updating the only semiconscious Andy on the status of the little girl she helped rescue in the show's opening episode, and the camera comes in close as she says that when she was down at the creek, "I heard voices, and I went to where they were singing. And I saw as they laid my poor fucking Bill in the ground." Her voice breaks on "in the ground" so that it's almost inaudible, but the accumulation of images makes clear that Jane's dialogue on the hill is as important as the Reverend's public speech. After a sob overtakes her description of Bill's funeral, she shifts her sight, literally. "There's a bird I've never seen before," she says softly, looking toward the trees. "Shall I talk about it to you?" In this moment, the act of narration becomes a point of reconstituting the self as a social being, and Jane is restored to the body of the camp, and to her position as Bill's mourner.

Jane's dialogue here also connects Andy's failing body to the community of others. Her first question, "Are you dead?" raises again the problem of knowledge constructed through the vulnerable body. But Jane answers the question of his body with a reference to the body of the camp: "There you are, choking and coughing, just like the rest of us." This trope of collective identity gains narrative power as the season progresses and Reverend Smith begins to deteriorate physically due to a brain tumor. The brain tumor that causes the seizures makes him "feel" that his flesh is rotting, that he's died, that he's a walking body. When Doc Cochran asks about his symptoms, he says, "Formerly, Doctor, when the Word took me as I read Scripture, people felt God's presence through me, and that was a great gift that I could give to them. Now the Word does not take me as I read, nor do I feel Christ's love, nor do those who listen hear it through me." The relationship Reverend Smith posits between the "Word" and the human body as conduit is an intensely communal figuration of religious experience, but it's also one of the keys to the way the show connects the body of the person to the body of the camp. When asked by the doctor if he's in pain, he says, "There is no pain. There are new smells that I smell, and parts of my body I can't feel, and his . . . and his love." The show posits the loss of "his love" as a part of the same trajectory that causes the loss of the Reverend's control over his body's boundaries and functions. But here, as elsewhere, this loss is viewed as communal, not individual. When he describes his physical ailments to Jane—the loss of control of an eye, a limb—he returns again to the loss of a connection to something beyond the discrete boundaries of the body. He tells Jane, "When I read the scriptures, I do not feel Christ's love as I used to." Jane leans toward the Reverend and asks, "Oh, is that so? That is too bad! Join the fuckin club of most of us." I'm interested here in the way the dialogue figures the minister's spiritual alienation as a confusion over language and what it means—what it causes the body to "feel"—but also in the fact that this alienation, while painful, isn't really alienation; it merely inaugurates the minister into the "fuckin club of most of us." Westerfelhaus and Lacroix argue that one of the "disquieting" aspects of *Deadwood* is that "Reverend Smith's prophetic voice is literally and figuratively snuffed out, and by the conclusion of *Deadwood*'s first season, the town has lost the man who had functioned as its moral conscience."[22] But his voice is most emphatically *not* silenced by his death, because his metaphor takes over the town; Al as well as Seth becomes its proxy. This is a form of the same strategy—a loosening of individual subjectivity, so that while characters come into town representing certain things for the viewer (virtue, commerce, exploitation), by the end no one figure is the discrete representative of anything.

At the end of the episode that contains Bill's funeral ("The Trial of Jack McCall"), the camera returns to Jane on the hillside where she continues to care for Andy. She starts humming "How Firm a Foundation," and her clumsy verbal markings of the missing words—"Da dum, de, da dum"—are drowned out as strings on the show's nondiegetic soundtrack start under her voice and eventually cover it.

The song begins in the graveyard as diegetic, with the many voices waiting to pick up the musical cue half a beat late, and it *becomes* nondiegetic. This movement back and forth across the lines of the show's diegesis is another example of its innovative mirroring of form and theory. Just as the song spreads, from the mourners at the gravesite to Jane on the hill to the show's own soundtrack, the show's trope of the failing body as the site of generative potential is not limited to the person of Reverend Smith. In the closing scene of the season (in an episode evocatively titled "Sold Under Sin"), the doctor has made a leg brace for Jewel (Geri Jewell), the physically disabled cook at Al's Gem Saloon. She convinces the doctor to dance with her, and as they twirl, she tells him, "Say I'm as nimble as a forest creature." Doc says, "You're as nimble as a forest creature," to this woman who for the first time, with the aid of the brace, is able to dance. But once again, the show refuses to see the body's potential failure as discrete to the individual person. Jewel looks up at the doc and says, "No, say it about yourself."

Milch's own reading of Reverend Smith's "parts of the body" speech returns to Milch's insistence that alienation from others is an illusion—though alienation from the self might be another matter.

> In the first season, the Reverend Smith says, "If the foot shall say, Because I am not the hand, I'm not of the body, is it therefore not of the body?" In other words, just because we misapprehend our nature, does it mean that we are alienated from the world? No, it means that we misapprehend our nature.

Crucially for our ideas about vulnerability and the way they enlist our consent to various forms of violence and erasure, this means that pain doesn't isolate the self from others, as Scarry argues—it clarifies the ways that vulnerability is always relational: in, of, and for others. In *Precarious Life,* Butler defines vulnerability as relational, as a function of our primary vulnerability "to others." *Deadwood* conceives of the community as itself a body and rewrites pain as a connecting, not isolating, spectacle. The show thus creates a tension between our visceral recoil as spectators of suffering and the way the show presents violence, as "no more and no less human, and no less prone to the accidental creation of attachment and meaning, than any other human behavior."[23] If violence connects instead of isolates, and if suffering is communal rather than individual, Milch's insistence that violence is "no more and no less human" than any other behavior turns the question of vulnerability toward the category of the "human" that we saw *Battlestar Galactica* take up around the question of torture.

While Westerfelhaus and Lacroix argue that "neither the town of Deadwood nor the surrounding countryside offers the series' characters physical or moral refuge,"[24] this misses the way that certain spaces in Deadwood and in the show's narrative do come to function as refuges—the hotel room where Trixie helps Alma kick her laudanum habit, the back of the hardware store where Sol helps Trixie "learn another way,"[25] and finally the hotel room where Calamity Jane and Joanie provide the show with its final image of community. Joanie returns to the room after witnessing Charlie stand up for an African American man's right to vote in the elections taking place on the street outside the room where Jane lies, drunk and despairing after an earlier misunderstanding with Joanie. Joanie sits on the bed and haltingly connects her growing romantic relationship with Jane to the years of love and loyalty between Jane, Charlie, and the missing Bill:

> I saw at the voting what I guess you knowed about Mr. Utter all these years, and Mr. Hickok must have knowed. What he's like in a tight one he didn't even need to be in. I want to be that to you. Even when we don't get along.

Joanie brings in Bill's robe and places it over Jane, embracing her. Wild Bill's role as the representative of the western as a genre means that his coat, which in *Deadwood*'s opening episode lay beneath Wild Bill in the back of the wagon that brought him to Deadwood, here returns as a signifier of Bill's love and Charlie's tacit acceptance of Jane and Joanie's relationship. The coat ultimately becomes a proxy for the viewer's relationship to vulnerability. At first, it seems to be the base of individual subjectivity. But by the end, it embraces the radical vulnerability that binds us to one another.

Afterword

FEMALE POWER AND TARANTINO'S *BASTERDS*

In the preceding chapters, we have seen the logic of female frailty dismantled, the iconography of dependence replaced, and the myth of the heroic individual challenged. In part, this work has depended on changing beauty standards that no longer figure muscle definition and femininity as opposites. By 2004, when writer/director Mary Harron put out a casting call for *The Notorious Bettie Page* (2005), set in the 1950s, she had to specify "no gym" to be assured of finding actors for the female roles without the athletic builds that have become the new millennium's standard. But, as post-9/11 television shows us, the debate about vulnerability can also move beyond bodies. If *Deadwood* and *Battlestar Galactica* ask us to think beyond our investment in discrete bodies and individual subjectivity, where does that leave the individual human being and the beating heart that *Macbeth* figured as central to the idea of the vulnerable? The vulnerable body is a point of contention for popular culture, but to see how the turn away from individual subjectivity can have rousing political consequences, we must return to *Buffy* and Iris Marion Young's ideas about throwing like a girl.

Buffy the Vampire Slayer, less a fantasy of supernatural strength than of women believing they have potential, makes its most unapologetically feminist statement in its final episode, "Chosen," when Buffy ceases to be "the one." The episode, which aired on May 20, 2003, uses a floating Steadicam shot to approach Sunnydale High School as the final, apocalyptic battle looms, in a visual allusion to the show's pilot episode. But this time, the camerawork sets us up for a different reversal of expectations. In the pilot episode, this cinematography was a tongue-in-cheek homage to slasher films, reversing our assumptions about the identities of stalker and prey. Here, the camera stalks toward the school long enough for the audience to register the prickly sense of dread, but then swerves and stabilizes, showing the band of friends striding toward the school, ready to wrest control of the show's narrative from the genre conventions that would contain it. The show is not interested in who lurks in the dark, waiting to victimize the woman onscreen, or even in what kind of power she as an individual can exert against him. The show's seventh season seems to set up a new set of questions: Which of the "potentials"—teenage girls marked as latent slayers—will inherit Buffy's power after her death? Will Buffy and her ragtag crew of friends and potentials win the final battle? But the episode's turning point, which uncloaks Buffy's plan to defeat the "first evil," reveals that these, too, are the wrong questions to ask. Intense fan speculation leading up to the final episode guessed that the finale would find a way to subvert the trope of isolated superhero that had always given the show its narrative tension. One popular fan theory speculated that the slayer power would somehow expire, and that Buffy would be forced to face down the apocalypse without her "power." Instead, the show reframed its central question. Throughout its run on the WB and then on UPN, *Buffy* had asked how a "normal" girl deals with being granted extraordinary power. Now, Buffy asks the assembled potentials: "Are *you* ready to be strong?"

Once Buffy and the rest of the show's protagonists enter the school to confront the threat lurking beneath its floors, the episode juxtaposes Buffy explaining her plan with its enactment. After repeating the series's founding mythology—in every generation, one slayer is born—Buffy interrupts the litany, dismantling the patriarchal assumptions on which this myth of heroic individualism has always rested. The slayer is alone "because a bunch of men who died thousands of years ago made up that rule." Breaking completely with the patriarchal power of the "Watchers' Council," against whom Buffy had chafed throughout the series, she narrates a plan to disperse the slayer power, engendering in every "potential" the power that thus far had been hers and Faith's alone. "I say we change the rule. I say my power should be *our* power." The montage that follows is a beautiful visual distillation of the collective identity formation I have suggested is the real innovation of television in the twenty-first century. Buffy's voice-over says, "From now on, any girl in the world who might be a slayer *will* be a slayer," as the camera shows a girl in Middle America standing at home plate waiting for the pitch in a softball game, biting her lip nervously. "Every girl who could have the power *will* have the power," she continues, as an African American teenager clutching schoolbooks puts her hand on a locker to steady herself. "Can stand up will stand up." We see the outlines of a dingy trailer and a man's hand, coming down to strike until a woman's hand reaches up and blocks his. She catches his arm and rises up into visibility in the frame—arresting the camera's gaze. This scene in the trailer was the last image the *Buffy* production crew shot, which Joss Whedon calls a fitting end to the seven-year-long project of making a feminist viewpoint visible in popular culture. But it's also an arresting image because the woman's worn tank top and heavyset frame identify her as precisely the kind of woman popular culture usually ignores. Showing the *Buffy* audience an image of her standing up and fighting back as Buffy comes to the climax of her speech serves as a rebuke to popular culture's obsession with privilege, and, frankly, to *Buffy*'s own focus on thin, conventionally attractive female characters. "Slayers, every one of us. Make your choice. Are you ready to be strong?"

These images—a black woman at school that alludes to the fight for school desegregation, a working-class woman fighting back against domestic violence, and a girl playing softball, waiting for the pitch—give *Buffy* a new, powerful iconography to replace the image of Buffy alone that ends the show's opening credit sequence. In this new iconography, power is diffused, our identification with a single protagonist given over to a series of women, learning to stand up. In the last shot of the sequence, the girl playing softball no longer looks nervous. She pulls the bat back farther and faces the pitcher with a deliberate half-smile—a smile on its way to becoming. This is the second series finale Joss Whedon wrote for *Buffy the Vampire Slayer.* The WB attempted to cancel the show at the close of its fifth season, which ended with "The Gift," an impressive, moving episode that nevertheless does little to challenge the myth of individual heroism that animates the superhero genre. It ends with Buffy sacrificing herself to save humanity; the episode's final shot is of Buffy's grave, which reads "Buffy Summers, 1981–2001. She saved the world. A lot." But in the spring of 2001, UPN bought the rights to the show, and Buffy dug up from under that headstone and into a sixth and seventh season that considerably darkened the show's quippy tone. This set the stage for a more compromised, more adult form of heroism for Buffy, but it also sets up the second ending, which uses Buffy's resurrection to challenge the trope of individual heroism.

Buffy is not the only early-twenty-first-century heroine to claw her way out of a grave on her way to the kind of heroism that is mistakenly labeled postfeminist. Beatrix Kiddo, reborn out of a four-year-long coma in *Kill Bill, Vol. 1* (2003), must fight her way out of a literal coffin in *Kill Bill, Vol. 2* (2004). As the previous chapters have argued, resistant vulnerability is not about sadistic pleasure in seeing pain inflicted on the female body. Tarantino is often accused of filming as if violence is a film-school exercise or a joke, so when Bill's brother shoots Beatrix in the chest with a shotgun full of rock salt and buries her alive, the feminist viewer rightly awaits the next development with skepticism. But Tarantino, so often walking the edge of lurid spectacle, uses the image of Beatrix in a coffin to show us something new. The camera reveals Beatrix entombed; the flashlight she holds shows us her bloodied torso as she eyes the closed top of the casket. Finally, the painful flashbacks that detailed Beatrix's training at the hands of misanthropic kung fu master Pai Mei start to pay off emotionally for the viewer. Uma Thurman's face lights in a determined half-smile as she puts up her hand to feel the smooth pine of the coffin lid, less than twelve inches from her face. "Okay, Pai Mei," she says softly, "Here I come." She uses the three-inch punch technique Pai Mei taught her, which involves standing in front of a wooden board and touching its surface with the edge of her fingers, then making a fist and punching the board without drawing her arm back. In theory a method for fighting in close quarters, the movement itself is eerily reminiscent of what Iris Marion Young details in her analysis of children's bodily movement when throwing a ball. Studies show that boys more often rotate their bodies sideways and bring the hand with the ball behind their shoulders before throwing it forward, which puts the weight of the body behind the ball, whereas girls are more likely to keep the body stationary and to push the arm holding the ball forward, which results in the weaker throw often mocked as "throwing like a girl." The three-inch punch offers the intriguing possibility that, rather than correcting the "feminine" style of bodily comportment—learning to "throw like a boy," as female softball players are coached to do—the female body can learn to put its full force behind a seemingly constrained movement. As triumphant music plays on the soundtrack and Beatrix punches her way out of the coffin, fighting like a girl becomes something powerful, and keeping your shoulders stationary and shooting out your hand is suddenly no longer the subject of a schoolyard taunt or a misogynist joke. It's literally the way to freedom.

The path to freedom is darker in *Inglourious Basterds* (2009), where Tarantino approaches the scene of the twentieth century's most defining crime, the Holocaust. Tarantino's most triumphant female hero—Shoshanna Dreyfus (Mélanie Laurent)—rises from two different graves. Tarantino's continual use of the resurrection trope seems to return us to the logic of the rape-revenge film, where the heroine must be utterly debased by the film in order to be reborn as the narrative's hero. But Tarantino's desire to rewrite the cultural script, to avoid portraying Jewish characters as victims, demands that he revise his usual squirm-inducing approach to punishing the female body. The long, tense opening sequence of *Inglourious Basterds,* set in 1941 in Nazi-occupied France, reveals the veneer of civility as perhaps more brutal than the stylized violence for which Tarantino is famous. Colonel Hans Landa (Christoph Waltz) questions a French farmer, Perrier LaPadite (Denis Ménochet), about a Jewish family suspected of hiding in the area. Landa, the "Jew-hunter," insists that he is effective in his task because he is "aware of what tremendous feats human beings are capable of once they abandon dignity." But Shoshanna emerges as inheritor of Beatrix Kiddo's title as heroine precisely because she *doesn't* abandon dignity. The "tremendous feats" of which the rape-revenge heroine is capable depend upon her earlier debasement, but here, Shoshanna authors her own power in the film from the moment she escapes from her living grave beneath LaPadite's floor. As Landa and LaPadite engage in a fraught verbal battle, the camera pans down LaPadite's leg and past the floorboards to show the audience what LaPadite tries so desperately to conceal—the Dreyfus family hidden beneath. The shot of the family shows us Shoshanna, her hand clamped over her mouth, her blue eyes illuminated by the line of light that shines through the floorboards. This cuts to a shot looking down on the floorboards that pulls back; Shoshanna's eyes and her father's are visible in the space beneath the boards, entombed. The hiding space turns literally into a grave when Landa's men open fire. We see Shoshanna moving beneath the floorboards from Landa's perspective, then running away from the house. But once the camera breaks with Landa's perspective to show her running, blood-spattered, in a medium shot toward freedom, we never again see her from any perspective but her own.

The Shoshanna storyline competes for attention throughout the film with the plotline following Brad Pitt's Lieutenant Aldo "the Apache" Raine and his "Basterds," a squad of American Jewish soldiers famous for "killing Nazis." But this storyline, the center of the film according to both its critics and to Tarantino himself, emerges as a farcical counterpoint to the ultimately moving story of Shoshanna's triumph. Pitt's hick-camp performance as Raine, along with the Basterds' comical bungling of their plot to kill Hitler, makes this plotline a mockery of U.S. ineffectual masculinity. The film plays Raine's penchant for scalping Nazi soldiers he's killed—and demanding a debit of one hundred scalps from each of his men—as a dark joke. Yet both this bloody token-gathering and the Basterds' practice of carving a swastika into the foreheads of any Nazis they leave alive reveals the film's obsession with guilt physically written on the body. Raine frames this explicitly as an anxiety about memory and about history. He asks a German private, the last surviving member of his squad, if he intends to take off his uniform if he survives the war. "Not only do I intend to take off my uniform, I intend to burn it," the boy says. As he prepares to carve a swastika into the private's forehead, Raine says, "We're gonna give you a little something you can't take off." The anxiety about whether the veteran can erase, expunge, or recover from the guilt and pain of war is the drama that animated *The Men, The Deer Hunter,* and *Battlestar Galactica.* Raine makes the mark of guilt literal, but rather than conflating the U.S. military with the horror of war, so often the strategy of post-Vietnam U.S. cinema, Tarantino leaves the "enemy" Nazis marked—like Cain, the Tennessee native Raine would likely point out. But in Tarantino's final calculation, film as an art form is marked with its origins in racist (D. W. Griffith) and fascist (Leni Riefenstahl) art. In *Basterds,* film is both the vehicle to triumph for the resistance and a proxy for its failure—complicit in the forms of affect and ways of seeing that led to the Holocaust, but also the conduit for Jewish triumph over the Nazis.

Pitt's Raine and his Basterds are not the authors of this triumph; for that, Tarantino returns to Shoshanna Dreyfus, hiding in Paris running a movie theater. The first time we see the theater, the marquee advertises Leni Riefenstahl in *The White Hell of Pitz Palu,* and we learn that her projectionist and lover is a black Frenchman, Marcel (Jacky Ido). Their plot to burn down the theater with the Nazi high command inside during the premiere of a Nazi propaganda film is Tarantino's attempt to construct an alternative to twentieth-century history but also to rewrite the story of our identification with the image onscreen. Attempting to work through the particular horror of a theater shooting in Aurora, Colorado, in 2012, during the midnight premiere of *The Dark Knight Rises,* Alyssa Rosenberg wrote: "We are vulnerable when we go to the movies, open to fear, and love, and disgust, and rapture, surrendering our brains and hearts to someone else's vision of the world."[1] The intellectual and emotional vulnerability Rosenberg here identifies as central to the experience of cinema is precisely the logic Tarantino uses within the film to fill Shoshanna's theater with Nazis. Fredrick Zoller (Daniel Brühl), the German soldier turned actor who stars in the propaganda film-within-the-film, argues for a theater packed full of Germans alone: "The only people who should be allowed in the room are people who will be moved by the exploits on the screen." Shoshanna is emphatically *not* a member of the group "who will be moved by the exploits on the screen," and her one moment of identification with Zoller's onscreen image implies that sympathy with the onscreen point of view is a trap for the female viewer. Zoller confronts Shoshanna in the projection booth during the screening, and she shoots him with a concealed pistol. But as he lies on the floor, apparently dead, she gazes out of the projection booth toward his image onscreen, his face in close-up. Her face softens and the film's soundtrack changes as she turns her gaze toward his body on the floor. But, of course, her sympathy is misplaced; she touches his shoulder, and he turns and shoots her. At the moment that Shoshanna begins to be moved by the image onscreen—to register the close-up as a marker of the fundamental humanness of the other—she is at her most vulnerable.

By the time Marcel is ready to carry out his part of the plan, Shoshanna is dead in the projection booth. But in this final example of resistant vulnerability, even death does not rob the female protagonist of her agency. Her own image on the screen, in a reel that she and Marcel have shot and cut into the propaganda film, resurrects Shoshanna. Her face appears on the screen, and her voice overtakes the soundtrack: "I have a message for Germany. That you are all going to die. And I want you to look deep into the face of the Jew who's going to do it. Marcel, burn it down." As Samuel L. Jackson's uncredited voice-over explains, the 35 millimeter nitrate film is itself explosive. As Shoshanna is reborn through her image on the screen, Marcel sets the reels on fire, having barred the door so that the Nazis cannot escape. Critics have rightly pointed out that this scene is a disturbing rewrite of historical Nazi atrocities against Jewish populations during the Holocaust. But Tarantino is after more than just a fantasy version of Europe's history during the twentieth century. In Tarantino's alternate history, the German high command dies in June 1944, ending the war eleven months early, but not ending its continuing hold on the artistic imagination. Having brought up Riefenstahl's name, Tarantino imagines the Third Reich annihilated by a burning film frame, but he cannot erase the influence of Riefenstahl's *Triumph of the Will* on American cinema, including his own. In this fantasy, cinema becomes both coffin and marquee for the most notorious war criminals of the twentieth century.

But the grisly scene of the theater fire is not the film's final image. Raine and one of the surviving Basterds, on orders to free the turncoat Colonel Landa, carve a swastika into Landa's forehead, marking him as they have marked other Nazi "survivors." The swastika scar operates as a historical and affective trace in the film. But Tarantino's own obsession with this marking and with the scalping of the dead Nazis is itself a cinematic trace of the racial conflict and genocide that mark American history. We might read this as further evidence of Tarantino's undisciplined pastiche of distinct historical traumas, but it also reworks the captivity-narrative tradition that has obsessed American culture from Mary Rowlandson's *A Narrative of the Captivity and Restoration of Mrs. Mary Rowlandson* (1682) through John Ford's *The Searchers* (1956) to the war films and westerns this book has analyzed. These fictions owe part of their emotional force to the captivity-narrative tradition and its long history as a site of anxiety about the female body. I have argued that if films like *Saving Private Ryan* imagine the captivity narrative with a missing man's body in the place of Mary Rowlandson—or *The Searchers*' Little Debbie—that replacement shifts our collective cultural ideas about vulnerability being gendered female. Female exceptionalism has deep roots in misogyny: we have long known this. Yet we have been unwilling to relinquish our stake—as both academics and consumers of popular culture—in the special vulnerability of the female body, even as we celebrate women's agency, women's bodies, and women's voices. Our insistence as feminists that violence against women matters has too often, in culture and in criticism, reinscribed the stubborn impression that women, like children, need special protection. But not all images of suffering women are created equal. Images of injury and pain don't have to inure us to violence against women—they can open us instead to a new precariousness not based on gender. This book argues not that we should care less about women but that we should care more about women, men, and the cultural narratives that keep us from seeing one another.

Notes

INTRODUCTION

1. Act 5, scene 7, lines 53–58, in *The Oxford Shakespeare*, http://www.bartleby.com.

2. See Raymond Williams, *The Long Revolution* (London: Chatto and Windus, 1961).

3. I do not mean "sentimental" as a pejorative term, merely a descriptive one for the ways that boundaries of race, class, and gender are crossed through sympathetic feeling. This term gives us a way to talk about the openness associated with vulnerability but also its reliance on traditionally gendered positions.

4. See Carol Clover, *Men, Women, and Chain Saws: Gender in the Modern Horror Film* (Princeton: Princeton University Press, 1992), particularly "Her Body, Himself."

5. See Rick Altman, *Film/Genre* (London: BFI, 1999) on the semantic/syntactic approach to film genre.

6. Iris Marion Young, "Throwing like a Girl: A Phenomenology of Feminine Body Comportment, Motility and Spatiality," *Human Studies* 3, no. 1 (1980): 137–156; 144, 153 quoted. Young argues that specifically "feminine" body comportment "is learned as the girl comes to understand that she is a girl . . . The girl learns actively to hamper her movements. She is told that she must be careful not to get hurt, not to get dirty, not to tear her clothes, that the things she desires to do are dangerous for her. Thus she develops a bodily timidity which increases with age. In assuming herself as a girl, she takes herself up as fragile" (153).

7. See Sherrie A. Inness, *Tough Girls: Women Warriors and Wonder Women in Popular Culture* (Philadelphia: University of Pennsylvania Press, 1999), and Dawn Heinecken, *The Warrior Women of Television: A Feminist Cultural Analysis of the New Female Body in Popular Media* (New York: Peter Lang, 2003). Carol Clover coined the term "final girl" to describe the tomboyish, triumphant heroines of slasher films such as *Halloween* (1979) and *Friday the 13th* (1980).

8. See Caroline Heldman, " 'The Hunger Games,' Hollywood, and Fighting Fuck Toys," April 5, 20120, http://carolineheldman.wordpress.com/2012/04/05/the-hunger-games-hollywood-and-fighting-fuck-toys/. In her analysis of Jennifer Lawrence's Katniss in *The Hunger Games,* Heldman identifies another example of what I call "resistant vulnerability."

9. See Judith Butler, *Precarious Life: The Powers of Mourning and Violence* (New York: Verso, 2004), and Laura Kipnis, *The Female Thing: Dirt, Sex, Envy, Vulnerability* (New York: Pantheon, 2006).

10. See Sarah Projansky, *Watching Rape: Film and Television in Postfeminist Culture* (New York: New York University Press, 2001), for an excellent discussion of how rape discourse operates historically and in the popular culture of 1980–2000.

11. Ibid., 30. Projansky is right that "representations of rape form a complex of cultural discourses central to the very structure of stories people tell about themselves and others" (3).

12. David Greven, *Manhood in Hollywood from Bush to Bush* (Austin: University of Texas Press, 2009), 44.

13. Yvonne Tasker and Diane Negra, eds., *Interrogating Postfeminism: Gender and the Politics of Popular Culture* (Durham: Duke University Press, 2007), 20.

14. Alyssa Rosenberg, "Ten Great Women Television Characters Created by Men," *Think Progress,* http://thinkprogress.org/alyssa/2011/09/27/329710/ten-great-women-television-characters-created-by-men/, a list that also includes Buffy and Starbuck.

15. See Laura Mulvey's seminal essay "Visual Pleasure and Narrative Cinema," *Screen* 16, no. 3 (1975): 6–18.

16. See, for example, David Savran, *Taking It Like a Man: White Masculinity, Masochism, and Contemporary American Culture* (Princeton: Princeton University Press, 1998), Peter Lehman, ed., *Masculinity: Bodies, Movies, Culture* (New York: Routledge, 2001), Kaja Silverman, *Male Subjectivity at the Margins* (New York: Routledge, 1992), and Gaylyn Studlar, *In the Realm of Pleasure: Von Sternberg, Dietrich, and the Masochistic Aesthetic* (New York: Columbia University Press, 1993).

17. Susan Jeffords's influential studies of Vietnam narratives and Hollywood masculinity have offered such readings of male suffering. Jeffords sees the spectacle of the suffering male body as a form of fetishistic display, a way for the (assumed) male viewer to contain his attraction to this intimate image of another man's body through a focus on spectacle and sadism. But while I find Jeffords's theorization of Vietnam and its gender relations compelling, her sense that the exploded bodies in films like *Platoon* lead to a "remasculinization" of America misses something about the place of pity in our reactions to this spectacle, particularly when popular culture turns, in the late 1990s, away from the Vietnam films Jeffords studies and toward World War II. Yvonne Tasker's work on action cinema is likewise important to framing the way the figure of the suffering body is talked about in film studies, particularly since her attention to "Hollywood's fighting heroines" reveals the paucity of our critical language when trying to describe gendered violence in popular film. The laudable seriousness with which Tasker treats popular films could benefit from the attention to vulnerability that I argue is key to understanding the "physical drama of power and powerlessness" that Tasker labels central to the construction of the action heroines of the 1980s. See Tasker, *Spectacular Bodies: Gender, Genre, and the Action Cinema* (New York: Routledge, 1993). Greven has usefully challenged "the ways in which critics have valorized masochism as a resistant mode of masculine subjectivity, [suggesting instead] that masochistic male sexuality often serves to bolster, rather than subvert, traditional masculinity" (*Manhood in Hollywood from Bush to Bush,* 7).

18. Jeffords's analysis of action films in the Reagan and Bush I eras contrasts the "hard body" identified with Reagan with the "soft" or "errant" body she sees as representative of Jimmy Carter. She then sees in early 1990s film a shift from male bodies to male emotions;

I suggest both that the body does not disappear from the picture in the 1990s, and that the "soft," "errant" body is figured in films like *Saving Private Ryan* as both normative and suffering in ways that destabilize our assumptions about male vulnerability.

19. For a compelling argument about gender, sexuality, and bodies onscreen, see Judith Halberstam, *Female Masculinity* (Durham: Duke University Press, 1998). What Halberstam wants to claim as the privileged space of "the unholy union of femaleness and masculinity" is, for her, most unadulterated (and therefore most powerful) when coupled with queer sexuality. But what I see happening in post–Cold War popular culture is not Halberstam's fusion of the female body and the concept of masculinity, but instead an *uncoupling* of bodies, male and female, from the assumptions the dominant culture makes about their vulnerability. Crucially, this means attention to popular films and television that Halberstam writes off to concentrate on the—in her view more transgressive—venue of gender performance art. I want to suggest that concentrating on the popular is particularly important in the post–Cold War moment, where popular culture seems to be trading in familiar images, but asks us to *respond* to them differently.

20. This is what allows Clover to argue that we shouldn't get too excited about the final girl because the position of power is still "male." See Clover, *Men, Women, and Chain Saws.*

21. See Elaine Scarry's *The Body in Pain: The Making and Unmaking of the World* (New York: Oxford University Press, 1985) for a forceful and humane analysis of torture, war, and the stories we use to construct both. Scarry also describes the way American culture seems invested in feeling about pain: that its effects on the human body and the human psyche are so extreme as to be utterly debilitating—"unmaking," in her terms. Scarry's argument diverges from mine in two important ways: 1) She focuses on the extremes of pain, the clearest example being torture. In my view, there is a tendency in the culture, especially when talking about women, to conflate greatly varying levels of pain with the all-encompassing pain that Scarry describes as "self-destroying." 2) Perhaps most crucially, Scarry talks about actual pain, while I focus on representations of pain. Scarry devotes considerable attention to words—the "language of pain" and the "language of agency"—arguing that pain "unmakes" in part because (in her view) it robs the victim of his voice. "To have pain is to have *certainty;* to hear about pain is to have *doubt*" (13, italics original). But for my purposes, pain, and crucially the visual representation of pain, isn't about subjects (as it is for Scarry) but about audiences.

22. Lisa Coulthard, "Killing Bill: Rethinking Feminism and Film Violence," in *Interrogating Postfeminism*, ed. Yvonne Tasker and Diane Negra (Durham: Duke University Press, 2007), 153–175.

23. We will have to wait (nervously, if his previous forays into historical filmmaking are any sign) for Quentin Tarantino's *Django Unchained* to see the black female body as the site around which male protective power gathers.

24. See Projansky, *Watching Rape,* for the ways that black female bodies are "persistently displaced."

25. Doug Petrie, episode commentary, "Fool for Love," *Buffy the Vampire Slayer*, season 5, *The Chosen Collection*.

26. Projansky outlines the history of rape as a form of terrorism against black women in the United States and the ways that American popular culture elides this history: "Overall, whiteness is by far the dominant racialization of rape in late-twentieth- century fictional films and television shows" (ibid., 161).

27. See Susan Faludi, *The Terror Dream: Fear and Fantasy in Post-9/11 America* (New York: Macmillan, 2007).

CHAPTER 1 — *THE FURIES, THE MEN,* AND THE METHOD

1. It is no surprise that the paperback cover for Susan Faludi's *The Terror Dream: Myth and Misogyny in an Insecure America* (New York: Picador, 2008), juxtaposes three silhouette images of iconic scenes, one taken from each of these genres—captivity narrative, western, and war film. At the top of the cover, a dancing Native American figure taunts a woman tied to a tree; occupying the cover's middle space, a cowboy holds a woman he has presumably just rescued in his arms as if she is a child; at the bottom of the cover, three soldiers on patrol march away from the smoking ruin of a city. These images sketch the cultural shorthand that American popular culture has used to define the body's vulnerability.

2. See June Naimas, *White Captives: Gender and Ethnicity on the American Frontier* (Chapel Hill: University of North Carolina Press, 1993).

3. Charles Bitsch and Claude Chabrol, "Interview with Anthony Mann," in the booklet accompanying the Criterion Collection DVD of *The Furies* (2008), 17. Borden Chase was the screenwriter for several Mann westerns, but not for *The Furies*.

4. Robin Wood, "*The Furies:* Mann of the Western," in the Criterion Collection booklet, 7, also available at http://www.criterion.com/current/posts/521-the-furies-mann-of-the-western (accessed November 12, 2012).

5. Wood identifies 1950, when Mann's *Winchester '73* as well as *The Furies* was released, as an important transitional moment in Mann's career (ibid.). *The Furies* was filmed before *Winchester '73* but released in August, a month after *Winchester '73,* which was Mann's first collaboration with Jimmy Stewart, who would go on to star in Mann-directed westerns *Bend of the River* (1950), *The Naked Spur* (1953), *The Far Country* (1954), and *The Man from Laramie* (1955).

6. See Mary Ann Doane, *The Desire to Desire: The Woman's Film of the 1940s* (Bloomington: Indiana University Press, 1987), and Molly Haskell, *From Reverence to Rape: The Treatment of Women in the Movies* (New York: Holt, Rinehart & Winston, 1974), for analyses of the genre.

7. See Marianne Conroy, "Acting Out: Method Acting, the National Culture, and the Middlebrow Disposition in Cold War America," *Criticism* 35, no. 2 (1993): 239–263, for a useful overview of this debate (240 quoted). She argues that the Method's status as a middlebrow

form stymies critical debate about its cultural meanings. Leo Braudy suggests that the Method *does* provide a substantive challenge to norms of masculine behavior: "In short, practices and people considered marginal by normal society became defined as central by a significant proportion of 50s artists in all fields" (" 'No Body's Perfect': Method Acting and 50s Culture," *Michigan Quarterly Review* 35, no. 1 (1996): 191–215, 200 quoted). Conroy argues that the Method—a flashpoint in postwar debates about American culture's embrace of the "middlebrow"—has the potential to democratize discussions of American taste, to position the film audience as something other than passive consumers (240).

8. For a useful history of the Method on the American stage and screen, see Braudy, "'No Body's Perfect,'" and Bruce McConachie, "Method Acting and the Cold War." *Theater Survey* 41, no. 1 (May 2000): 47–67.

9. See Conroy, "Acting Out," for an excellent brief history of the Actors Studio and its debt to Stanislavski. For an overview of the interpersonal dynamics between Kazan, Lewis, Crawford, and Strasberg at the Actors Studio after their departure from the Group Theatre, and on the differences between Strasberg's Method and Stanislavski's System, see McConachie, "Method Acting and the Cold War," 50–51.

10. See Braudy, " 'No Body's Perfect,'" 199.

11. See McConachie on the ideological consequences of the Method's continued dominance in acting classrooms and the American theater and film industries: "To expect that any mainstream discourse about acting could overcome and counter the dominant ideological contradictions of any period is unrealistic. That Strasberg's "method" should continue to exert such influence in acting training and performance in the twenty-first century, however, is a curious fact that speaks both to the inherent conservatism of practical pedagogy in the arts and to the durability of cold war thinking in the culture" (65).

12. Braudy, " 'No Body's Perfect,'" 194.

13. Stanwyck earned these four nominations for her performances in *Stella Dallas* (1938), *Ball of Fire* (1942), *Double Indemnity* (1945), and *Sorry, Wrong Number* (1949). She never won an Oscar for Best Actress, though she was awarded an Honorary Academy Award in 1982 "for superlative creativity and unique contribution to the art of screen acting."

14. See Naremore, *Acting in the Cinema* (Berkeley and Los Angeles: University of California Press, 1988), and Richard Dyer, *Stars* (London: British Film Institute, 2008), particularly Naremore's description of the "shift from a semiotic to a psychological conception of performance" between 1880 and 1920 (52).

15. Naremore, *Acting in the Cinema,* 53.

16. "Despite the fact that film acting has usually been explained in roughly Stanislavskian terms, the players in classic Hollywood frequently relied upon an untutored application of the principles Delsarte . . . tried to systematize" (ibid., 63).

17. Ibid., 199.

18. Ibid., 49, 43.

19. Howard Hampton, *Born in Flames: Termite Dreams, Dialectical Fairy Tales, and Pop Apocalypses* (Cambridge: Harvard University Press, 2006), 53, 55.

20. Though the lineage I trace from this film differs from Hampton's, I share his sense that *The Furies* offers a welcome change from the "aesthetic distance" he argues that contemporary extremity onscreen offers to the "hip audience" (ibid., 6).

21. Naremore explains "expressive objects," a term he gets from Pudovkin, as "moments when the human subject and the theatrical object come into contact" and seem to meld into one being (ibid., 85).

22. This placement of the necklace is an eerie prefiguring of the noose TC will place around Juan's throat.

23. Ezra Goodman, *Los Angeles Daily News,* Dec. 1, 1949.

24. Joseph Breen to Hal Wallis, May 18, 1949, MPAA Production Code Administration Records, Margaret Herrick Library, Academy of Motion Picture Arts and Sciences.

25. The PCA file on *The Furies* contains a long, entertaining description of PCA demands that "open-mouth" kisses be cut from the film and the increasing frustration from the film's producers over PCA interference. This back-and-forth appears to have ended in a series of practical jokes played by the film's production crew on the PCA inspectors: "With regards Item 3, the open-mouthed kiss, Mr. Wallis would be led, upon his return to the office, to show us his private collection of open-mouth kisses taken from other films, among which he guaranteed he had a couple of beauties which would top anything we saw in his picture. Consequently, would we please not ask him to remove the open-mouth kiss from his picture, because he would not do it." This taunting culminates in a PCA complaint about "information from an unimpeachable source" describing Wallis Productions "laughing behind our backs around the Paramount lot, and, in effect, making fools of us." After John Mock promises to make cuts to the kissing scenes, and then produces a new cut of the film with only a few frames removed, "We told him we thought he was taunting us . . . [and] told him, in anger, that we resented such adolescent carryings-on." "Memo for the Files," January 25, 1950, description by J.A.V. of a series of conversations between John Mock and Joseph Breen, Herrick Library.

26. See especially Savran, *Taking It like a Man;* Susan Jeffords, *Hard Bodies: Hollywood Masculinity in the Reagan Era* (New Brunswick: Rutgers University Press, 1994) and *The Remasculinization of America: Gender and the Vietnam War* (Bloomington: Indiana University Press, 1989); and Greven, *Manhood in Hollywood from Bush to Bush.*

27. See Richard Maltby, *Hollywood Cinema* (Oxford: Blackwell Publishers, 1995), on Hitchcock's use of safe and unsafe space in *Psycho* (1960). I refer here to the generic fissure this moment represents, but also to its disorienting camerawork and unsettling effect.

28. Niven Busch, *The Furies* (1948), reprint ed. included with Criterion Collection DVD, 127–29, 138, 140.

29. Ibid., 140.

30. Audio commentary, Criterion Collection DVD. The film's paratexts suggest that the Juan/Vance relationship was drastically cut in the editing room.

31. On affective memory in Method acting, see Cynthia Baron and Sharon Marie Carnicke, *Reframing Screen Performance* (Ann Arbor: University of Michigan Press, 2008). Baron and Carnicke point out Lee Strasberg's importance to disseminating this idea in the United States: "Strasberg popularized the use of affective memory and the substitution of actors' personal experience for characters' circumstances and objectives" (26). See also Naremore, *Acting in the Cinema,* 61.

32. Braudy rightly notes that this phenomenon is not limited to the aftermath of World War II: "With the end of World War II—perhaps with the ending of every war until women become an equal part of the military—a master historical narrative defining and even guaranteeing masculinity abruptly vanishes" (" 'No Body's Perfect,'" 201). I take up this trope in greater detail in the next chapter's analysis of Vietnam films. Braudy's evocative formulation—"until women become an equal part of the military"—mirrors my own sense that women's increasingly equality in the armed services has the potential to shift the cultural calculus around the representation of vulnerability.

33. See Jeremy Byman, *Showdown at High Noon: Witchhunts, Critics, and the End of the Western* (Lanham, MD: Scarecrow Press, 2004).

34. See Naremore, *Acting in the Cinema,* on the distinction between "theatrical" and "aleatory" performance, which he labels acting and accident (14).

35. Kristen Hatch, "1951: Movies and the New Faces of Masculinity," in *American Cinema of the 1950s,* ed. Murray Pomerance (New Brunswick: Rutgers University Press, 2008), 57. This article offers a cogent discussion of Marlon Brando and Montgomery Clift as the two early-1950s performers most emblematic of the "new" masculinity in postwar American cinema.

36. Ibid., 58.

37. On critics' descriptions of Brando, see Michael T. Schuyler, "He 'Coulda Been a Contender' for Miss America: Feminizing Brando in *On the Waterfront,*" *Canadian Review of American Studies* 41, no. 1 (2001): 97–113; for discussion of Brando's sexual ambiguity, see Ryan, "Contenders," *Sight & Sound,* Aug. 2007, 36–40.

38. Hatch, "1951: Movies and the New Faces of Masculinity," 58.

39. Braudy, " 'No Body's Perfect,'"198.

40. Hatch, "1951: Movies and the New Faces of Masculinity," 52.

41. McConachie offers a useful history of the Method in relation to American performers' self-representation during the tumultuous early 1950s: "The problem for the historian of "the Method" is not its slow emergence out of the ignorance of the past, but its sudden success in cold war America" ("Method Acting and the Cold War," 47). For an important analysis of the Method's ideological import in the 1950s, when it gains cultural dominance, see Conroy, "Acting Out."

42. Ted Anderson writing in the Paralyzed Veterans of America's News-Bulletin, viewed in the Herrick Library's collection of clippings and reviews of *The Men* (miscellaneous #49, f. 653).

43. See McConachie for a lucid discussion of the debate between proponents of the Method and defenders of the high-theatrical style: "Throughout the 1950s, English opponents of 'The Method,' including Tyrone Guthrie and Michael Redgrave, and their American allies in academia and the press, attacked the Actors Studio for muddying the distinction between high and popular culture through sloppy diction, overwrought emotionalism, and actorly self-indulgence at the expense of the play" ("Method Acting and the Cold War," 62).

44. See Conroy, "Acting Out."

45. Herrick Library, *The Men,* miscellaneous #49, f. 653.

46. Naremore, *Acting in the Cinema,* 212.

CHAPTER 2 VICTIMIZED, VIOLENT, AND DAMNED

1. Peter McInerney, "Apocalypse Then: Hollywood Looks Back at Vietnam," *Film Quarterly* 33, no. 2 (Winter 1979–1980), 24.

2. Charles Foran, "Celluloid Wars: VIETNAM," *Queen's Quarterly* 112 (Summer 2005): 255–265.

3. Bruce Spear, "Political Morality and Historical Understanding in *Casualties of War,*" *Literature/Film Quarterly* 20, no. 3 (1992), 246.

4. The list of scholars critiquing the film's politics is long. See, for example, Michael Klein, "Historical Memory, Film, and the Vietnam War," in *From Hanoi to Hollywood,* ed. Linda Dittman and Gene Michaux (New Brunswick: Rutgers University Press, 1990), 29–38; Marsha Kinder, "Political Game," *Film Quarterly* 32, no. 4 (Summer 1979): 14–16; and Ernest Callenbach, "Phallic Nightmares," *Film Quarterly* 32, no. 4 (Summer 1979): 18–22, who compares Cimino to D. W. Griffith (18). Richard Slotkin labels the film (along with *Full Metal Jacket*) "critical of American involvement in the war," while John Hellmann defends it against charges of racism. Slotkin, "Unit Pride: Ethnic Platoons and the Myths of American Nationality," *American Literary History* 13, no. 3 (Autumn 2001): 492; Hellmann, "Vietnam and the Hollywood Genre Film: Inversions of American Mythology in *The Deer Hunter* and *Apocalypse Now,*" *American Quarterly* 34, no. 4 (Autumn 1982): 418–439.

5. Peter McInerney suggests that the film's ability to be read as "a rough blessing of macho homoeroticism" and, simultaneously, "a racist flag-waver" is "the secret of the film's enormous power" ("Apocalypse Then," 30). Leslie Fiedler argues that (in 1990) he has yet to find a Vietnam War film that "mythicized for all audiences, popular and elite . . . the defeat in Vietnam of not just our forces but our illusions" but thinks that *The Deer Hunter* "come[s] close to performing that formidable task; in part because [it is] sufficiently ambiguous to reflect the doubts which these days undercut the one-time certainties of the

most hawkish and dovish"; "Mythicizing the Unspeakable," *Journal of American Folklore* 103 (Oct.–Dec. 1990): 393.

6. See Hellmann, "Vietnam and the Hollywood Genre Film," on the ways that Michael represents the "disturbing traits" of the western hero as well as his positive ones: "Indeed, the narcissistic, promiscuous, and pistol-flashing Stanley, who is Michael's antagonist, is also the dark reflection of Michael's repressed self, just as the outlaw is the mirror image of the western hero" (422). Frank Burke goes so far as to suggest that "Michael is not a 'hero' in any other than a stereotypical and self-destructive sense"; "In Defense of *The Deer Hunter;* or, The Knee Jerk Is Quicker than the Eye," *Literature/Film Quarterly* 11, no. 1 (1983): 22.

7. In my view, the best salvos in these debates have been Peter Lehman in 1983, Robin Wood in 1986, and Sylvia Shin Huey Chong in 2005. Lehman, " 'Well, What's It like over There? Can You Tell Us Anything?': Looking for Vietnam in *The Deer Hunter,*" *North Dakota Quarterly* 51, no. 3 (1983): 31–41; Wood, *Hollywood from Vietnam to Reagan* (New York: Columbia University Press, 1986); Chong, "Restaging the War: *The Deer Hunter* and the Primal Scene of Violence," *Cinema Journal* 44, no. 2 (Winter 2005): 89–106.

8. "The bizarre truth about *The Deer Hunter* is that it doesn't and can't *really* represent Vietnam, the South Vietnamese people, or the Viet Cong . . . [When the veteran in the bar says "Fuck it" to Michael's question] it is as if for a moment a character speaks the major ideological problem of the film. Cimino can no more show Vietnam than the Green Beret can speak it" (Lehman, " 'Well, What's It like over There,'" 136).

9. Chong, "Restaging the War," 90.

10. Marsha Kinder is representative of those critics who argue that Cimino presents Clairton nostalgically in contrast to his lurid, disorienting portrayal of Vietnam: "[The film] suggests the reason the war is so grim is that it draws Americans away from their wholesome small-town life . . . away from the communal rituals of festive weddings, exhilarating hunts, and somber funerals. It draws them to treacherous jungles where they are subjected to inhuman atrocities committed by an alien race" ("Political Game," 14). I will suggest that the Clairton sequences are far more complex in their presentation of class and gender than Kinder acknowledges. See Don Francis, "The Regeneration of America: Uses of Landscape in *The Deer Hunter,*" *Literature/Film Quarterly* 11, no. 1 (1983): 16–21, for another vein of this argument. While Kinder sees Clairton and the mountains as part of the same piece (small-town America, idealized male bonding), Francis argues that they are a duality (machine and garden) and that Cimino sends them to Vietnam to reconcile by "commit[ing] cultural suicide" (17).

11. Wood, *Hollywood from Vietnam to Reagan,* 288. Wood points out that the film's focus on loss includes Michael as well as Nick and Steven—Nick loses his life and Steven his legs, but Michael loses what Wood calls his "charismatic authority" (276). Susan Jeffords makes a fairly convincing case that Nick is the father of Angela's baby, which certainly complicates the image of easy brotherhood that many ascribe to these early scenes, but for my purposes the film's characterization of Linda is even more crucial (*Remasculinization of America,* 94–102).

12. See Kathleen Brady, John Briggs, and Edward A. Hagan, "The Enemy Is 'Us': Misconstruing the Real War in *The Deer Hunter* and Other Post-Vietnam War Narratives," in *Dressing Up for War: Transformations of Gender and Genre in the Discourse and Literature of War,* ed. Aránzazu Usandizaga and Andrew Monnickendam (Amsterdam: Rodopi, 2001), 257–269, for one of the few sustained readings of the film's female characters and its critique of male violence: "Cimino's film has been misunderstood both because it appropriates the war story genre without being a genre film and because its central focus on misogyny as a necessity of American masculinity seems to run counter to our expectations and perceptions of this genre" (257).

13. Wood's analysis of the Mike / Linda / Nick triangle: "The narrative of *The Deer Hunter* is posited on, largely motivated by, the love to two men for each other, but this, far from being a problem, is assumed to be unequivocally positive and beautiful; therefore, the film is compelled to permit the spectator to pretend that its sexual implications do not exist" (*Hollywood from Vietnam to Reagan,* 291).

14. In one of the few references to Walken's performance, Michael Dempsey suggests that Nick is "sketchily written but eerily acted by Christopher Walken"; "Hellbent for Mystery," *Film Quarterly* 32, no. 4 (Summer 1979): 13. The quality Dempsey labels "eerie" is central to my argument here about vulnerable masculinity and its connection to the feminine. Marsha Kinder calls this quality "vagueness," but attributes it to the character's "personality" rather than Walkens's performance: "Whenever Nick is moving to the music or relaxing with the boys, it's hard to watch anyone else on screen (even De Niro), but there is an odd vagueness at the center of his personality" ("Political Game," 15).

15. Richard Kamber, in one of the few analyses of the film focused exclusively on class, identifies Nick's "The whole thing is right here. I love this fuckin' place" as the crucial line in the film: "This unfashionable sentiment informs the entire production"; "Taming *The Deer Hunter:* A Working Class Movie Without Middle Class Condescension," *Cresset* 44, no. 1 (1980): 29.

16. Ernest Callenbach calls the Michael / Nick dynamic central to the film's emotional dynamic: in scenes between Michael and Nick, "Cimino and his actors manage a kind of intimacy between men which is rarely seen on film" ("Phallic Nightmares," 20).

17. Chong, "Restaging the War," 94–94. Peter Lehman calls the film "stylistically schitzophrenic," arguing that "the entire Vietnam sequences seem like two big, hysterical tears in an otherwise classical, realist text" (" 'Well, What's It like over There,'" 133).

18. Wood argues, "The rejection of the film on political grounds is in fact closely involved with the issue of realism and the confusions that almost invariably attend the use of that term" (*Hollywood from Vietnam to Reagan,* 242). Brady, Briggs, and Hagan argue that "critics have judged the film by standards of realism that do not apply to the kind of representation that Cimino is making" ("The Enemy Is 'Us,'" 258).

19. Wood, *Hollywood from Vietnam to Reagan,* 243.

20. Wood argues that "the first Russian roulette sequence invites us to identify, not only with the diverse reactions of Mike, Nick, and Steven, but at moments with the Vietcong leader, simply on the basis of his youth and vulnerability" (ibid., 244). Chong suggests that identification is not split among protagonists so much as diverted onto the action itself: "The profusion of perspectives during the first Russian roulette scene is particularly disorienting, so that identification is diverted from both the characters and the camera and onto the action" ("Restaging the War," 97).

21. Chong, "Restaging the War," 100.

22. For critiques of this sequence, see Kinder, "Political Game," and Michael Klein, "Historical Memory, Film, and the Vietnam War," in *From Hanoi to Hollywood,* ed. Linda Dittmar and Gene Michaux (New Brunswick: Rutgers University Press, 1990), 29–38. Kamber insists that "far from being an expression of recalcitrant jingoism, as some critics have charged, this final scene is a gently ironic depiction of baffled mourners reaching out for words that they themselves cannot command" ("Taming *The Deer Hunter,*" 30). While I find Kamber's description of the song as a kind of ritual convincing, I agree with Peter Lehman that the scene provides a "sad and desperate image" (" 'Well, What's It like over There,'" 133), and with Wood, who sees the ending (and the film's tone throughout) as "the emotional commitment to values simultaneously perceived as obsolete" (*Hollywood from Vietnam to Reagan,* 256). Fiedler asserts: "Nor is this a sentimental cop-out, as some have charged, much less a piece of covert irony, as others embarrassed by such charges have argued. Singing it, the aging survivors pledge allegiance to the traditional values to which their parents had earlier painfully learned to assimilate: the values of a middle-aged middle America, symbolized not just by the flag they bless, but the church, home, marriage, and the family to which they have returned" ("Mythicizing the Unspeakable," 395). For a perspective on the ending similar to Fiedler's, see Hellmann, "Vietnam and the Hollywood Genre Film."

23. See Jeffords, *Remasculinization of America.* Janet C. Moore suggests instead that "the film is less about a so-called Vietnam experience than it is about the war film conventions that reproduce the warrior ideology they pretend to disclaim"; "For Fighting and for Fun: Kubrick's Complicitous Critique in *Full Metal Jacket,*" *Velvet Light Trap* 31 (Spring 1993): 40. Thus the debate about gender in the film comes to resemble the debate about race in *The Deer Hunter,* with the film's defenders suggesting that it's *not* primarily about Vietnam. Moore, for example, considers *Full Metal Jacket* a "useful feminist work insofar as, and only insofar as, it is also seen as postmodern, nonrealist, autotheorized fiction" (*Hollywood from Vietnam to Reagan,* 40).

24. James Naremore, "Stanley Kubrick and the Aesthetics of the Grotesque," *Film Quarterly* 60, no. 1 (Fall 2006): 4–14.

25. As Thomas Doherty puts it, "This is a film short on reaction shots and nearly bereft of eyeline matches: the vantage is distancing, almost anti-septic, as scrubbed-down as the squad's ghostly white barracks lavatory"; "Full Metal Genre: Stanley Kubrick's Vietnam Combat Movie," *Film Quarterly* 42, no. 2 (Winter 1988–1989): 27.

26. Michael Pursell, "*Full Metal Jacket:* The Unravelling of Patriarchy," *Literature/Film Quarterly* 16, no. 4 (1988): 229. Moore takes a similar tack, arguing that "the expected emotional affect is flattened and defamiliarized" (*Hollywood from Vietnam to Reagan,* 40).

27. This effect has often been noted—see especially James Naremore's analysis of the "moral and emotional disequilibrium" that "confuses both our intellectual and emotional responses" ("Stanley Kubrick and the Aesthetics of the Grotesque," 10). In the opening barracks scene, particularly, Naremore argues that "the clarity, symmetry, and aura of discipline . . . are in uneasy conflict with the slightly weird exaggeration of space, and with Hartman's loud, hyperbolic performance" (11).

28. Michael Klein, for example, suggests that "in the first section of the film our sympathies are directed against a brutal, middle-aged, and extremely unattractive right-wing drill sergeant, a figure few in the audience would identify with" ("Historical Memory, Film, and the Vietnam War," 29). While I believe that pleasure in this part of the film works in a more complicated way than Klein acknowledges, he is right to imply that sympathy and identification are impossible to untangle from one another in the first half of the film.

29. See Thomas Doherty: "Sgt. Hartman is a poet laureate of verbal vulgarity. . . . such a virtuoso of vile invective that the main response to his torrents of abuse is delight in a master at work" ("Full Metal Genre," 26–27).

30. Naremore, "Stanley Kubrick and the Aesthetics of the Grotesque," 13.

31. Richard Rambuss, "Machinehead," *Camera Obscura* 14, no. 3 (Sept. 1999): 100.

32. Rambuss suggests the moment where Cowboy forces Joker to "do it" is a sign that "the machine does not function . . . until every part has done its part" (ibid.).

33. Susan White, "Male Bonding, Hollywood Orientalism, and the Repression of the Feminine in Kubrick's *Full Metal Jacket,*" in *Inventing Vietnam: The War in Film and Television,* ed. Michael Anderegg (Philadelphia: Temple University Press, 1991), 209.

34. White argues that "Pyle's limpid demand for love from Joker, his masochistic enjoyment of the first harsh words from the sergeant, reflect his unique inability, in this group, to shake the menace of the unmasculine" (ibid., 207). I argue that Pyle's eleventh-hour rebirth as a hardbody is one of the film's most antirealist elements.

35. See Ron Magid, "*Full Metal Jacket:* Cynic's Choice," *American Cinematographer,* Sept. 1987, 74–84, on the way director of photography Douglas Milsome lights and shoots this scene to create both a sense of "pain and horror" as well as a "combination of naturalism and stylization" (79).

36. Rambuss, "Machinehead," 101.

37. Doherty, "Full Metal Genre," 28.

38. See Rambuss, "Machinehead," 108–109, for an analysis of male vulnerability in *Full Metal Jacket*. It is primarily the performances (apart from D'Onofrio's) that prevent me from seeing the film as an example of the construction of male vulnerability onscreen.

Rambuss is right to point out how ridden the film's dialogue is with references to the penetration of the male body, though the film does (as Rambuss also points out) triangulate this through the presence of Vietnamese women.

39. See Rambuss, arguing against Jeffords's analysis of the scene, for some compelling points about the ambiguity of the sniper's death, though I disagree with his assertion that the film version "empties the scene of male bravura" (ibid., 117). Paula Willoquet-Maricondi argues that the scene shows "Kubrick criticiz[ing] the whole process of masculinization by showing that it involves not only the defeat of an "other" (female or otherwise) but, more fundamentally, the defeat of the very self"; "Full-Metal-Jacketing; or, Masculinity in the Making," *Cinema Journal* 33, no. 2 (Winter 1994): 6. John Newsinger reads the scene as a form of "magnificent" irony: "These tough, macho fighting men to whom all Vietnamese women are apparently available, these products of the American war machine, have been put through the grinder by a young woman. This is the most radical statement of any of the Vietnam War films. Kubrick challenges the whole ethos of the masculine warrior, calls into question their mastery of the world"; " 'Do You Walk the Walk?': Aspects of Masculinity in Some Vietnam War Films," in *You Tarzan: Masculinity, Movies, and Men,* ed. Pat Kirkham and Janet Thumim (New York: St. Martin's Press, 1993), 133.

40. Klein, "Historical Memory, Film, and the Vietnam War," 33.

41. See, for example, Michael Pursell: "The symbolic and linguistic universes create the physical one, and it is the slaughter of the woman that turns Joker into a full Marine, living out the 'Born to Kill' slogan written across his head" ("*Full Metal Jacket:* The Unravelling of Patriarchy," 222). Thomas Doherty sees this as a retreat from any critique of the military machine: "[By the end of the film], Marines have died, but in a way not all that far from *The Sands of Iwo Jima,* the Marine tradition is upheld. Consecrated in the blood of the innocent, Joker attains a kind of purifying transcendence: 'I'm in a world of shit, yes, but I am alive and I am not afraid'" ("Full Metal Genre," 30).

42. Rambuss, "Machinehead," 110.

43. White, "Male Bonding, Hollywood Orientalism, and the Repression of the Feminine," 212.

44. Timothy Corrigan, *A Cinema Without Walls: Movies and Culture After Vietnam* (New Brunswick: Rutgers University Press, 1991), 44.

45. Newsinger, " 'Do You Walk the Walk?'" 135.

46. Greven calls *Casualties of War* "the greatest Vietnam War film ever made"; *Manhood in Hollywood from Bush to Bush* (Austin: University of Texas Press, 2009), 53. Newsinger suggests that it is "arguably the grimmest Vietnam War film" (" 'Do You Walk the Walk?'" 134).

47. See Greven for an analysis of Penn's "extraordinary, terrifying, moving performance," which he suggests "[fuses] the horrifying and the humorous . . . with a current of vulnerability that only intensifies the fury the character exhibits" (ibid., 62–63, 65).

48. See Greven for an analysis of the way that Meserve's rescue feminizes Eriksson; *Manhood in Hollywood from Bush to Bush*, 62–63.

49. Eben J. Muse's analysis of the camerawork in the rape scene suggests that "when Meserve leaves the middle horizon and walks toward the camera, he passes the foreground horizon and continues to move toward the camera, thus separating the lone abstainer from even voyeuristic complicity"; "The Land of Nam: Romance and Persecution in Brian DePalma's *Casualties of War*," *Literature/Film Quarterly* 20, no. 3 (1992): 209.

50. Greven, *Manhood in Hollywood from Bush to Bush*, 80; see 73 for Eriksson's gaze as an example of the "masochistic gaze."

51. Ibid., 69. See also Robert Eberwein, " 'As a Mother Cuddles a Child': Sexuality and Masculinity in World War II Combat Films," in *Masculinity: Bodies, Movies, Culture*, ed. Peter Lehman (New York and London: Routledge, 2001), 131, for a reading of Diaz's vulnerability in this scene.

52. Greven, *Manhood in Hollywood from Bush to Bush*, 66.

53. Ibid., 72.

54. Susan Fraiman, *Cool Men and the Second Sex* (New York: Columbia University Press, 2003), 25.

55. See Greven, *Manhood in Hollywood from Bush to Bush*, for a reading of the "cherry" as an example of "non-volitional suffering" (74).

56. Fraiman, *Cool Men and the Second Sex*, 25.

CHAPTER 3 — THE BODY AT WAR

1. Nancy Collins, "More Demi Moore," *Vanity Fair*, Aug. 1991, 100, 142.

2. Jennet Conant, "Demi's Birthday Suit," *Vanity Fair*, Aug. 1992, 118.

3. Judith Halberstam, *Female Masculinity* (Durham: Duke University Press, 1998), 40.

4. These are not, of course, separate questions; films are complex negotiations of production necessity, the competing artistic aims of screenwriter, director, and producer, individual directorial and acting choices, and the contending forces in culture that shape the way controversial images are produced and understood.

5. For the details of Moore's recruitment of Scott as director, see Paul M. Sammon, *Ridley Scott: The Making of His Movies (Close Up)* (New York: Da Capo Press, 1999).

6. On the political and theoretical contexts of Vietnam representation during the 1970s and 1980s, see Susan Jeffords, *The Remasculinization of America: Gender and the Vietnam War* (Bloomington: Indiana University Press, 1989). Jeffords, building on work that John Ellis, Teresa de Lauretis, and others have done on audience identification in film, describes the suffering male body in Vietnam films as a form of "fetishistic display." See also Robin Wood, *Hollywood from Vietnam to Reagan* (New York: Columbia University Press, 1986).

7. See Robert Eberwein, " 'As a Mother Cuddles a Child': Sexuality and Masculinity in World War II Combat Films," in *Masculinity: Bodies, Movies, Culture,* ed. Peter Lehman (New York and London: Routledge, 2001), 149–166, for the ways WWII combat films negotiated this focus on the male body while preserving midcentury ideals of masculinity.

8. Ian Nathan, "Apocalypse Then," *Empire*, Oct. 1998, 102.

9. See Neal Gabler, " 'Private Ryan' Satisfies Our Longing for Unity," *Los Angeles Times,* Aug. 9, 1998; Anthony Giardina, "Are We Not Men? Nineties Preoccupations with Manhood Are Fueling Our Obsession with World War II," *GQ*, May 1999, 137–144; and Richard Goldstein, "World War II Chic," *Village Voice,* Jan. 19, 1999, 43–47. Albert Auster argues that the film, coming after "the low-key American victories in the Cold War and the Gulf War, was a perfect anodyne for the somewhat equivocal victory of those triumphs"; "*Saving Private Ryan* and American Triumphalism," *Journal of Popular Film and Television* 30, no. 2 (2002): 99.

10. According to Congressional Research Service statistics, 147 American service personnel died in combat during the first Gulf War; *American War and Military Operations Casualties: Lists and Statistics* (Washington: CRS, 2004), 23, available at http://www.fas.org/sgp/crs/natsec/RL32492.pdf.

11. See Philippa Gates, " 'Fighting the Good Fight': The Real and the Moral in the Contemporary Hollywood Combat Film," *Quarterly Review of Film and Video* 22, no. 4 (2005): 297–310. Gates traces three phases of Vietnam War films for their attitudes toward realism and the figure of the American soldier.

12. See Sylvia Shin Huey Chong, "Restaging the War: *The Deer Hunter* and the Primal Scene of Violence," *Cinema Journal* 44, no. 2 (Winter 2005): 89–106, on the connection between war photography and film violence in *The Deer Hunter.* See also Edward Rothstein, "Rescuing the War Hero from 1990's Skepticism," *New York Times,* Aug. 3, 1998, on the ways Vietnam and its cultural legacy provide the context for WWII films like *Patton* (1970) and *A Bridge Too Far* (1977).

13. John Hodgkins, "In the Wake of Desert Storm: A Consideration of Modern World War II Films," *Journal of Popular Film and Television* 30, no. 2 (2002): 76.

14. Goldstein, "World War II Chic," 43.

15. Giardina, "Are We Not Men?" 137.

16. See Aaron B. O'Connell, "Saving Private Lynch: A Hyperreal Hero in an Age of Postmodern Warfare," *War, Literature and the Arts* 17, no. 1–2 (2005): 33–52, on the importance of the captivity-narrative tradition to films like *Saving Private Ryan.* The trope of the missing child is especially relevant to the vulnerability system I explore in Spielberg's film. For the ways that this discourse influenced the narrative of PFC Jessica Lynch's rescue from Iraq in 2003, see ibid., 38.

17. Nathan, "Apocalypse Then," 102. See Lester Friedman, *Citizen Spielberg* (Champaign: University of Illinois Press, 2006) for an admirably detailed analysis of the Omaha Beach sequence and its importance to Spielberg's interest in the WWII combat genre.

18. See Andrew Wallenstein, "Many Reinforce War Film: Affils Grapple with 'Great Debate,'" *Hollywood Reporter,* Nov. 12, 2004, 1, 95, on this election-year debate. Much press attention also focused on the boot camp the actors attended, run by Dale Dye, and the "real" suffering they endured to ensure their portrayals were as accurate as possible—article after article praised them as "gallant men who endured sheer hell for the sake of absolute realism" (Nathan, "Apocalypse Then," 101). Tania Modleski critiques this impulse, which she calls "the alibi of the real," saying of *Saving Private Ryan* and *Schindler's List* (Spielberg, 1993): "Realism becomes a perfect alibi for indulging in morally dubious pleasures, assuring us that we're not just having a little sadistic fun but participating in the solemn act of bearing witness"; "The Context of Violence in Popular Culture," *Chronicle of Higher Education* 47, no. 53 (April 27, 2001): B15.

19. Michael Hammond argues that the film's audio is crucial to its "underlying obbligato of melancholy": "This undertone exists not only in the musical score but in the tone of anguished voices and viscerally felt noises which heightens the consequence of weaponry and make poignant fear, suffering, and loss"; "*Saving Private Ryan*'s 'Special Affect,'" in *Action and Adventure Cinema,* ed. Yvonne Tasker (London and New York: Routledge, 2004), 153.

20. Ina Rae Hark, "Animals or Romans: Looking at Masculinity in *Spartacus,*" in *Screening the Male: Exploring Masculinities in Hollywood Cinema,* ed. Steven Cohan and Ina Rae Hark (London: Routledge, 1993), 151.

21. Gary Kamiya, "Total War," *Salon,* June 30, 1998, http://www.salon.com/1998/06/30/review_109/.

22. David Denby, "Heroic Proportions," *New York Magazine,* July 27, 1998, 44.

23. Friedman argues, "Retrospectively, one realizes that Ryan was not present on the beach that day in June 1944, so what initially seemed like a first-person remembrance becomes a third-person account, a conjectured narrative pieced together long after most of the events depicted in the story actually transpired" *(Citizen Spielberg,* 224).

24. Burns wrote, directed, and starred in *The Brothers McMullen* (1995) and *She's the One* (1996). Vin Diesel and Giovanni Ribisi gained stature in the 2000s, but at the time of *Saving Private Ryan*'s release, the two were little known.

25. This scene's setting in an abandoned church is appropriate to what Fred See identifies as Spielberg's impulse to "reinstall domestic holiness" into the fractured worlds his films present; "Steven Spielberg and the Holiness of War," *Arizona Quarterly* 60, no. 3 (2004): 115. But here, while the stories about home are intended to attach violent death to the sphere of domestic holiness, the narratives themselves are punctuated by a sense of cruelty and loss at odds with the salvific tone they create.

26. As Tania Modleski puts it, "It's all in the context—in the way the film allows us to understand what we're seeing, in the questions it poses about the place of violence in our culture and about the viewer's own investment in the erotics of violence" ("Context of Violence in Popular Culture," B15). It is here, during Wade's death scene, that Spielberg

most needs a different context for this violence than the male vulnerability established by the beach landing and Carpazo's death scene.

27. Kamiya, "Total War."

28. *Saving Private Ryan* shooting script, Margaret Herrick Library.

29. Goldstein reads this scene differently, seeing Upham as a "stand-in for the Boomer's self-contempt" ("World War II Chic," 47).

30. Joe Morgenstern labels the epilogue "a clumsily sentimental, flag-waving coda that drains integrity from the work as a whole"; "Battle Rages Ahead but Plot Drags Behind in *Saving Private Ryan,*" *Wall Street Journal,* July 24, 1998, W3. There is near-consensus among film critics on the frame's narrative fecklessness, even among those who praise the film.

31. Mervyn Rothstein, "No Apologies, No Regrets," *Cigar Aficionado,* Sept. 1996, 152.

32. On the trope of trauma in Vietnam narratives, see especially Jeffords, *The Remasculinization of America.*

33. See, for example, Malcolm Farr, "Drive to Call Up GI Janes," *Daily Telegraph*, November 20, 2009, 18; and Kelly Twedell, "GI Janes Jump In on Action; Flex Muscles in Camp for Spouses at Fort Bragg," *Washington Times*, July 23, 2009, B02.

34. Kenneth Turan, "Shipping Out with Demi," *Los Angeles Times*, Aug. 22, 1997, articles .latimes.com/1997/aug/22/entertainment/ca-24686.

35. See Yvonne Tasker, *Spectacular Bodies: Gender, Genre, and the Action Cinema* (New York: Routledge, 1993), and Susan Jeffords, *Hard Bodies: Hollywood Masculinity in the Reagan Era* (New Brunswick: Rutgers University Press, 1994), on this trope in action cinema.

36. Cynthia Fuchs argues that the buddy film moves "from conflict to resolution (between the two men or between them and a hostile command structure), a narrative continuum which contains initial axes of racial, generational, political, and ethnic difference under a collective performance of extraordinary virility"; "The Buddy Politic," in *Screening the Male: Exploring Masculinities in Hollywood Cinema,* ed. Steven Cohan and Ina Rae Hark (London: Routledge, 1993), 195. *G.I. Jane* complicates this by presenting Urgayle first as part of a hostile command structure, then revealing that the command structure is not hostile at all, once the evils of "gender norming" have been excised.

37. William Leith, "Boom to Bust: Demi Moore, Nakedly Ambitious," *Observer* review section, Sept. 20, 1996, 20.

38. On male masochism in action films, see David Savran, *Taking It like a Man: White Masculinity, Masochism, and Contemporary American Culture* (Princeton: Princeton University Press, 1998; Tasker, *Spectacular Bodies;* and Jeffords, *Hard Bodies.*

39. Caris Davis, "Age of Innocence," *Sunday Times* (London), August 4, 1996, 10–11.

40. Here, too, *G.I. Jane* steers away from both the logic and the iconography of most previous tough-women action films. Tasker analyzes "possession of the gun as a symbol of power for women" in films like *Thelma and Louise,* arguing that "within Hollywood's symbolic system possession of a gun is a potent symbol of power, partly drawing from

an American context in which the freedom to bear arms is constructed as a right of the citizen" (*Spectacular Bodies,* 26). I argue that in most action narratives with female protagonists, and certainly in *G.I. Jane,* this strategy has more to do with the common conception of guns as a physical equalizer than with Second Amendment ideas of citizenship. But, curiously, *G.I. Jane* does not participate in the same kind of visual coding as the James Cameron films. To be sure, her skill and speed at assembling the weapon provides a pleasurable moment, but it is only this short section of the montage that uses gun iconography to empower O'Neil. Usually, the film insists that she does not need this kind of empowerment—even without the equalizing power of guns, O'Neil can compete with the male recruits.

41. Amy Taubin, "Dicks and Jane," *Village Voice,* August 26, 1997, 73.

42. See Susan Fraiman, *Cool Men and the Second Sex* (New York: Columbia University Press, 2003), 23–27, on *Casualties of War.*

43. Turan, "Shipping Out."

44. Newberry shouts, "O'Neil, tell him somethin' or I will!" and she insists "Don't you tell him shit!"

45. In a 2001 piece in the *Observer* (London), Mark Morris quotes *Thelma and Louise* screenwriter Callie Khouri: "I thought when Louise shot that guy there'd be dead silence in the theatre. That scene was written carefully: it was an attempted rape, and I wanted to make what she did wrong. And yet people cheered. I was stunned." Khouri's perspective here highlights the complex interplay between intention, spectatorship, and cultural iconography that is always at work in the reception of popular film. But Khouri's argument about the controversy surrounding *Thelma and Louise* points out how invested Ridley Scott has been since the early 1990s in creating an iconography of female power: "Bad guys get killed in every goddamn movie that gets made. And that guy was the bad guy and he got killed. It was only because a woman did it that there was any controversy at all. If a guy had come out and saved their asses and shot that guy and said: 'Run, quick,' do you think there would have been a fucking moment of controversy?" Mark Morris, "Girls Just Want to Have Guns," *Observer* (London), July 15, 2001.

46. Anthony Lane, "Arms and the Woman," *New Yorker,* Sept. 8, 1997, 86.

47. When the secretary of the navy threatens DeHaven's Senate seat, DeHaven agrees to frame O'Neil for homosexual conduct; she is temporarily removed from SEAL training.

48. Jerry O'Brien, "Women in SEALs Training? Get Real," *Los Angeles Times,* Sept. 1, 1997, articles.latimes.com/1997/sep/01/entertainment/ca-27826.

49. Tasker, *Spectacular Bodies,* 152.

50. See Lizette Alvarez, "GI Jane Breaks the Combat Barrier," *New York Times,* Aug. 15, 2009, www.nytimes.com/2009/08/16/us/16women.html?ref=lizettealvarez&_r=0.

51. Jeanine Basinger, *The World War II Combat Film: Anatomy of a Genre* (Middletown, CT: Wesleyan University Press, 2003), xii.

CHAPTER 4 — MATTHEW SHEPARD'S BODY AND THE POLITICS OF QUEER VULNERABILITY IN *BOYS DON'T CRY* AND *THE LARAMIE PROJECT*

1. Andrew Sullivan, "Afterlife," *New Republic,* Nov. 22, 1999, 6.

2. JoAnn Wypijewski, "A Boy's Life: For Matthew Shepard's Killers, What Does It Take to Pass as a Man?" *Harper's,* Sept. 1999, 64.

3. See Jennifer Petersen on Shepard's physical slightness as one of the most often-reported facts about him: "Almost every initial story noted [his height and weight] whereas reports of his age varied or were often absent"; "The Mourning Public: Grief and Identification in an Anti-Gay Murder," paper presented at the annual meeting of the International Communication Association, San Francisco, May 23, 2007, 14, available at http://www.allacademic.com/meta/p172460_index.html. See also Brian L. Ott and Eric Aoki: "The news media's devotion to drama virtually insured that sensationalistic descriptions of Matthew Shepard's body would lead every story"; "The Politics of Negotiating Public Tragedy: Media Framing of the Matthew Shepard Murder," *Rhetoric and Public Affairs* 5, no. 3 (Fall 2002): 485.

4. For the clearest articulations of the "internalized homophobia" reading of the film, see Rachel Swan, "Boys Don't Cry," *Film Quarterly* 54, no. 3 (Spring 2001): 47–52; and Melissa Rigney, "Brandon Goes to Hollywood: *Boys Don't Cry* and the Transgender Body in Film," *Film Criticism* 28, no. 2 (2003): 4–23. For an alternative reading of the film's gender and sexuality politics, see Brenda Cooper, who argues that "the film can serve a liberatory function whereby the privileged subjectives of heterosexuality and hegemonic masculinity are dismantled, while female masculinity and gender fluidity are privileged and normalized" (49); "*Boys Don't Cry* and Female Masculinity: Reclaiming a Life and Dismantling the Politics of Normative Heterosexuality," *Critical Studies in Media Communication* 19, no. 1 (March 2002): 44–63.

5. Cynthia Fuchs, "*Boys Don't Cry,*" *PopMatters,* http://www.popmatters.com/film/boys-dont-cry.html.

6. See Swan, "*Boys Don't Cry,*" 51.

7. Ibid., 47.

8. See Rigney, "Brandon Goes to Hollywood." On the theory of female masculinity that informs Rigney's and Cooper's arguments, among others, as well as my own thinking on *GI Jane,* see Halberstam, *Female Masculinity.*

9. Rigney reads the erotics of Brandon's performance as a function solely of his interactions with female characters: "The masculinity that Brandon is associated with is an erotic masculinity, one that forms the basis of heterosexual female fantasy . . . It appears that Hollywood has found another ladies man, one who apparently charms young women on the screen as well as in life" ("Brandon Goes to Hollywood," 17). In my view, Brandon's appeal to characters like Lana is about how what "young women" want *isn't* the kind of masculinity represented by John.

10. See Swan, "*Boys Don't Cry*," for references to John as the film's "villain" and Karina Eileraas for a reading of the exposure scene: "Their actions reassert male dominance over a woman (or, in their words, a 'lying bitch'), and violently engrave her body with their power and authority as a *theoria* of knowers and truth-tellers. Lotter and Nissen delight in forcefully exposing Brandon Teena's genitals, which they equate with her 'true' gender identity"; "The Brandon Teena Story: Rethinking the Body, Gender Identity, and Violence Against Women," *Michigan Feminist Studies* 16 (2002): 91.

11. Michele Aaron argues that the reveal scene's composition "invoke[s] not the simple martyrdom of Christ/Brandon but the complicity of the spectators (both inside and outside the frame)."; "Pass/fail," *Screen* 42, no. 1 (2001): 94.

12. Halberstam, "The Transgender Gaze in *Boys Don't Cry*."

13. Ibid.

14. See Swan: "This assault on his usurped 'male' body aims to punish Brandon for transgressing the long-cherished conception of gender as a reflection of sex and the rapists act as agents of a 'natural' order that dates back to Adam and Eve. We may see this rape as the moment in which John and Tom castrate Brandon, thereby restoring his vagina as a female orifice" ("*Boys Don't Cry*," 49–50). For a similar reading, see Rigney: "The rape fixes Brandon's sex as female and operates to control Brandon, forcing upon him the status of object rather than subject, female rather than male" ("Brandon Goes to Hollywood," 9).

15. David M. Jones, "Hegemonic Whiteness and the Humboldt Murders: *Boys Don't Cry*, Historical Memory, and the Ghostly Absence (Presence) of Phillip De Vine," in *Coming Out to the Mainstream: New Queer Cinema in the 21st Century*, ed. JoAnne C. Juett and David M. Jones (Newcastle upon Tyne: Cambridge Scholars Publishing, 2010), 181. Jones's primary aim is to examine the erasure of Phillip De Vine, an African American man who was killed in the attack along with Brandon and Lisa Lambert (the film's Candace).

16. Ott and Aoki, "Politics of Negotiating Public Tragedy," 484–485.

17. See Petersen for an analysis of the debate about Shepard's place in LGBT organizing and the concern about the whitening of queer politics: "While Matthew Shepard was mourned as a national loss, that is, as a sort of nationally representative body, some of the very things that enabled his iconicity raise issues regarding his place in political activism and organizing" ("Mourning Public," 8).

18. While *The Laramie Project* has often been criticized as sentimental and universalizing, I do not use the term "sentimental" as a pejorative artistic judgment but instead as a reference to the cross-category identification that is the moral project of sentimental literature.

19. Jay Baglia and Elissa Foster, "Performing the 'Really' Real: Cultural Criticism, Representation, and Commodification in *The Laramie Project*," *Journal of Dramatic Theory and Criticism* 19, no. 2 (2005): 139.

20. See Thomas R. Dunn on the use of public memory in the Shepard case and the argument for "an extended perspective of queer counterpublic memories"; "Remembering Matthew Shepard: Violence, Identity, and Queer Counterpublic Memories," *Rhetoric and Public Affairs* 13, no. 4 (2010): 611. (611). Dunn suggests that "to challenge the memory of Shepard as an isolated victim, the queer counterpublic circulated memories of Shepard that sought to turn him into a symbolic victim of antigay violence" (618).

21. See Jim Burroway, "Today in History: Armbands and Scarecrows," *Box Turtle Bulletin,* Oct. 10, 2008, for a narrative of both parades.

22. See Scott W. Hoffman, " 'Last Night, I Prayed to Matthew': Matthew Shepard, Homosexuality, and Popular Martyrdom in Contemporary America," *Religion and American Culture: A Journal of Interpretation* 21 (Winter 2011): 121–164, on Shepard's history as a "secular saint" in American public discourse.

23. The shot that leads into *The Laramie Project*'s scene from *Angels in America* shows Jonas Slonaker and one of the TTP writers sitting in an open field, looking out over the Wyoming landscape in the fading light. This shot is eerily similar to what will become an iconic image from Ang Lee's 2005 film *Brokeback Mountain.* See Amy Tigner, who suggests that the story of Shepard's death "illustrates the sublimated fear of homosexuality inherent in typical Western homosocial relationships and the potential violence associated with such fear"; "*The Laramie Project:* Western Pastoral," *Modern Drama* 45, no. 1 (Spring 2002): 140.

CHAPTER 5 — THE VIOLATED BODY AFTER 9/11

1. On July 7, 2009, the Sci-Fi Channel rebranded itself "SyFy." Although none of SyFy's other original programming has matched *Battlestar Galactica*'s critical acclaim, *BG*'s home on basic cable afforded it greater freedom to take artistic and political risks than is available to shows on network television.

2. Jane Mayer, "Whatever It Takes: The Politics of the Man Behind '24,'" *New Yorker*, February 19, 2007, http://www.newyorker.com/reporting/2007/02/19/070219fa_fact_mayer.

3. See Douglas L. Howard, " 'You're Going to Tell Me Everything You Know': Torture and Morality on Fox's *24*," in *Reading* 24: *TV Against the Clock,* ed. Steven Peacock (New York: I. B. Tauris, 2007), 133–148, for the ways that torture scenes have become more graphic and more frequent as the seasons progress.

4. Paul Cantor calls this effect in *24* "double time," a concept he adapts from Renaissance scholarship; *Gilligan Unbound: Pop Culture in the Age of Globalization* (New York: Rowman and Littlefield, 2003). See also Jacqueline Furby, "Interesting Times: The Demands *24*'s Real-Time Format Makes on its Audience," in Peacock, *Reading* 24: *TV Against the Clock,* 59–70.

5. Quoted in Mayer, "Whatever It Takes."

6. See David Luban, "Liberalism, Torture, and the Ticking Bomb," *Virginia Law Review* 91, no. 6 (Oct. 2005): 1425–1461, for an analysis of the ticking-bomb scenario in the "torture

memos" and a convincing argument that this scenario amounts to an "intellectual fraud" (1452). The United Nations Convention Against Torture, General Assembly resolution 39/46, Dec. 10, 1984, is available online at http://untreaty.un.org/cod/avl/ha/catcidtp/catcidtp.html; part 1, article 2, section 2 quoted.

7. Quoted in Mayer, "Whatever It Takes."

8. Scott Higham and Joe Stephens, "New Details of Prison Abuse Emerge; Abu Ghraib Detainees' Statements Describe Sexual Humiliation and Savage Beatings," *Washington Post,* May 21, 2004, A1.

9. Luban, "Liberalism, Torture, and the Ticking Bomb," 1449.

10. Mayer, "Whatever It Takes."

11. See Amy Kaplan, "Where is Guantanamo?" *American Quarterly* 57, no. 3 (September 2005): 831–858, for an analysis of the Marine Naval Station's position as both a part of and apart from the United States and the consequences of this legal limbo for the prisoners currently held there.

12. See Doran Larson, "Machine as Messiah: Cyborgs, Morphs, and the American Body Politic," *Cinema Journal* 36, no. 4 (Summer 1997): 57–75, on the ways that the cyborg works in the Vietnam context as well: "How Vietnam hangs over this and other man versus machine movies is not mysterious: the programmed minions of a machinelike totalitarian state take advantage of the self-reliant human Americans who play by the rules imposed by constitutional democracy" (71).

13. It is here that Grace Park's casting as Boomer/#8 becomes particularly important to my reading of *Battlestar Galactica* in the context of Vietnam.

14. On Starbuck's shifting gender associations over the course of the series, see Patrick B. Sharp, "Starbuck as 'American Amazon': Captivity Narrative and the Colonial Imagination in *Battlestar Galactica,*" *Science Fiction Film and Television* 3, no. 1 (2010): 57–78.

15. Luban, "Liberalism, Torture, and the Ticking Bomb," 1445.

16. "Flesh and Bone" contains a subplot in which the *Galactica* crew examines a captured Cylon raider. Chief Tyrol (Aaron Douglas) muses: "If you treat this thing more like an animal than a machine, that actually works." There's an obvious comparison between the Raider and Leoben, but while the Raider is one step into the uncanny valley of the human (a sleek fighter jet with organs and sinews and blood inside), Leoben is a step farther—physically indistinguishable from the humans holding him prisoner.

17. Judith Butler, *Precarious Life: The Powers of Mourning and Violence* (New York: Verso, 2004), 26.

18. Ibid., xiv.

19. The existential status of imaginary #6 is a subject of fierce debate among *Battlestar Galactica* fans—on the fan message boards she is often called "Chip Six," reflecting the theory that she's the result of a computer chip the Cylons have embedded in Baltar's

brain. The plasticity and exaggerated sexuality of this "version" of Six are most important to my reading of "Pegasus" and its investment in Cylon vulnerability.

20. Executive producer Ron Moore put an extended version of "Pegasus" on the season 2 DVD, including an extensive commentary track detailing the fight between *Battlestar Galactica*'s producers and the network over the explicitness of the rape scene. Even SyFy (formerly the Sci-Fi Channel), whose smaller and more specialized audience base usually allows for greater creative freedom than is available on broadcast television, seems reluctant to portray military officers as rapists.

21. See Karen Engle, "Feminism and Its (Dis)contents: Criminalizing Wartime Rape in Bosnia and Herzegovina," *American Journal of International Law* 99 (October 2005): 778–816, on the debate among feminist activists over the International Criminal Tribunal for the former Yugoslavia and how rape would be defined as a war crime. Engle's caution that defining rape as a gendered crime paints women as always civilians and always victims is central to my question about the place of female vulnerability in our cultural conversations about war. For a series of analyses of rape and international law, see Alexandra Stiglmayer, ed., *Mass Rape: The War Against Women in Bosnia-Herzegovina* (Lincoln: University of Nebraska Press, 1994).

22. Christine Helliwell, " 'It's Only a Penis': Rape, Feminism, and Difference," *Signs* 25, no. 3 (Spring 2000): 812. See also Sharon Marcus on how rape "feminizes" women: "The entire female body comes to be symbolized by the vagina, itself conceived of as a delicate, perhaps inevitably damaged and pained inner space"; "Fighting Bodies, Fighting Words," in *Feminists Theorize the Political,* ed. Judith Butler and Joan W. Scott (London: Routledge, 1992), 398.

23. See Susan Fraiman on the ways that this is a raced as well as a gendered construct: "By fetishizing the white woman as the quintessential victim of rape, it ignores the rape of Black women altogether, by white and Black men both."; *Cool Men and the Second Sex* (New York: Columbia University Press, 2003), 71. See Fraiman also on the "white chivalric fallacy [that] is inevitably at work in imperialist U.S. wars waged against a racial Other" (ibid.).

24. Judith Halberstam, "Automating Gender: Postmodern Feminism in the Age of the Intelligent Machine," *Feminist Studies* 17 (Autumn 1991), 454.

CHAPTER 6 — VULNERABILITY BY PROXY

1. Daniel Worden, "Neo-liberalism and the Western: HBO's *Deadwood* as National Allegory," *Canadian Review of American Studies* 39, no. 2 (2009): 228.

2. See Worden: "Thus the desirable human condition is one of stark individualism, free from any mode of collective belonging, be it in the form of debt, employment, or even fraternal membership in Merrick's proposed club" (ibid., 230). While Worden offers a compelling reading of the comic sequence where Merrick tries to set up his "club," I see a very different ethic at work in the series as a whole.

3. Ibid., 236, 240.

4. Westerfelhaus and Lacroix coin this term in reference to Max Gluckman's "rituals of rebellion," arguing rituals of disquiet emerge in post-9/11 American culture to "subvert

narrative comfort and cathartic closure"; "Waiting for the Barbarians: HBO's *Deadwood* as a Post-9/11 Ritual of Disquiet," *Southern Communications Journal,* 74, no. 1 (Jan.–March 2009): 20–21.

5. Milch frequently defends the show's profanity as "realistic" to the historical context, in spirit if not in letter. See Joseph Millichap, "Robert Penn Warren, David Milch, and the Literary Contexts of *Deadwood,*" in *Reading* Deadwood: *A Western to Swear By,* ed. David Lavery (New York: I. B. Tauris, 2006), 106.

6. See Erin Hill, " 'What's Afflictin' You?' Corporeality, Body Crises, and the Body Politic in *Deadwood,*" in Lavery, *Reading* Deadwood: *A Western to Swear By,* on the ways that crises "in which the body and its limitations take center stage" (171) structure the show's conception of the body politic.

7. Ibid., 174.

8. Milch has spoken in several interviews about this "St. Paul gets collared" pitch. See Mark Singer, "The Misfit: How David Milch Got from *NYPD Blue* to *Deadwood* by Way of an Epistle of St. Paul," *New Yorker,* Feb. 14, 2005, 192–205; and also David Lavery, "Introduction: *Deadwood,* David Milch, and Television Creativity" in Lavery, *Reading* Deadwood: *A Western to Swear By,* 2.

9. Milch, *Deadwood: Stories of the Black Hills* (New York: Melcher Media, 2006), 11.

10. Ibid., 41.

11. *Deadwood,* like many other long-form television narratives of the early twenty-first century, is full of such paratexts—DVD commentaries, featurettes, and extras that feature series creators offering historical background or narrative analysis. The status of these paratexts in terms of a show's "canon" remains a fascinating and under-undertheorized aspect of television studies.

12. Westerfelhaus and Lacroix, "Waiting for the Barbarians," 28.

13. For a reading of *Deadwood*'s opening credits, see Amanda Ann Klein, " 'The Horse Doesn't Get a Credit': The Foregrounding of Generic Syntax in Deadwood's Opening Credits," in Lavery, *Reading* Deadwood: *A Western to Swear By, 93–100.* Though I disagree with Klein's reading of the credits sequence, which she believes "efficiently established the central syntax of the Western genre, namely the archetypal struggle between civilization and savagery" (95), her essay provides a useful account of the western's operation in film and television. For a reading of the opening credits that attempts to place *Deadwood* squarely within the genre, see David Drysdale, " 'Laws and Every Other Damn Thing': Authority, Bad Faith, and the Unlikely Success of *Deadwood,*" in ibid., 136.

14. See Jason Mittell, *Genre and Television: From Cop Shows to Cartoons in American Culture* (New York: Routledge, 2004), on *The Untouchables:* "The latter program, like the era's popular westerns, placed crime into period dramas, linking clear dualistic justice to earlier moments in American history" (149). *Deadwood* is one of the first TV westerns to *not* be "emotionally anachronistic."

15. The western has never been the whitewashed, celebratory genre many assume it is—as Linda Mizejewski points out about *Stagecoach* (1939): "John Wayne and the settlers escape the supposedly savage Indians only to ride into a shabby, honky-tonk white-folks settlement blighting the wilderness. The achingly beautiful landscape and its sad ruination by a perfectly likable John Wayne sum up the Western's contradictions and melancholy soul"; *Hardboiled and High Heeled: The Woman Detective in Popular Culture* (New York: Routledge, 2004), 15.

16. See Singer, "Misfit," on this point, which Milch makes often in the episode commentaries and other features available on the show's DVDs.

17. Ibid., 192.

18. Ibid., 193.

19. This becomes one of the show's most often-discussed tropes, since Al's famous soliloquies on his violent past, his sexual abuse as a child, and his plans for the camp all occur while he receives fellatio. These "blow-job monologues" are the subject of emotional debate about the show's gender politics. Though this debate fails to consider the vulnerability of Al's anatomy in these situations, the foot-scraping scene I discuss is more important to my purposes. I suspect that cultural critics' reflective assumptions about the importance of sex makes the vulnerability of Al's penis more important than the vulnerability of his feet. But I want to suggest that *Deadwood,* particularly in the Al/Trixie relationship, reimagines the importance of different kinds of intimacy and vulnerability.

20. Ibid., 87, 88.

21. In "Pimp and Whore: The Necessity of Perverse Domestication in the Development of the West," in Lavery, *Reading* Deadwood: *A Western to Swear By,* 145–156, G. Christopher Williams argues Al and Trixie's "symbolic marriage" can be read as a metaphor for the development of community in the series. Others take a darker view of Al's relationships with women; see Kim Akass, "You Motherfucker: Al Swearengen's Oedipal Dilemma," ibid., 23–31, on what she sees as the show's "misogyny."

22. Westerfelhaus and Lacroix, "Waiting for the Barbarians," 34.

23. Milch, *Deadwood,* 153.

24. Westerfelhaus and Lacroix, "Waiting for the Barbarians," 35.

25. In the show's second and third seasons, Trixie forms a relationship with Sol, who teaches her bookkeeping, and she transitions from Al's employee to an independent agent, announcing in the third season, "I ain't exclusive to [Al] no more."

AFTERWORD

1. Alyssa Rosenberg, "The Shootings at 'The Dark Knight Rises' in Colorado," July 20, 2012, *ThinkProgress,* http://thinkprogress.org/alyssa/2012/07/20/553901/the-dark-knight-rises.

Bibliography

Aaron, Michele. "Pass/fail." *Screen* 42, no. 1 (2001): 92–96.

Akass, Kim. "You Motherfucker: Al Swearengen's Oedipal Dilemma." In *Reading* Deadwood: *A Western to Swear By,* edited by David Lavery, 23–31. New York: I. B. Tauris, 2006.

Altman, Rick. *Film/Genre.* London: BFI, 1999.

Alvarez, Lizette. "G.I. Jane Breaks the Combat Barrier." *New York Times,* Aug. 15, 2009.

Auster, Albert. "*Saving Private Ryan* and American Triumphalism." *Journal of Popular Film and Television* 30, no. 2 (2002): 98–104.

Baglia, Jay, and Elissa Foster. "Performing the 'Really' Real: Cultural Criticism, Representation, and Commodification in *The Laramie Project.*" *Journal of Dramatic Theory and Criticism* 19, no. 2 (2005): 127–145.

Baron, Cynthia, and Sharon Marie Carnicke. *Reframing Screen Performance.* Ann Arbor: University of Michigan Press, 2008.

Basinger, Jeanine. *The World War II Combat Film: Anatomy of a Genre.* Middletown, CT: Wesleyan University Press, 2003.

Bitsch, Charles, and Claude Chabrol. "Interview with Anthony Mann." In booklet accompanying Criterion Collection DVD of *The Furies* (2008).

Black, Joel. *The Reality Effect: Film Culture and the Graphic Imperative.* New York: Routledge, 2002.

Brady, Kathleen, John Briggs, and Edward A. Hagan. "The Enemy Is 'Us': Misconstruing the Real War in *The Deer Hunter* and Other Post–Vietnam War Narratives." In *Dressing Up for War: Transformations of Gender and Genre in the Discourse and Literature of War,* edited by Aránzazu Usandizaga and Andrew Monnickendam, 257–269. Amsterdam: Rodopi, 2001.

Braudy, Leo. " 'No Body's Perfect': Method Acting and 50s Culture." *Michigan Quarterly Review* 35, no. 1 (1996): 191–215.

Burke, Frank. "In Defense of *The Deer Hunter;* or, The Knee Jerk Is Quicker than the Eye." *Literature/Film Quarterly* 11, no. 1 (1983): 22–27.

Burroway, Jim. "Today in History: Armbands and Scarecrows." *Box Turtle Bulletin,* Oct. 10, 2008.

Butler, Judith. *Precarious Life: The Powers of Mourning and Violence.* New York: Verso, 2004.

Callenbach, Ernest. "Phallic Nightmares." *Film Quarterly* 32, no. 4 (Summer 1979): 18–22.

Cantor, Paul A. *Gilligan Unbound: Pop Culture in the Age of Globalization.* New York: Rowman and Littlefield, 2003.

Carson, Tom. "And the Leni Riefenstahl Award for Rabid Nationalism Goes to . . . A Reconsideration of *Saving Private Ryan*." *Esquire*, March 1999, 70–74.

Chong, Sylvia Shin Huey. "Restaging the War: *The Deer Hunter* and the Primal Scene of Violence." *Cinema Journal* 44, no. 2 (Winter 2005): 89–106.

Clover, Carol. *Men, Women, and Chain Saws: Gender in the Modern Horror Film*. Princeton: Princeton University Press, 1992.

Cohan, Steven, and Ina Rae Hark, eds. *Screening the Male: Exploring Masculinities in Hollywood Cinema*. London: Routledge, 1993.

Congressional Research Service. *American War and Military Operations Casualties: Lists and Statistics*. Washington: CRS, 2004. http://www.fas.org/sgp/crs/natsec/RL32492.pdf.

Conroy, Marianne. "Acting Out: Method Acting, the National Culture, and the Middlebrow Disposition in Cold War America." *Criticism* 35, no. 2 (1993): 239–263.

Cooper, Brenda. "*Boys Don't Cry* and Female Masculinity: Reclaiming a Life and Dismantling the Politics of Normative Heterosexuality." *Critical Studies in Media Communication* 19, no. 1 (March, 2002): 44–63.

Corrigan, Timothy. *A Cinema Without Walls: Movies and Culture After Vietnam*. New Brunswick: Rutgers University Press, 1991.

Coulthard, Lisa. "Killing Bill: Rethinking Feminism and Film Violence." In *Interrogating Postfeminism*, edited by Yvonne Tasker and Diane Negra, 153–175. Durham: Duke University Press, 2007.

Dando, Christina. "Range Wars: The Plains Frontier of *Boys Don't Cry*." *Journal of Cultural Geography* 23 (Fall/Winter 2005): 91–113.

Davis, Caris. "Age of Innocence." *Sunday Times* (London), Aug. 4, 1996, 10–11.

Dempsey, Michael. "Hellbent for Mystery." *Film Quarterly* 32, no. 4 (Summer 1979): 10–13.

Denby, David. "Heroic Proportions." *New York Magazine*, July 27, 1998, 44–45.

Dittmar, Linda, and Gene Michaud, eds. *From Hanoi to Hollywood: The Vietnam War in American Film*. New Brunswick: Rutgers University Press, 1990.

Doherty, Thomas. "Full Metal Genre: Stanley Kubrick's Vietnam Combat Movie." *Film Quarterly* 42, no. 2 (Winter 1988–1989): 24–30.

Drysdale, David. " 'Laws and Every Other Damn Thing': Authority, Bad Faith, and the Unlikely Success of *Deadwood*." In *Reading* Deadwood: *A Western to Swear By*, edited by David Lavery, 133–144. New York: I. B. Tauris, 2006.

Dunn, Thomas R. "Remembering Matthew Shepard: Violence, Identity, and Queer Counterpublic Memories." *Rhetoric and Public Affairs* 13, no. 4 (2010): 611–651.

Dunne, John Gregory. "Virtual Patriotism: Feeling Good About War." *New Yorker*, Nov. 16, 1998, 98–102.

Dyer, Richard. *Stars*. London: British Film Institute, 2008.

Eberwein, Robert. " 'As a Mother Cuddles a Child': Sexuality and Masculinity in World War II Combat Films." In *Masculinity: Bodies, Movies, Culture,* edited by Peter Lehman, 149–166. New York and London: Routledge, 2001.

Eileraas, Karina. "The Brandon Teena Story: Rethinking the Body, Gender Identity, and Violence Against Women." *Michigan Feminist Studies* 16 (2002): 85–118.

Engle, Karen. "Feminism and Its (Dis)contents: Criminalizing Wartime Rape in Bosnia and Herzegovina." *American Journal of International Law* 99 (October 2005): 778–816.

Faludi, Susan. *The Terror Dream: Fear and Fantasy in Post-9/11 America.* New York: Macmillan, 2007.

Fiedler, Leslie A. "Mythicizing the Unspeakable." *Journal of American Folklore* 103 (Oct.–Dec. 1990): 390–399.

Foran, Charles. "Celluloid Wars: VIETNAM." *Queen's Quarterly* 112 (Summer 2005): 255–265.

Fraiman, Susan. *Cool Men and the Second Sex.* New York: Columbia University Press, 2003.

———."Geometries of Race and Gender: Eve Sedgwick, Spike Lee, Charlayne Hunter-Gault." *Feminist Studies* 20 (Spring 1994): 67–84.

Francis, Don. "The Regeneration of America: Uses of Landscape in *The Deer Hunter.*" *Literature/Film Quarterly* 11, no. 1 (1983): 16–21.

Friedman, Lester. *Citizen Spielberg.* Champaign: University of Illinois Press, 2006.

Fuchs, Cynthia. "Boys Don't Cry" (review). *PopMatters.* http://www.popmatters.com/film/boys-dont-cry.html.

Furby, Jaqueline. "Interesting Times: The Demands *24*'s Real-Time Format Makes on its Audience." In *Reading 24: TV Against the Clock,* edited by Steven Peacock, 59–70. New York: I. B. Tauris, 2007.

Gabler, Neal. " 'Private Ryan' Satisfies Our Longing for Unity." *Los Angeles Times,* Aug. 9, 1998.

Gates, Philippa. " 'Fighting the Good Fight': The Real and the Moral in the Contemporary Hollywood Combat Film." *Quarterly Review of Film and Video* 22, no. 4 (2005): 297–310.

Giardina, Anthony. "Are We Not Men? Nineties Preoccupations with Manhood Are Fueling Our Obsession with World War II." *GQ,* May 1999, 137–144.

Girard, René. *Violence and the Sacred.* Trans. Patrick Gregory. Baltimore: Johns Hopkins University Press, 1977.

Goldstein, Richard. "World War II Chic." *Village Voice,* Jan. 19, 1999, 43–47.

Greven, David. *Manhood in Hollywood from Bush to Bush.* Austin: University of Texas Press, 2009.

Haffenreffer, David, and J. J. Ramberg. *Money and Markets.* CNN, Feb. 25, 2004.

Haggith, Toby. "D-Day Filming—For Real: A Comparison of 'Truth' and 'Reality' in *Saving Private Ryan* and Combat Film by the British Army's Film and Photographic Unit." *Film History* 14, no. 3–4 (2002): 332–353.

Halberstam, Judith. "Automating Gender: Postmodern Feminism in the Age of the Intelligent Machine." *Feminist Studies* 17 (Autumn 1991): 439–460.

———. *Female Masculinity.* Durham: Duke University Press, 1998.

———. "The Transgender Gaze in *Boys Don't Cry.*" *Screen* 42, no. 3 (2001): 294–298.

Hall, Stuart. "Notes on Deconstructing 'The Popular.'" In *People's History and Socialist Theory,* edited by Raphael Samuel, 227–240. London: Routledge & Kegan Paul, 1981.

Hammond, Michael. "*Saving Private Ryan*'s 'Special Affect.'" In *Action and Adventure Cinema,* edited by Yvonne Tasker, 153–166. London and New York: Routledge, 2004.

Hampton, Howard. *Born in Flames: Termite Dreams, Dialectical Fairy Tales, and Pop Apocalypses.* Cambridge: Harvard University Press, 2006.

Haraway, Donna. "A Cyborg Manifesto." In *The Cultural Studies Reader,* 2nd ed., edited by Simon During, 271–291. New York: Routledge, 1993.

Hatch, Kristin. "1951: Movies and the New Faces of Masculinity." In *American Cinema of the 1950s,* edited by Murray Pomerance, 43–64. New Brunswick: Rutgers University Press, 2005.

Heinecken, Dawn. *The Warrior Women of Television: A Feminist Cultural Analysis of the New Female Body in Popular Media.* New York: Peter Lang, 2003.

Helliwell, Christine. " 'It's Only a Penis': Rape, Feminism, and Difference." *Signs* 25, no. 3 (Spring 2000): 789–816.

Hellmann, John. "Vietnam and the Hollywood Genre Film: Inversions of American Mythology in *The Deer Hunter* and *Apocalypse Now.*" *American Quarterly* 34, no. 4 (Autumn 1982): 418–439.

Henderson, Lisa. "The Class Character of *Boys Don't Cry.*" *Screen* 42, no. 3 (2001): 299–303.

Hertzberg, Henrik. "Theatre of War." *New Yorker,* July 27, 1998, 30–33.

Higham, Scott, and Joe Stephens. "New Details of Prison Abuse Emerge; Abu Ghraib Detainees' Statements Describe Sexual Humiliation and Savage Beatings." *Washington Post,* May 21, 2004, A1.

———. "Punishment and Amusement; Documents Indicate 3 Photos Were Not Staged for Interrogation." *Washington Post,* May 22, 2004, A1.

Hill, Erin. " 'What's Afflictin' You?': Corporeality, Body Crises and the Body Politic in *Deadwood.*" In *Reading* Deadwood: *A Western to Swear By,* edited by David Lavery, 23–31. New York: I. B. Tauris, 2006.

Hodgkins, John. "In the Wake of Desert Storm: A Consideration of Modern World War II Films." *Journal of Popular Film and Television* 30, no. 2 (2002): 74–85.

Hoffman, Scott W. " 'Last Night, I Prayed to Matthew': Matthew Shepard, Homosexuality, and Popular Martyrdom in Contemporary America." *Religion and American Culture: A Journal of Interpretation* 21 (Winter 2011): 121–164.

Holmlund, Chris. *Impossible Bodies: Femininity and Masculinity at the Movies.* New York: Routledge, 2002.

———. *Running Scared: Masculinity and the Representation of the Male Body.* Philadelphia: Temple University Press, 1993.

Howard, Douglas L. " 'You're Going to Tell Me Everything You Know': Torture and Morality on Fox's *24*." In *Reading 24: TV against the Clock,* edited by Steven Peacock, 133–147. New York: I. B. Tauris, 2007.

Inness, Sherrie A., ed. *Action Chicks: New Images of Tough Women in Popular Culture.* New York: Palgrave Macmillan, 2004.

———. *Tough Girls: Women Warriors and Wonder Women in Popular Culture.* Philadelphia: University of Pennsylvania Press, 1999.

Jeffords, Susan. *Hard Bodies: Hollywood Masculinity in the Reagan Era.* New Brunswick: Rutgers University Press, 1994.

———. *The Remasculinization of America: Gender and the Vietnam War.* Bloomington: Indiana University Press, 1989.

Jones, David M. "Hegemonic Whiteness and the Humboldt Murders: *Boys Don't Cry,* Historical Memory, and the Ghostly Absence (Presence) of Phillip De Vine." In *Coming Out to the Mainstream: New Queer Cinema in the 21st Century,* edited by JoAnne C. Juett and David M. Jones, 174–216. Newcastle upon Tyne: Cambridge Scholars Publishing (2010).

Kamber, Richard. "Taming *The Deer Hunter:* A Working Class Movie Without Middle Class Condescension." *Cresset* 44, no. 1 (1980): 27–30.

Kamiya, Gary. "Total War." *Salon,* June 30, 1998. http://www.salon.com/1998/06/30/review_109/.

Kaplan, Amy. "Where Is Guantanamo?" *American Quarterly* 57, no. 3 (September 2005): 831–858.

Kaufman, Moisés, and members of the Tectonic Theater Project. *The Laramie Project.* New York: Vintage Books, 2001.

Kinder, Marsha. "Political Game." *Film Quarterly* 32, no. 4 (Summer 1979): 14–16.

Kipnis, Laura. *The Female Thing: Dirt, Sex, Envy, Vulnerability.* New York: Pantheon, 2006.

Kitses, Jim. Audio commentary, *The Furies*, Criterion Collection DVD (2008).

Klein, Amanda Ann. " 'The Horse Doesn't Get a Credit': The Foregrounding of Generic Syntax in *Deadwood's* Opening Credits." In *Reading* Deadwood: *A Western to Swear By,* edited by David Lavery, 93–100. New York: I. B. Tauris, 2006.

Klein, Michael. "Historical Memory, Film, and the Vietnam War." In *From Hanoi to Hollywood,* edited by Linda Dittmar and Gene Michaux, 29–38. New Brunswick: Rutgers University Press, 1990.

Krulak, Charles C., and Joseph P. Hoar. "It's Our Cage, Too—Torture Betrays Us and Breeds New Enemies." *Washington Post,* May 17, 2007, A17.

Larson, Doran. "Machine as Messiah: Cyborgs, Morphs, and the American Body Politic." *Cinema Journal* 36, no. 4 (Summer 1997): 57–75.

Lavery, David. "Introduction: *Deadwood,* David Milch, and Television Creativity." In *Reading* Deadwood: *A Western to Swear By,* edited by David Lavery, 1–10. New York: I. B. Tauris, 2006.

Lehman, Peter, ed. *Masculinity: Bodies, Movies, Culture.* New York: Routledge, 2001.

———. "'Well, What's It Like Over There? Can You Tell Us Anything?': Looking for Vietnam in *The Deer Hunter.*" *North Dakota Quarterly* 51, no. 3 (1983): 31–41.

Leith, William. "Boom to Bust: Demi Moore, Nakedly Ambitious." *Observer* review section, Sept. 20, 1996, 20.

Littlewood, Roland. "Military Rape." *Anthropology Today* 13, no. 2 (April 1997): 7–16.

Luban, David. "Liberalism, Torture, and the Ticking Bomb." *Virginia Law Review* 91, no. 6 (Oct. 2005): 1425–1461.

Magid, Ron. "*Full Metal Jacket:* Cynic's Choice." *American Cinematographer,* Sept. 1987, 74–84.

Maltby, Richard. *Hollywood Cinema.* Oxford: Blackwell Publishers, 1995.

Marcus, Sharon. "Fighting Bodies, Fighting Words." In *Feminists Theorize the Political,* edited by Judith Butler and Joan W. Scott, 385–40. London: Routledge, 1992.

Mardorossian, Carine M. "Toward a New Feminist Theory of Rape." *Signs* 27, no. 3 (Spring 2002): 743–775.

Margulies, Ivone, ed. *Rites of Realism: Essays on Corporeal Cinema.* Durham: Duke University Press: 2003.

Mayer, Jane. "Whatever It Takes." *New Yorker,* Feb. 19, 2007. http://www.newyorker.com/reporting/2007/02/19/070219fa_fact_mayer.

McConachie, Bruce. "Method Acting and the Cold War." *Theater Survey* 41, no. 1 (May 2000): 47–67.

McInerney, Peter. "Apocalypse Then: Hollywood Looks Back at Vietnam." *Film Quarterly* 33, no. 2 (Winter 1979–1980): 21–32.

Milch, David. *Deadwood: Stories of the Black Hills.* New York: Melcher Media, 2006.

Millichap, Joseph. "Robert Penn Warren, David Milch, and the Literary Contexts of *Deadwood.*" In *Reading* Deadwood: *A Western to Swear By,* edited by David Lavery, 101–114. New York: I. B. Tauris, 2006.

Mittell, Jason. *Genre and Television: From Cop Shows to Cartoons in American Culture.* New York: Routledge, 2004.

Mizejewski, Linda. *Hardboiled and High Heeled: The Woman Detective in Popular Culture.* New York: Routledge, 2004.

Modleski, Tania. "The Context of Violence in Popular Culture." *Chronicle of Higher Education* 47, no. 53 (April 27, 2001): B15.

———. *Feminism without Women: Culture and Criticism in a "Postfeminist" Age.* New York: Routledge, 1991.

Moore, Janet C. "For Fighting and for Fun: Kubrick's Complicitous Critique in *Full Metal Jacket.*" *Velvet Light Trap* 31 (Spring 1993): 39–47.

Morgenstern, Joe. "Battle Rages Ahead but Plot Drags Behind in *Saving Private Ryan.*" *Wall Street Journal,* July 24, 1998, W3.

Mulvey, Laura. "Visual Pleasure and Narrative Cinema." *Screen* 16, no. 3 (1975): 6–18.

Muse, Eben J. "The Land of Nam: Romance and Persecution in Brian DePalma's *Casualties of War.*" *Literature/Film Quarterly* 20, no. 3 (1992): 205–212.

Nathan, Ian. "Apocalypse Then." *Empire,* Oct. 1998, 100–114.

Naremore, James. *Acting in the Cinema.* Berkeley and Los Angeles: University of California Press, 1988.

———. "Stanley Kubrick and the Aesthetics of the Grotesque." *Film Quarterly* 60, no. 1 (Fall 2006): 4–14.

Neale, Steve. "Action-Adventure as Hollywood Genre." In *Action and Adventure Cinema,* edited by Yvonne Tasker, 71–83. New York and London: Routledge, 2004.

Newsinger, John. " 'Do You Walk the Walk?': Aspects of Masculinity in Some Vietnam War Films." In *You Tarzan: Masculinity, Movies, and Men,* edited by Pat Kirkham and Janet Thumim, 126–136. New York: St. Martin's Press, 1993.

O'Connell, Aaron B. "Saving Private Lynch: A Hyperreal Hero in an Age of Postmodern Warfare." *War, Literature and the Arts* 17, no. 1–2 (2005): 33–52.

Ott, Brian L., and Eric Aoki. "The Politics of Negotiating Public Tragedy: Media Framing of the Matthew Shepard Murder." *Rhetoric and Public Affairs* 5, no. 3 (Fall 2002): 483–505.

Petersen, Jennifer. "The Mourning Public: Grief and Identification in an Anti-Gay Murder." Paper presented at the annual meeting of the International Communication Association, San Francisco, May 23, 2007. Available at http://www.allacademic.com/meta/p172460_index.html.

Petrie, Doug. Episode commentary, "Fool for Love," *Buffy the Vampire Slayer: The Chosen Collection,* season 5.

Prince, Stephen, ed. *Screening Violence.* New Brunswick: Rutgers University Press, 2000.

Projansky, Sarah. *Watching Rape: Film and Television in Postfeminist Culture.* New York: New York University Press, 2001.

Pursell, Michael. "*Full Metal Jacket:* The Unravelling of Patriarchy." *Literature/Film Quarterly* 16, no. 4 (1988): 218–225.

Rabinowitz, Dorothy. "Summer of War: It's D-Day at the Movies." *Wall Street Journal,* July 31, 1998.

Rambuss, Richard. "Machinehead." *Camera Obscura* 14, no. 3 (Sept. 1999): 97–123.

Richardson, Joan. "*Deadwood:* Unalterable Vibrations." *Hopkins Review* 3, no. 3 (Summer 2010): 376–405.

Rigney, Melissa. "Brandon Goes to Hollywood: *Boys Don't Cry* and the Transgender Body in Film." *Film Criticism* 28, no. 2 (2003): 4–23.

Rothstein, Edward. "Rescuing the War Hero from 1990's Skepticism." *New York Times,* Aug. 3, 1998.

Ryan, Paul. "Contenders." *Sight & Sound,* Aug. 2007, 36–40.

Sammon, Paul M. *Ridley Scott, Close Up: The Making of His Movies.* New York: Da Capo Press, 1999.

Savran, David. *Taking It Like a Man: White Masculinity, Masochism, and Contemporary American Culture.* Princeton: Princeton University Press, 1998.

Scarry, Elaine. *The Body in Pain: The Making and Unmaking of the World.* New York: Oxford University Press, 1985.

Schuyler, Michael T. "He 'Coulda Been a Contender' for Miss America: Feminizing Brando in *On the Waterfront.*" *Canadian Review of American Studies* 41, no. 1 (2001): 97–113.

See, Fred. "Steven Spielberg and the Holiness of War." *Arizona Quarterly* 60, no. 3 (2004): 109–141.

Sharp, Patrick. "Starbuck as 'American Amazon': Captivity Narrative and the Colonial Imagination in *Battlestar Galactica.*" *Science Fiction Film and Television* 3, no. 1 (2010): 57–78.

Shaviro, Steven. *The Cinematic Body.* Minneapolis: University of Minnesota Press, 1993.

Silverman, Kaja. *Male Subjectivity at the Margins.* New York: Routledge, 1992.

Singer, Mark. "The Misfit: How David Milch Got from *NYPD Blue* to *Deadwood* by Way of an Epistle of St. Paul," *New Yorker,* Feb. 14, 2005, 192–205.

Slocum, J. David, ed. *Violence and American Cinema.* New York: Routledge, 2001.

Slotkin, Richard. "Unit Pride: Ethnic Platoons and the Myths of American Nationality," *American Literary History* 13, no. 3 (Autumn 2001): 469–498.

Sobchack, Vivian. *The Address of the Eye: A Phenomenology of Film Experience.* Princeton: Princeton University Press, 1992.

———. *Carnal Thoughts: Embodiment and Moving Image Culture.* Berkeley and Los Angeles: University of California Press, 2004.

Spear, Bruce. "Political Morality and Historical Understanding in *Casualties of War.*" *Literature/Film Quarterly* 20, no. 3 (1992): 243–248.

Stiglmayer, Alexandra, ed. *Mass Rape: The War against Women in Bosnia-Herzegovina.* Lincoln: University of Nebraska Press, 1994.

Studlar, Gaylyn. *In the Realm of Pleasure: Von Sternberg, Dietrich, and the Masochistic Aesthetic.* New York: Columbia University Press, 1993.

Suid, Lawrence H. *Guts and Glory: The Making of the American Military Image in Film.* Lexington: University Press of Kentucky, 2002.

Sullivan, Andrew. "Afterlife." *New Republic,* Nov. 22, 1999. (6)

Swan, Rachel. *"Boys Don't Cry." Film Quarterly* 54, no. 3 (Spring 2001): 47–52.

Tasker, Yvonne. *Spectacular Bodies: Gender, Genre, and the Action Cinema.* New York: Routledge, 1993.

———. *Working Girls: Gender and Sexuality in Popular Cinema.* New York: Routledge, 1998.

Tasker, Yvonne, and Diane Negra, eds. *Interrogating Postfeminism: Gender and the Politics of Popular Culture.* Durham: Duke University Press, 2007.

Tigner, Amy. *"The Laramie Project:* Western Pastoral." *Modern Drama* 45, no. 1 (Spring 2002): 138–156.

Wallenstein, Andrew. "Many Reinforce War Film: Affils Grapple with 'Great Debate.'" *Hollywood Reporter,* Nov. 12, 2004, 1, 95.

Warshow, Robert. *The Immediate Experience: Movies, Comics, Theatre, and Other Aspects of Popular Culture.* Cambridge: Harvard University Press, 2001.

Westerfelhaus, Robert, and Celeste Lacroix. "Waiting for the Barbarians: HBO's *Deadwood* as a Post-9/11 Ritual of Disquiet." *Southern Communications Journal,* 74, no. 1 (Jan.–March 2009): 18–39.

White, Patricia. "Girls Still Cry." *Screen* 42, no. 2 (2001): 217–221.

White, Susan. "Male Bonding, Hollywood Orientalism, and the Repression of the Feminine in Kubrick's *Full Metal Jacket.*" In *Inventing Vietnam: The War in Film and Television,* edited by Michael Anderegg, 204–230. Philadelphia: Temple University Press, 1991.

Williams, G. Christopher. "Pimp and Whore: The Necessity of Perverse Domestication in the Development of the West." In *Reading* Deadwood: *A Western to Swear By,* edited by David Lavery, 145–156. New York: I. B. Tauris, 2006.

Williams, Linda. *Hard Core: Power, Pleasure, and the "Frenzy of the Visible."* Berkeley and Los Angeles: University of California Press, 1989.

Williams, Raymond. *The Long Revolution.* London: Chatto and Windus, 1961.

Willis, Sharon. *High Contrast: Race and Gender in Contemporary Hollywood Films.* Durham: Duke University Press, 1997.

Willoquet-Maricondi, Paula. "Full-Metal-Jacketing; or, Masculinity in the Making." *Cinema Journal* 33, no. 2 (Winter 1994): 5–21.

Wood, Robin. *Hollywood from Vietnam to Reagan*. New York: Columbia University Press, 1986.

———. "*The Furies:* Mann of the Western." In booklet accompanying Criterion Collection DVD, *The Furies* (2008), also available at http://www.criterion.com/current/posts/521-the-furies-mann-of-the-western (accessed November 12, 2012).

Worden, Daniel. "Neo-liberalism and the Western: HBO's *Deadwood* as National Allegory." *Canadian Review of American Studies* 39, no. 2 (2009): 221–246.

Wypijewski, JoAnn. "A Boy's Life: For Matthew Shepard's Killers, What Does It Take to Pass as a Man?" *Harper's,* Sept. 1999, 61–74.

Young, Iris Marion. "Throwing like a Girl: A Phenomenology of Feminine Body Comportment, Motility and Spatiality." *Human Studies* 3, no. 1 (1980): 137–156.

Index

About the Author

Sarah Hagelin is an assistant professor of English and director of film studies at the University of Colorado, Denver, where she specializes in film, television, and twentieth-century American literature and culture. She received her PhD from the University of Virginia and has had essays featured in *The War Body on Screen* (2008) and the forthcoming *National Responses to the Holocaust.*